HYGIENE
A Salon
Handbook

Second Edition

Phillip Hatton

BSc (Hons), MIBiol, CBiol, MIT, MRIPHH, PGCE, Dip Ed Man.

b

**Blackwell
Science**

Copyright © Phillip Hatton 1986, 1991

Blackwell Science Ltd
Editorial Offices:
Osney Mead, Oxford OX2 0EL
25 John Street, London WC1N 2BL
23 Ainslie Place, Edinburgh EH3 6AJ
238 Main Street, Cambridge
  Massachusetts 02142, USA
54 University Street, Carlton
  Victoria 3053, Australia

Other Editorial Offices:
Arnette Blackwell SA
1, rue de Lille, 75007 Paris
France

Blackwell Wissenschafts-Verlag GmbH
Kurfürstendamm 57
10707 Berlin, Germany

Blackwell MZV
Feldgasse 13, A-1238 Wien
Austria

First Edition published by Collins
  Professional and Technical Books 1986
Reprinted by BSP Professional Books 1988
Second Edition published 1991
Reprinted by Blackwell Science 1993, 1994

Set by Best-set Typesetter Ltd
Printed and bound in Great Britain
by Hartnolls Ltd, Bodmin, Cornwall

DISTRIBUTORS

Marston Book Services Ltd
PO Box 87
Oxford OX2 0DT
(*Orders:* Tel: 01865 791155
    Fax: 01865 791927
    Telex: 837515)

USA
  Blackwell Science, Inc.
  238 Main Street
  Cambridge, MA 02142
  (*Orders*: Tel: 800 759-6102
        617 876-7000)

Canada
  Oxford University Press
  70 Wynford Drive
  Don Mills
  Ontario M3C 1J9
  (*Orders*: Tel: 416 441-2941)

Australia
  Blackwell Science Pty Ltd
  54 University Street
  Carlton, Victoria 3053
  (*Orders*: Tel: 03 347-5552)

A catalogue record for this book is available
from the British Library

ISBN 0-632-02815-7

HYGIENE
A Salon
Handbook

Other books of interest

COLOURING
A Salon Handbook
Lesley Hatton, Phillip Hatton and Alisoun Powell
0 632 01922 0

PERMING AND STRAIGHTENING
A Salon Handbook
Second Edition
Lesley Hatton and Phillip Hatton
0 632 03316 9

CUTTING AND STYLING
A Salon Handbook
Lesley Hatton and Phillip Hatton
0 632 01851 8

FOUNDATION HAIRDRESSING
Lesley Hatton and Phillip Hatton
0 632 02613 8

AFRO HAIR
A Salon Handbook
Phillip Hatton
0 632 02285 X

HAIR AND BEAUTY BUSINESS MANAGEMENT
Second Edition
Annette Mieske
0 632 03823 3

SETTING UP YOUR OWN SALON
National Hairdressers' Federation
0 632 03889 6

HOW TO WIN CLIENTS
AND INTERPRET THEIR NEEDS
A Hairdresser's Guide
Ian Mistlin
0 632 03891 8

To my mother

Contents

Preface

The second edition of this textbook on hygiene has been extended so that beauty therapists, as well as hairdressers, will find it a useful supportive text in their training.

Questions have been placed throughout the text in this edition, rather than at the end of chapters, so that the book can be used for independent learning. The questions work through the content of each chapter in a step-by-step manner, so that you will immediately know if you do not understand something. The final chapter is a set of brief revision notes that should get a student through any examination with a hygiene content.

A new chapter on caution in the hairdressing salon has been included to make the hairdresser more aware of the dangers associated with the chemicals that they use. The other new chapter is on caution in the beauty therapy salon, dealing with a wide range of the services used in beauty.

The chapter on first aid is important as everyone should know what to do in an emergency. Kept in the salon, this book will be an invaluable guide on all aspects of safety and hygiene. You should be able to give correct advice to clients with scalp problems, and your opinions will be valued if they are correct. The book tries to answer most of the questions that I have been asked over the years in salons and by my students in college.

Like the first edition, the book is as up to date as possible. Although it is a serious and important subject, I hope that you will enjoy reading the book and will come back to it as the need arises.

Phillip Hatton

1

The Skin and Hair

1.1 The structure and functions of the skin

The skin consists of two layers, the epidermis and dermis. Underneath lie the subcutaneous tissues.

The skin is one of the largest organs of the body. Its weight, including fat, is one-eighth of a normal individual's body weight. The average area of skin at birth is 2500 square centimetres and this increases to 18 000 square centimetres in an adult man. The skin, excluding fat, of an average man weighs some 4.8 kg (about 10 pounds), while that of a woman weighs 3.2 kg (about 7 pounds). It is attached loosely over most of the trunk of the body, but tightly on the palms of the hands and soles of the feet.

The diagram of the skin in Figure 1.1 is a generalised vertical section, showing everything that might be present in the skin. Some of the parts shown in the diagram will be absent in some areas because there are two main types of skin: 'hairy' and 'glabrous'. Hairy skin covers most of the body and characteristically possesses hair follicles to which sebaceous glands are attached. The skin of the palms and soles, however, lacks hair follicles and sebaceous glands and this is called glabrous skin. The epidermis of glabrous skin is also particularly thick.

The skin forms a waterproof barrier. The horny layer of the epidermis is responsible for this property, the sebum playing a much smaller role in waterproofing than most people imagine. The skin is also protective, forming a barrier against physical traumas.

The skin owes its colour to red haemoglobin in the blood vessels, yellow carotenoids in subcutaneous fat and the dark brown pigment melanin. Melanin is produced in special cells called melanocytes, found in the epidermis (see Section 1.2). This is produced in response to ultra-violet radiation, present in natural sunlight, which produces burning and cellular damage when it is absorbed by the skin cells. The melanin absorbs the ultra-violet radiation before it can penetrate to the living cells; if it does not, the skin burns. Skin colour is determined genetically and environmentally. Various degrees of pigmentation occur in different ethnic

1

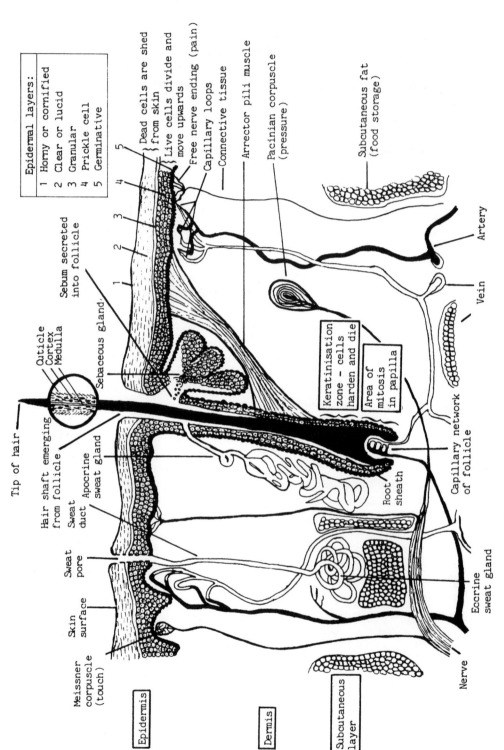

Fig. 1.1   Generalised vertical section of the skin.

groups but the differences are in the amount of melanin produced and *not* in the number of melanocytes present. Besides the sun, hormones can also increase pigmentation, as many pregnant women discover. Endocrine glands can malfunction to produce darkly pigmented skin. (This occurs, for instance, in Addison's disease in which the adrenal cortex is damaged). Skin cancer is a common disease in light-skinned races who are exposed to strong sunlight, the Scots and Irish having a high rate of skin cancer when they emigrate to countries with strong sunshine, such as Australia or Africa. Some individuals are born without the ability to produce melanin in their bodies – a congenital condition known as albinism.

The skin contains a number of nerves which detect changes in the surrounding environment and relay this information to the brain. These are called sensory nerves and are shown in Figure 1.1. There are two main networks of nerves in the dermis, one just below the epidermis and one in the lower dermis. Branches from these are capable of detecting heat, cold, pain and pressure (touch). A few nerve endings for pain enter the epidermis. Motor nerves which bring about movement of elastic tissue are also found in the skin. They cause the dilation of blood vessels, the raising of hairs when the arrector pili muscle is stimulated, and the secretion of sweat.

The temperature of the body in a healthy individual is kept constant at around 37°C. This temperature is very important for the normal functioning of the body. If the temperature drops, the biochemical reactions that keep our body 'ticking over' slow down, resulting in death from hypothermia. If the temperature increases by several degrees, the enzymes that make these biochemical reactions occur are changed, so that they cannot work properly anymore. This eventually results in death. If you put an egg in a frying pan and gently heat it, there comes a point when the increase in temperature makes the clear egg white actually turn white. At this point the structure of the protein in the egg white has been changed. As enzymes are made of protein their structure is changed by an increase in temperature and they cannot work properly (when the structure of a protein is changed in this way we refer to it as being denatured). This is why the high temperatures of fevers are so dangerous and must be brought down.

Body temperature too high

Two main changes occur when the body temperature is too high, involving the blood vessels of the skin and sweating. The blood vessels near the skin surface dilate (enlarge) so that the skin becomes red and heat is brought from the middle of the body to the skin surface where it can be lost more easily. This loss is simple, from the hot skin surface to the cooler air (clothing would slow it down). When you are hot sweating increases, so beads of sweat can normally be felt on the skin. Sweat cools the skin when it evaporates (turns from water into water vapour). This change from a liquid to a gas requires energy, which is supplied from the heat of the body. Simply wiping your forehead with a handkerchief will dry the skin, but will not take energy from the skin.

Body temperature too low

Four changes occur when the body temperature drops below 37°C. The first two are the opposite of what has just been described above. The blood vessels near the skin surface constrict (get smaller), keeping heat in the middle of the body, so it is not lost at the skin surface so easily (the skin usually becomes paler). Sweating will be reduced, so less heat is lost by the evaporation of sweat.

The third change involves the arrector pili muscle which makes the hair stand on end, so that an insulating layer of air is trapped next to the skin surface. This 'tricks' the body as the air next to the skin is warmed, and the heat is lost more slowly to the warmed layer of air than it would be to the cooler surrounding air. Wearing several thin layers of clothing instead of one thick layer works in much the same way, as several insulating layers of warmed air become trapped.

The fourth and final reaction of the skin when the body temperature drops is to shiver. Shivering is the movement of muscles in the skin, which produces heat to help warm the body. So, if you start shivering after swimming don't feel embarrassed, it will stop once you have warmed up!

The skin is a barrier against infection. It has an acid pH of between 4.5 and 5.5 in normal skin, with an average of about 5.4, and this inhibits the growth of bacteria. Fungi are controlled by sebum, which inhibits their growth. If the skin is damaged so that blood flows, the process of clotting will seal the opening.

Vitamin D, which controls the take-up of calcium in bones, is produced by the action of ultra-violet radiation (in sunlight, for instance) on the epidermis. A deficiency of vitamin D can cause rickets.

The skin plays a small role in excretion, as sweat contains waste products such as urea and lactic acid. The subcutaneous layer is a storage area for fat, which we lose slowly when we diet. The skin contains a lot of water, which we lose quickly in vigorous exercise. If you lose five pounds in weight during a game of squash it is almost all due to water loss (dehydration). Having a drink will put back much of the weight instantly.

About one-fifth of dietary protein is required to maintain the formation of new keratin for the skin, hair and nails. An average adult requires about 50 g (1½–2 ounces) of protein daily, so 10 g is used in the daily production of new keratin.

In countries where there is famine (or in the slimming disease, anorexia nervosa) the quality of hair is one of the first things to suffer. An orange band is often seen on hair affected by a lack of dietary protein. This is because the hair can no longer produce melanin. Protein must be present in the diet every day as it cannot be stored by the body. This is because of the nitrogen it contains, which is poisonous to the body. If extra protein is taken in one day the excess is converted by the body into energy. Nitrogen is excreted from the body as urea in urine.

All proteins are made up of amino acids. There are 22 different amino acids present in foods which contain protein. The body digests protein and breaks it down to these individual amino acids. They can then be rearranged by the body to make new protein for growth and replacement of body cells. Some amino acids can be synthesised by the body if they are not present in the diet; these are called nonessential amino acids. The ones which must be taken in the diet because they cannot be synthesised are called essential amino acids. Sources of protein such as meat, fish and eggs contain all the essential amino acids, so are called first class proteins. Other sources of protein such as vegetables, pulses and cereals do not contain all the essential amino acids, so are called second class proteins. To obtain all the essential amino acids a vegetarian must eat several sources of second class proteins, or their diet will be deficient in some amino acids.

Questions 1.1

1 What are the two layers of the skin called?
2 What is glabrous skin and where is it found?
3 What type of skin covers most of the body?
4 Which part of the skin is most important in waterproofing?
5 To what does the skin owe its colour?
6 Name the pigment responsible for producing the differences in skin colour of different ethnic groups.
7 What is the function of the pigment in protecting the skin?
8 Why are there sometimes pigmentation changes in pregnant women?
9 Who is most likely to suffer from skin cancer and why?
10 What is albinism?
11 What do the sensory nerves of the skin detect?
12 What are the functions of motor nerves in the skin?
13 What is the normal temperature of the body and why is it important that it is kept constant?
14 How is body temperature maintained?
15 What is the pH of skin?
16 Is this pH acid or alkaline?
17 How does this help stop infection?
18 What produces vitamin D in the epidermis?
19 What can a deficiency of vitamin D cause?
20 What is stored in the subcutaneous layer?
21 How much protein does an adult require each day?
22 How much of the protein that we eat is used to form new keratin?
23 Why must protein be taken in the diet every day?
24 What are essential and non-essential amino acids?
25 What is the difference between first and second class proteins?
26 Why must a vegetarian have several sources of protein in their diet?

1.2 The epidermis

The epidermis consists of several layers of cells. The lower layer is continually dividing, pushing cells towards the surface. These upper layers are protective and by the time the cells have reached here they have died. There are very few nerves in the epidermis and no blood vessels. The actual thickness of the epidermis may vary from 0.1 mm to 2 mm depending on the part of the body where it is found. It is thin on the eyelids and abdomen, and thick on the soles of the feet and palms of the hands. The main functions of the epidermis are to protect the underlying tissues from infection, dirt and injury; to form a waterproof barrier; and to prevent excessive water loss. Read the next section in conjunction with Figure 1.2 which shows the types of cell present in the epidermis.

(1) *The horny layer (stratum corneum)*
     This outer upper layer consists of flat dead scales of keratin which are gradually shed by friction, i.e. when the skin is rubbed with towels or the hair is brushed. If this horny or cornified layer were stripped off, water loss from the skin would be increased some twenty times. Cells stay in this layer for only fourteen days before being shed.

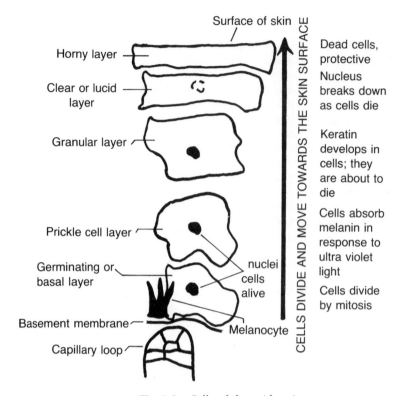

Fig. 1.2 Cells of the epidermis

(2) *The clear layer (stratum lucidum)*
These flattened cells have no nuclei and contain the protein keratin. The melanin granules are destroyed here so that the layer becomes clear. (This destruction of melanin does not happen in black skin.) Because they have no nuclei the cells are dead.

(3) *The granular layer (stratum granulosum)*
In this layer the nuclei of the cells are broken down, resulting in the death of the cells. The protein keratin is laid down here. This layer may be thought of as a transitional layer between the outer dead cells and the inner living, dividing cells.

(4) *The prickle cell layer (stratum spinosum)*
The cells in this layer have fine threads connected to the cells around them. These 'spiny outgrowths' may play some part in absorbing melanin granules into the cells. Together with the germinating layer below, this layer is sometimes called the Malpighian layer.

(5) *The germinative layer (stratum germinativum)*
This is often called the basal layer. The regularly arranged cells are constantly dividing by mitosis to form the new cells which push the older ones upwards. The germinative layer is continuous around the hair follicles, sebaceous glands and sweat glands. Although this may appear to be part of the dermis, it is in fact a downgrowth of the epidermis. Large branched cells called melanocytes

produce the pigment melanin here. The production of this pigment is protection against ultra-violet rays present in sunlight; the pigment absorbs the radiation.

It takes twenty-eight days for a cell to pass from the germinative to the horny layer (epidermal transit time). This is decreased to five days in psoriasis, resulting in the cells of the horny layer retaining their nuclei.

Questions 1.2

1   How many layers of cells are there in the epidermis?
2   Draw and label a simple diagram to show the layers of the epidermis.
3   In which areas of the body is the epidermis at its thinnest?
4   In which areas of the body is the epidermis at its thickest?
5   What are the functions of the epidermis?
6   In which layer of the epidermis can you find flat dead scales of keratin?
7   How are the flat dead scales removed from the skin?
8   Why is the stratum lucidum called the clear layer?
9   What is the difference between black and white skins in the stratum lucidum?
10   Are the cells in the stratum lucidum dead or alive?
11   Why is the stratum granulosum thought of as a transitional layer?
12   Are the cells in the stratum spinosum dead or alive?
13   How are the older cells in the germinating layer pushed upwards?
14   What is the function of the melanocytes in the germinating layer?
15   What is the epidermal transit time?
16   What happens to this time in psoriasis?

1.3   The dermis

The dermis has an average thickness of about 3 mm and may be divided into two layers.

The *papillary or upper layer* joins the epidermis in a series of ridges called dermal papillae. It is these ridges which are responsible for fingerprints. These papillae are well supplied with blood vessels to take essential nourishment to the growing cells of the epidermis. These blood vessels also constrict and dilate in response to the body temperature (constricting if cold and dilating if hot). This layer is continuous around the hair follicles. The papillary layer consists of white non-elastic fibres of the protein collagen, together with some yellow elastic fibres known as connective tissue and resembling a woven fabric.

Immediately below this layer is the *reticular layer*, which contains a dense network of collagen fibres arranged in layers. Between these collagen fibres are networks of elastic fibres which allow the skin to stretch and then return to normal size – as in pregnancy and weight loss. These fibres can increase in length by 100% and still return to their original size. These is a jelly-like 'ground substance' which absorbs water to make the skin turgid (the cells are full of water which makes them rigid and hard to touch, rather like an overfilled hot water bottle). This ground substance is composed of a variety of carbohydrates, proteins and lipids, the most important of which are mucopolysaccharides.

The dermis contains three different cell types:

(1) *Phagocytic cells*
    Phagocytes are white blood cells which surround and digest foreign matter which has entered the skin, such as bacteria. They are an important line of defence against infection.
(2) *Fibroblasts*
    Fibroblasts are concerned with the secretion of mucopolysaccharides for the ground substance and also the secretion of collagen fibres.
(3) *Mast cells*
    Mast cells secrete heparin and histamine when the skin is damaged. The heparin delays the clotting of blood and is used in medicine to prevent clotting. Histamine causes dilation of the blood vessels to bring extra blood to an injured area to aid repair. It is responsible for many of the effects associated with inflammation – irritation and other skin disorders. This is why anti-histamine tablets are taken by those who suffer from allergies, to reduce these effects.

Also found in the dermis are the nerve endings for pain, light touch, deep pressure, heat and cold. One network of nerve endings is found just below the epidermis and another in the lower dermis. As can be seen from Figure 1.1, there are Meissner's touch corpuscles just below the epidermis and Pacinian pressure corpuscles deeper in the dermis. Pain receptors are found as branched nerve endings in the upper and lower dermis. They slightly penetrate the lower epidermis. Temperature receptors are found in the middle of the epidermis as branched nerve endings. The function of these nerves is to relay sensory information to the brain so that the body can react to potential hazards, such as sharp or hot objects.

The glands of the skin, although found in the dermis, are actually downgrowths of the epidermis.

Questions 1.3

1   What is the average thickness of the dermis?
2   Name the two layers of the dermis.
3   How does the dermis join the epidermis?
4   Where can this be seen on the skin?
5   How are the cells of the epidermis nourished by the dermis?
6   What does the papillary layer consist of?
7   What are white fibres made of?
8   What do the yellow elastic fibres resemble?
9   Describe the function of the elastic fibres in weight loss or pregnancy.
10 What is the function of the jelly-like 'ground substance' that can be found in the dermis?
11 How many different cell types are found in the dermis?
12 What is the function of the phagocytic cells?
13 What is the function of the fibroblasts?

14   What is the function of heparin and where is it secreted?
15   Why are anti-histamines taken by some people?
16   What are the functions of the nerve endings found in the dermis?
17   Where in the skin are they found?

1.4   The glands of the skin

A gland is an organ which takes materials from the blood and transforms them into new substances which pass from the gland as a secretion. The glands of the skin pass their secretions into ducts from which they eventually end up on the skin surface. The three types of glands are shown in Figure 1.1.

Sebaceous glands

Sebaceous glands secrete sebum. Sebum is the major ingredient of the lipid (fatty material) which covers the skin and hair. Sebaceous glands are usually found attached to the sides of hair follicles but the large glands of the face open directly on to the skin surface. The glands are found on all areas of skin except the palms and soles and between the fingers and toes. The greatest concentration of the glands (between 400–900 glands per square centimetre) are found on the scalp, face, upper chest and shoulders. These are known as *seborrhoeic areas*.

Sebum is composed of glycerides, free fatty acids, wax esters, squalene and cholesterol. This oily secretion provides protection against fungal infections as it inhibits their growth. Sebaceous gland activity is controlled by the androgens – the male hormones – which are produced in the male testes and to a lesser extent in the female ovaries and adrenal glands, so women also develop active sebaceous glands. The effect of male hormones on these glands is linked to the development of acne at puberty in adolescent males and females (see Section 2.3).

Sebaceous glands are holocrine – that is, they break down their own cells to produce their secretions. The small cells on the outside of the gland move towards the centre. During this time they fill with lipid material and increase in size. At the opening into the hair follicle, the cell walls rupture to release the sebum. The loss of cells must be balanced by the production of new cells for the secretion of sebum to continue.

Eccrine sweat glands

Eccrine sweat glands are numerous in the skin and are found over most of the body surface. They have a tubular spiral duct lined with epidermal cells extending from their visible opening in the epidermis down into the dermis itself, where the tube becomes coiled and convoluted into a ball. This tubular gland secretes odourless sweat which rises up the duct to be released on the skin surface. The evaporation of sweat has a cooling effect but these glands secrete not only when the body is hot; they also respond to ultra-violet radiation, emotional stress and fevers. Sweating is controlled by the nervous system.

Although the composition of sweat is often quoted as 98% water and 2% sodium chloride, the sodium chloride content varies considerably. There are also small amounts of urea, amino acids and sugars in eccrine sweat.

The glands are most numerous on the palms of the hands and soles of the feet. Nervous sweating of these two areas is common – excessive sweating is called 'hyperidrosis'. Even in cool temperate climates we lose at least one litre (almost two pints) of sweat each day. Because the sweat evaporates from the whole skin surface over twenty-four hours we do not notice it. For this reason it is termed 'insensible' perspiration. In hot weather we sweat a lot more to help cool the body. This is called 'sensible' perspiration. Sweating during exercise can deplete the body of salt so that cramp develops. This is why long distance runners take salt tablets. Older textbooks refer to eccrine sweat glands as 'suderiferous' glands.

Stale eccrine sweat only really smells on the feet. Regular changing of socks or tights, together with regular washing of feet, is essential to help control this.

Aprocine sweat glands

These glands are associated with hair follicles in a number of areas such as the pubic region, armpits and nipples. They begin to develop and secrete sweat at puberty, and are under both hormonal and nervous control. The fresh secretion is milky and does not have any noticeable odour. The odour known as 'body odour' or B.O. develops once bacteria begin to break down the sweat. It is controlled by the use of deodorants and anti-perspirants (see Section 9.6). Older textbooks refer to these glands as 'odoriferous' glands.

Questions 1.4

1 What is the function of a gland?
2 How do secretions reach the skin surface?
3 What do the sebaceous glands secrete?
4 What are sebaceous glands attached to?
5 Which areas of the body do not have any sebaceous glands?
6 What are seborrhoeic areas?
7 What does sebum provide protection against?
8 What controls the activity of sebaceous glands?
9 How is acne linked to sebaceous gland activity?
10 Why are sebaceous glands also described as holocrine glands?
11 Where are eccrine sweat glands found?
12 How does sweat reach the skin surface?
13 What is the function of sweat?
14 What is sweating controlled by?
15 Where are the most eccrine sweat glands found?
16 What is sweat composed of?
17 What is hyperidrosis?
18 What does the term 'insensible' perspiration mean?
19 What does the term 'sensible' perspiration mean?
20 Why do long distance runners take salt tablets?
21 Does eccrine sweat usually smell?
22 Where are aprocine sweat glands found?
23 When do they start to secrete sweat?

24   What are apocrine glands under the control of?
25   How does body odour (B.O.) develop?
26   What can be used to control body odour?

1.5   *Your skin and how to look after it*

According to the classifications popularised by women's magazines there are four basic skin types: normal, dry, oil and combination. When women buy make-up or other beauty products there is often a descriptive label referring to one of these skin types. Remember that your skin type will vary with age and your state of health.

'Normal skin' is what everyone would like to possess but few of us do. Normal skin is fine-textured, smooth and rarely breaks out in spots. It retains its quality well with age but will probably become drier after thirty.

'Dry skin' does not retain moisture well. It dehydrates either because of a lack of sebum or because of the effects of heat (sun, wind and house heating). Dry skin is unlikely to develop spots, the pore openings being very small. This type of skin tends to age and develop wrinkles early.

'Oily skin' is due to over-active sebaceous glands. It shines because of the film of sebum that is always present. It also tends to break out in spots, and acne is often present. The skin pores are usually large and the hair is often oily and lank. Oily skin ages more slowly and develops fewer wrinkles. It may, however, be your skin type only in your teens and twenties, when it is heavily influenced by androgens (male hormones).

'Combination skin' is a mixture of oily and dry skin, the oily skin being in the shape of a 'T' (across the forehead and down the middle of the face).

Everyday skin care is important no matter what skin type you have. The most important principle is that the skin should be kept clean, without removing so much of the sebum that it becomes too dry. Your cleanser choice will therefore depend on the oiliness of your skin. Oily skins should be cleansed with a mild soap and water. To avoid roughening the skin, use warm water rather than hot (hot water would cause the blood vessels to dilate and the skin to redden), blot the skin dry with your towel and do not rub it. For dry skin, soap and water can be too powerful and a cleansing cream or lotion should be used instead. This will lift off dirt, dead skin cells and make-up without degreasing the skin. If the skin becomes too dry after washing, use a 'moisturiser'. This is an emollient cream or lotion, which provides protection for the skin from water loss. Moisturisers do not put water into the skin as the name suggests, but form a barrier to reduce water loss.

Preparations are marketed which claim to 'feed' the skin with 'natural' substances such as collagen or placental extracts. They may also claim to rejuvenate the skin by removing lines and wrinkles. This is misleading, since skin can only be nourished through its blood supply and lines can only be removed by cosmetic surgery. No one can escape the ravages of time, and how quickly the skin shows it depends on heredity (what skin your parents have) and exposure to weather (long-term exposure to sunlight definitely speeds up ageing). All you can do is delay the ageing process.

Most women use a combination of three types of cosmetics for their daily beauty routine: a cleanser, toner and moisturiser. As has already been said, the cleanser removes dirt, make-up and also, in the case of oily skin, sebum. The word 'toning' refers to freshening and tightening of the skin. Toners are 'astringent' – that is, they evaporate quickly to cool the skin and make the tiny skin muscles contract. Many contain alcohol which removes sebum so, if you have dry skin, look for a product without alcohol in it. A moisturiser is only really necessary if the skin is dry or has had the sebum removed by cleansing (after using soap). It leaves an oily film to help restrict water loss.

For many people, one of the pleasures of working is to be able to afford a holiday in the sun. For those with fair skins this often results in the pain of sunburn. The skin reddens and can peel and blister. Sunlight can also cause long-term damage. It can age the skin prematurely by damaging the supporting tissue or cause the development of skin tumours, including cancer. Cancer is most likely to develop in fair-skinned people who are exposed to a lot of sun. Sailors appear to be one of the groups of people at most risk. The growths mainly occur in those regions of the body that receive the greatest amount of light, such as the neck, head, arms and hands. The growths can usually be removed easily, skin cancer being generally completely curable if dealt with in time. Black people are noted for their resistance to this type of skin cancer, indicating that dark pigmentation protects them from the harmful effects of sunlight.

Sunburn is caused by UVB, the medium wavelength of ultra-violet radiation which is present in sunlight. It penetrates and damages the skin cells, thus causing the 'burning'. The body's natural protective reaction is to deposit melanin in the skin. This is why people from areas of the world with the strongest sunlight (and long daylight hours) have the darkest skin, while people from areas with weaker sunlight (and shorter daylight hours) have the fairest skin. If you have fair skin you can easily be burnt. *When you go into the sun you should restrict the first exposure to about twenty minutes.* Unfortunately for most people, this golden rule is often ignored and reddened skin is usually the result rather than a tan. On each subsequent day of the holiday, gradually increase the exposure to sunlight. Children and bald men are extremely susceptible to burning.

If you take sufficient care while sunbathing it is unnecessary to use suntan creams and lotions, which generally do not speed up the natural tanning process. Some products which claim to accelerate tanning, however, contain substances, such as oil of bergamot, which make the skin more sensitive to sunlight so that it tans more quickly. Doubts exist about their safety over a period of time.

Sunscreens and sunblocks will afford some protection against burning. Sunscreens contain an ingredient which is opaque to UVB which causes sunburn. It does, however, allow UVA, the longer wavelength of ultra-violet radiation which causes tanning without sunburn, to pass through. Sunscreens are available in the form of lotions, creams, mousses and oils.

Sunblocks contain an ingredient which is opaque to both types of ultra-violet rays, so it not only reduces the risk of burning but also prevents tanning. These are available in the form of lotions, creams, mousses and oils.

Some suncreams are emollients and only offer protection against the drying effects of the sun and wind. Remember that if you swim much of your suntan product will be washed off, so it is important to reapply as required if protection is to be maintained. Also, remember that a suntan does not develop instantaneously. The skin will change colour some time after you have been in the sun. So if someone tells you that you are turning red, there will be some later burning even if you get out of the sun immediately. If you do get burnt, taking a cool shower or bath will help reduce pain. Calamine lotion is very cooling and excellent for sunburn. If the skin blisters try not to break them, as they protect against infection.

Sunburn occurs in four stages:

(1) Minimal erythema (erythema is a term for redness of skin) is produced by twenty minutes' exposure of fair skin to sun on a typically British summer's day. It is a slight red or pink coloration of the skin. Obviously, this effect is speeded up in hot climates.
(2) Vivid erythema is produced by fifty minutes' exposure to the sun, producing a bright red coloration but no pain.
(3) Painful burning accompanied by vivid erythema is produced by one hundred minutes' exposure to sun.
(4) Blistering burning is produced by two hundred minutes' exposure to sun. It produces vivid erythema, a high level of pain, blistering and peeling.

You can get sunburnt on a cloudy day, or by the reflection of sunlight off sand or snow. Going on a winter holiday to ski is a sure way of getting a tan. Sunbeds do not burn because they use tubes which produce only UVA. Sunlamps, however, usually produce UVB which can burn; this radiation can also cause conjunctivitis (inflammation of the mucous membrane covering the eyeball) so follow the manufacturer's instructions. Goggles should be worn with both sunbeds and sunlamps or the eyes could be damaged – perhaps seriously.

Fake tanning creams and lotions produce a 'tan' which can look natural. It is important to find the product that suits your skin by 'patch testing' different brands. Some may give a more yellow to orange colour on certain skins. Tablets have been marketed which will produce a tan in the skin, working by depositing pigment, but many people have to discontinue their use when the palms of their hands turn orange!

Black skins can also get burnt by the sun, although it is unlikely because of the amount of melanin present. Black skin is also more resistant to the ageing process brought about by sunlight, because of the protection afforded by the melanin.

Questions 1.5

1   What are the four basic skin types?
2   What causes changes in skin type?
3   Give a brief description of the four basic skin types.
4   What do you consider your type to be?
5   What is the most important principle of everyday skin care?
6   Why is warm rather than hot water used on the skin?
7   What type of cleanser is most suitable for oily skin?
8   What type of cleanser is most appropriate for dry skin?
9   How does a moisturiser help to protect the skin?
10 How is the skin nourished?

11   How can lines and wrinkles be removed from the skin?
12   What is the ageing of skin caused by?
13   What effect does an astringent have on the skin?
14   Which cosmetic preparations have an astringent action?
15   What short and long-term damage can sunlight cause to the skin?
16   Which wavelength of ultra-violet radiation causes sunburn?
17   How can someone with fair skin avoid sunburn?
18   Which wavelength of ultra-violet radiation causes the skin to tan?
19   What is the action of a sunscreen?
20   What is the action of a sunblock?
21   What does an emollient suncream offer protection against?
22   How would you treat sunburn?
23   What are the four stages of sunburn?
24   Why do you not get sunburn with a sunbed?
25   Why can you get sunburn with a sunlamp?
26   Why should goggles be worn when using either a sunbed or a sunlamp?

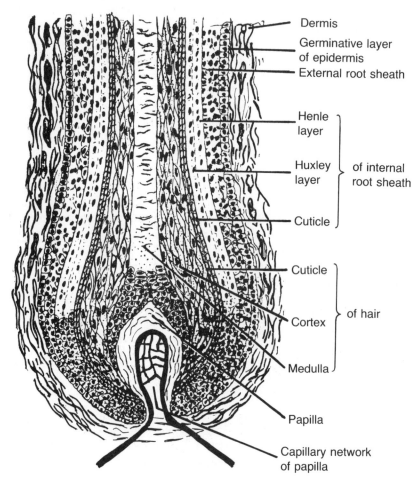

Fig. 1.3(a)   Longitudinal section of a hair in a follicle.

27   What other methods are there of tanning the skin?

28   Why is black skin more resistant to the ageing process?

1.6   The structure of the hair and hair follicle

The hair is composed of a dead protein called keratin. The hair itself is arranged in three layers, an outer cuticle, middle cortex and central medulla. If the hair is coloured, it is due to the presence of pigments – either melanin (black-brown) or pheomelanin (red-yellow). If these are lacking, the hair is white. Canities is the term given to grey hair. It is an illusion created by the mixture of white and coloured hairs. Individual 'grey' hairs do not exist.

Hair grows from a follicle, as is shown in both longitudinal and cross section in Figure 1.3. The walls of the follicle form the outer root sheath of the hair. The lower part of the follicle widens out to form the hair bulb which contains the germinal matrix, the source of hair growth. Dermal tissue projects into the follicle base to form the dermal papilla, and this has a network of capillary blood vessels to supply oxygen, energy and the amino acids needed for growth. Melanocytes are present in the upper part of the papilla, producing pigment granules which are distributed throughout the cortex.

In the follicle the hair is surrounded by an inner root sheath which has three layers. Henlé's layer is one cell thick and lies next to the outer root sheath. Huxley's layer is two or three cells thick and is in the middle of the sheath. The cuticle of this inner root sheath interlocks with the cuticle of the hair. Both the hair and the inner

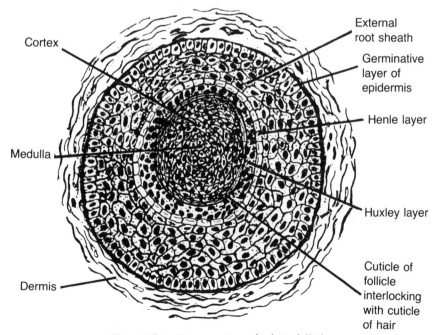

Fig. 1.3(b)   Cross section of a hair follicle.

root sheath grow at the same rate. But the inner root sheath breaks down about two-thirds of the way up the follicle, so only the hair emerges past the skin surface. Uncut hairs have a pointed tip.

Questions 1.6

1	What is the hair made of?
2	What are the three layers of the hair?
3	Name the black-brown pigment of the hair.
4	Name the red-yellow pigment of the hair.
5	What colour is the hair if there is no pigment present?
6	What is the term used to describe grey hair?
7	What causes the hair to look grey?
8	Where does the hair grow from?
9	Where is the hair bulb?
10	Why is the hair bulb important to hair growth?
11	Why are melanocytes present in the papilla?
12	What is the function of the inner root sheath?
13	How would you know if a hair had been cut?

1.7 The hair growth cycle

Each hair follicle undergoes a cycle of activity. The hair grows to a maximum length, then hair growth ceases and the hair is shed and replaced. The growth cycle has three distinct phases:

(1) *Anagen*: the period of active growth   *Active*
                                                                              ↓
(2) *Catagen*: the period of breakdown and change   *Collapsing*
                                                                              ↓
(3) *Telogen*: the resting stage before resumption of growth   *Tired*

(Remember this sequence by the mnemonic *ACT*)

Read the next section in conjunction with Figure 1.4.

(1) *Anagen*
    The epidermal cells surrounding the dermal papilla form the germinal matrix or root of the hair. These cells are constantly dividing, and as new cells are formed they push the older ones upwards where they begin to change shape. By the time the cells are about one-third of the way up the follicle they are dead and fully keratinised. A scalp hair will grow actively for between one and a half and seven years (three years being an average growth period). The average growth rate is about 1.25 cm per month (roughly a half inch). On average 85% of follicles are in anagen.
(2) *Catagen*
    This is the end of the active growth period, and is marked by changes occurring in the follicle. The hair stops growing and becomes detached from the base of

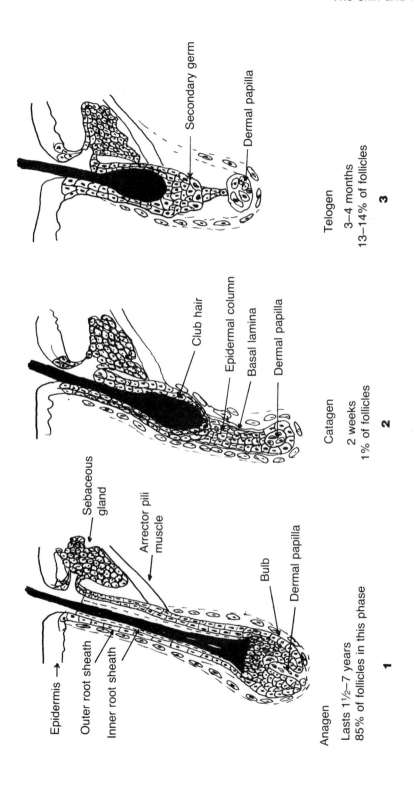

Secondary germ

Dermal papilla

Telogen
3–4 months
13–14% of follicles

3

Club hair

Epidermal column

Basal lamina

Dermal papilla

Catagen
2 weeks
1% of follicles

2

Epidermis →

Outer root sheath

Inner root sheath

Sebaceous gland

Arrector pili muscle

Bulb

Dermal papilla

Anagen
Lasts 1½–7 years
85% of follicles in this phase

1

Fig. 1.4   The hair growth cycle. (1) Anagen. (2) Catagen. (3) Telogen.

the follicle forming a club hair. The hair bulb begins to break down, resulting in the follicle becoming shorter. A small section of the outer root sheath remains in contact with the group of cells which formed the hair papilla. This period of breakdown or change lasts two weeks. As the inner root sheath breaks down, the hair remains in the follicle because of its shape. On average, 1% of follicles are in catagen.

(3) *Telogen*

The section of remaining root sheath still in contact with the papilla is known as the secondary or root germ. It is from this germ that a new hair can grow. The shortened follicle rests for three to four months. The hair may be brushed out at this time or at the onset of anagen. On average, 13 to 14% of follicles are in telogen.

After telogen, the cycle returns to anagen and the root germ begins to grow downwards and forms a new bulb around the dermal papilla. It is the lower end of the germ which forms the new bulb, producing a new hair. The upper part of the germ forms the new cells which lengthen the follicle below the club hair. The new hair may push the old hair out. You may see two hairs in a follicle. The hair will again appear as in the first diagram in Figure 1.4.

The average daily loss of hairs is between sixty and one hundred hairs a day. If the loss is over one hundred hairs daily, hair loss will exceed replacement – and you become bald. During the year you may notice a 'moult' of extra hair loss in the autumn or spring (this is related to change of daylight).

There are some rare cases of individuals (both male and female) who lose all their hair regularly every seven years, as their growth cycle is not continuous. They remain bald for about four months and then hair regrows.

- Hair growth is fastest from the age of sixteen to the late twenties. New hairs grow faster and the growth rate slows down with increasing length (almost half the rate when the hair is a metre long).
- Does cutting hair make it grow faster? All experiments say *no*.
- Irritation (due to sunburn, dermatitis or drugs) *can* increase growth rate and cause hair to grow in areas where hair would not normally be found.
- The hair growth rate can be slowed down during illness and pregnancy, by a lack of thyroid hormone and as a side-effect of the contraceptive pill.
- Hair grows faster in summer because of the ultra-violet in sunlight which speeds up cell division.

Figure 1.5 shows the average number of hairs on the scalp, according to the natural colour of the hair.

Questions 1.7

1   What does ACT stand for?
2   What happens in the three phases of the hair growth cycle?
3   How are older cells pushed up through the hair follicle?
4   When do the cells become fully keratinised?

Hair colour	Number of hairs
Natural blonde	140,000
Natural red	90,000
Natural brown	110,000
Natural black	108,000

Fig. 1.5   Average number of hairs on the scalp, according to the colour of the hair.

5   For how long will a scalp hair grow actively?
6   What is the average growth rate of the hair?
7   How many hairs are lost on average each day?
8   How does the time of year affect hair loss?
9   At what age is hair growth fastest?
10   Does cutting the hair speed up growth?
11   What can cause hair growth in areas where it does not normally grow?
12   What could cause hair growth to slow down?
13   How does the number of hairs on the scalp vary with natural hair colour?

1.8   The nails

The nails grow in a similar way to the hair, by the mitosis (cell division) of cells in the germinating layer of the epidermis. Like the hair, the cells are filled with keratin and die. This is why it does not hurt to cut hair or nails, because they are dead.

The nail consists of a plate of hard keratin which is produced by mitosis in the matrix at the base of the nail. Part of the matrix can be seen through the translucent nail plate as the pale area called the lunula or half moon. The colour of the nail is due to the blood vessels of the dermis beneath the nail plate. The cuticle is an extension of the horny layer of the epidermis. It prevents germs entering the skin at the nail fold (see Figure 1.6).

Fingernails grow more rapidly than toenails, as you can tell if you compare how many times you need to cut them both. It would take between three and six months to regrow completely a fingernail that was lost, and even longer for a toenail. As the nail grows it moves along a groove on either side of the nail. Folds of skin overlap the sides and base of the nail to protect the nails from infection.

Nails should be kept clean as the dirt that can accumulate underneath them provides a breeding ground for germs. Nails should also be kept short so that they do not scratch the client's scalp or catch in the hair. Hairdressers use strong detergents in shampoos which remove oil from nails, leaving them brittle and more susceptible to infection, such as ringworm. Nail varnish offers protection against this, as it coats the nail with a plastic resin. Ingredients such as glycerol keep the plastic coating soft and prevent flaking. Nail varnish removers can also cause nails to become brittle, so an oily remover should be used (nail varnish remover simply dissolves the plastic so it can be wiped off).

A number of disorders can affect the nails:

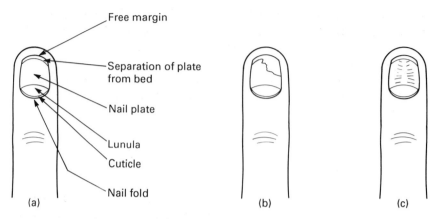

Fig. 1.6 (a) The structure of a nail. (b) Onycholysis. (c) Longitudinal groove.

Paronychia This is inflammation of the tissue around the nail, which can be caused by damage to the cuticle, especially if manicure tools are not sterile. An abscess or whitlow may result as the nail fold becomes red, tender and swollen. Pus may exude from the nail fold if gentle pressure is applied. This is an occupational hazard to people who frequently immerse their hands in water. It is essential to keep the hands as dry as possible and avoid manicuring your nails. If it persists, seek medical advice.

Onycholysis This is the separation of the nail plate from the nail bed which may result from an accident, or as the result of ringworm, infection, psoriasis, thyroid disease or dermatitis (see Figure 1.6). Medical advice should be sought if it is not due to an accident.

Koilonychia This term applies to a concave dip in the nail surface, like the inside of a spoon. The nails are thin and soft. It is usually a sign of iron-deficiency but can be due to repeated exposure to strong detergents. Seek medical advice.

Onychogryphosis This term refers to curving and thickening of the nail. It is usually due to damage such as might result from having the fingernail trodden on or slammed in a car door. See a chiropodist, as in severe cases the nail may have to be removed.

Ridges These may be longitudinal or transverse across the nail plate, and may be seen in psoriasis, eczema and fungal infection. Seek the advice of a chiropodist or doctor if you are worried about fungal infection.

Grooves These are usually longitudinal and may be due to physical or chemical damage. Picking at the cuticle produces the groove shown in Figure 1.6. Cuticle removers which contain caustic chemicals such as sodium hydroxide can cause this type of damage chemically. Try to eliminate the cause of the grooving.

Beau's lines These are caused in some people by severe illnesses which can also affect the matrix of the nail. The date of the illness can be estimated from the position of the line, which is a transverse groove across the nail.

Brittle nails These are nails which are easily split or break at the free edge. Brittle nails are caused by frequent use of detergent or solvents (including nail varnish remover). Keep hands dry, wear rubber gloves, and wear nail varnish which contains nylon fibres to strengthen the nail. Eating gelatin is unlikely to do anything to strengthen the nails although many people 'swear' by it. The protein will be broken down into amino acids by the body like all other proteins, so has no special property that enables it to strengthen the nails.

Soft nails Nails can be softened by constant immersion in water or by contact with alkaline chemicals. Perm lotions and relaxers will soften the nails in the same way as the hair during processing. Wear rubber gloves and keep the hands dry.

Discoloured nails Yellow nails may be due to psoriasis (Section 3.1) or ringworm (Section 2.5), which cause thickening of the nail plate. They may also be caused by smoking or staining by nail varnish. A blue-black area under the nail is due to physical damage that has caused bleeding and clotting of blood under the nail. Hitting your nail with a hammer produces what is commonly called 'black man's pinch'. Small white spots on the nails are common and are due to air pockets in the keratin. These may be due to nail damage causing a portion of the nail to separate from the nail bed. There is no remedy and the spots must be allowed to grow out. They are not caused by calcium deficiency as many people believe.

A number of products are available for the nails. Nail hardeners consist of formaldehyde resins, which help prevent nail breakage and peeling. Many people buy nail hardeners in an attempt to grow their nails longer. Many people, however, become allergic to these resins, resulting in swelling of the skin around the nail. Use nail hardeners with care and follow the instructions provided.

If you have been carefully growing your nails but the calamity of a split occurs, all is not lost! Nail menders can be applied which coat the nail with several layers of nylon or rayon fibres. Each coat is allowed to dry before the next is applied. Many people have used 'super glue' to mend their broken nails with good results.

Artificial or false nails have enabled many people to develop long nails instantly, without the inconvenience of waiting for them to grow. There are two major types: ones which are 'painted' on and ones which are glued on.

Paint-on nails consist of a plastic polymer and a hardener which are mixed just before application. They are brushed over the nail as a thick liquid which hardens and becomes firmly attached to the nail. The chemicals can cause dermatitis and as the nail must grow out with the natural nail, great care must be taken. Try one nail first as it cannot be removed.

False nails can be attached to the natural nails by the use of adhesives. The artificial nail is glued in place and filed to shape. Since the nail underneath can soften, these nails should not be left in place for more than a few days. There is a danger of moisture getting under the false nail, which not only causes softening, but makes the nail susceptible to infection. Nails are also available which can last for months without removal. These must be well-fitted to avoid softening of the nail underneath.

Questions 1.8

1   How are the nails and hair alike?
2   Draw a simple labelled diagram of the nail.
3   What is the colour of the nail due to?
4   What is the function of the cuticle?
5   How do you know which type of nail grows quickest?
6   How should the hairdresser care for her nails?
7   What is paronychia?
8   How is paronychia caused?
9   What is onycholysis?
10   How can onycholysis be caused?
11   What is koilonychia?
12   What are the possible causes of koilonychia?
13   What is onychogryphosis?
14   How can onychogryphosis be caused?
15   When might ridges be seen on the nails?
16   What are the causes of grooving in the nails?
17   What are Beau's lines?
18   How can the hairdresser avoid brittle nails?
19   What causes soft nails?
20   Why are nails sometimes discoloured?
21   What are nail hardeners and why must they be used with care?
22   How can broken nails be repaired?
23   Describe the two main types of false nail.
24   What are the dangers of having false nails?

2
Infectious Diseases

2.1 What is an infectious disease?

An infectious disease is a disease that can be passed to other people by the transfer of micro-organisms. Contagious diseases are simply diseases that can be 'caught', directly by contact with an infected person or indirectly by contact with an infected object. Contagious diseases are therefore also infectious.

There are three groups of micro-organisms that can cause infectious diseases: bacteria, fungi and viruses. These micro-organisms may spread from one infected individual to others by two methods:

(1) *By direct contact with the infected person:*
  (a) By touching an infected area of the body – for example, by kissing.
  (b) By droplet infection, in which air-borne droplets from the infected person are inhaled. These droplets may be produced during sneezing, coughing, spitting or talking. Colds and influenza are spread by this method, especially in poorly ventilated, overcrowded conditions.
(2) *By indirect contact with an infected article* such as a towel or brush. Some infections are spread indirectly in food.

The body has a number of ways of protecting itself against disease. The skin has an acid pH which helps inhibit the growth of micro-organisms. The respiratory tract is lined with mucus, hairs and tiny cilia to trap any micro-organisms that are breathed in. The stomach secretes hydrochloric acid as part of the digestive process and this will kill some micro-organisms taken in with food.

Once micro-organisms are inside the body, wandering white blood cells will recognise them as 'foreign' bodies and try to ingest them. This process is known as phagocytosis, with the white blood cells literally 'eating' the micro-organisms. White blood cells attack any object in the skin that they recognise as foreign, such as splinters or even an ingrowing toenail. As they attack it pus is formed and extra blood flow causes the area to inflame.

Pus is the remains of dead bacteria, white blood cells and lymph. Lymphocytes will produce antibodies against the infection. These combine with the micro-organism, rather like two pieces of a jig-saw, and make it harmless. For many infections the lymphocytes carry a 'memory', so that after an initial first exposure they can quickly produce antibodies for subsequent infections. This is the purpose of vaccination or immunisation, where a modified form of the micro-organism is injected into an individual to produce a memory population of antibodies. This modified form of micro-organism does not produce the disease. The body also produces antitoxins which counteract the effects of poisons produced by bacteria. This mode of defence is important in blood poisoning.

Raising the body temperature is another method of fighting infection, as it speeds up the chemical reactions used to attack the micro-organisms.

Antibiotics such as penicillin are chemical substances produced by micro-organisms that will inhibit the growth of other micro-organisms. They can fight infections caused by bacteria and fungi but not viruses, as viruses invade the cells of the host.

The spread of infection can be minimised by hygienic daily routines, both for yourself and in the salon (see Chapters 5, 6 and 9).

Questions 2.1

1   What is an infectious disease?
2   Name the three micro-organisms that cause infectious diseases.
3   In what two ways can these micro-organisms be passed from one person to another?
4   Give examples of how infection could be spread in the salon.
5   How does the body protect itself from disease?
6   How does the body protect itself once a foreign body enters the skin?
7   What is pus and how is it formed?
8   How do lymphocytes work in fighting infection?
9   What is the purpose of vaccination or immunisation?
10   What diseases have you been vaccinated against?
11   What are antitoxins?
12   How does a rise in body temperature help to fight infection?
13   How do antibiotics work?
14   Why are viruses not killed by antibiotics?
15   How can the spread of infection be minimised?

2.2   Bacteria

Bacteria are minute, single-celled organisms. The human body carries a number of bacteria, many of which are harmless, but some can cause disease. The harmless bacteria are described as *non-pathogenic*, whereas the disease causing bacteria are described as *pathogenic*. The term 'pathogen' is used to describe any type of micro-organism that causes infection.

Bacteria are too small to be seen with the naked eye, so are looked at with the aid

Cocci are the *spherical or round* bacteria. In adverse conditions they are able to protect themselves by forming tough outer coats. In this condition they are known as *spores*.

When round bacteria are seen to be in clumps, they are called *staphylococci*. These are the type of bacteria which cause acne, boils and barber's rash.

When round bacteria are seen to be in chains, they are called *streptococci*. These are the type of bacteria which cause impetigo and sore throats.

Rod-shaped bacteria are known as *bacilli*. They cause some serious diseases, including diphtheria and typhoid.

These *spiral*-shaped bacteria are known as *spirochaetes*. The venereal disease syphilis is caused by bacteria from this group.

These *comma*-shaped bacteria are known as *vibrios*. They cause one major disease which is of importance to man – cholera.

Fig. 2.1   Bacteria cannot be seen with the naked eye; it is neccessary to use a microscope. Bacteria may be classified according to their shape and the major groups are indicated above.

of a microscope. Bacteria are classified according to their shape; the major groups, together with examples of diseases that they cause, are illustrated in Figure 2.1.

In favourable conditions bacteria reproduce themselves by splitting into two. This *cell division* is called *mitosis*. The first bacterium produces two identical cells from the first parent cell, the two divide to form four, the four divide to form eight, and so on. This can happen every twenty minutes and can carry on indefinitely in the correct conditions. Six conditions are necessary:

(1) A supply of food.
(2) Moisture (dryness can prevent growth).
(3) A suitably warm temperature. Most bacteria grow well at body temperature (37°C) but can be killed by higher temperatures (usually above 70°C). Low temperatures stop or slow down bacterial growth. This is why we store food in cold conditions, because bacteria will quickly multiply in warmth and 'spoil' the food.
(4) A supply of oxygen. Bacteria that need atmospheric oxygen are classified as *aerobic*. If bacteria can exist without oxygen they are classified as *anaerobic*.
(5) Darkness. Bacteria are killed by ultra-violet radiation which is present in natural sunlight.
(6) Slightly alkaline conditions, a pH of between 7 and 8. They do not grow well at the natural acid-balanced pH of the skin and hair (which have a pH of about 5.4).

All six of these conditions are provided by the blood, so great care must be taken to stop bacteria entering the bloodstream. If they do, blood poisoning can develop rapidly.

In adverse conditions some types of bacteria (also fungi, see Section 2.4) form spores. This is a way of surviving when other bacteria would die. The spore develops within the individual bacterium and produces a resistant outer wall. This spore wall thickens and eventually the spore is released from the parent cell. This is shown in Figure 2.2. A mature spore can exist in a dormant state for a long period of time. It is resistant to heat, cold, drying and even disinfectants. Once a suitable environment is available the spore germinates and the spore wall splits to release a bacterial cell. Spores are the last to be killed during sterilisation.

The bacteria that cause tetanus (Clostridium tetani) form spores which are found in the soil. If someone is cut by a dirty object, or dirt enters a wound, tetnus can

Fig. 2.2 The formation of a spore. The spore appears inside the parent cell as a small area which gradually increases in size. The spore wall thickens until the spore is eventually released from the parent cell.

develop. The bacteria produce a toxin which causes violent muscle spasms and eventual death. Tetanus can be prevented by vaccination, for which booster injections are given every five years and immediately after a suspect injury, such as a cut on a rusty blade. Temporary immunity can be given to someone who has not been vaccinated, by an injection of antitoxin. Hairdressers and beauty therapists should be vaccinated against tetanus as they will cut themselves occasionally, and even though the tetanus spores should not really be found in a clean salon they might be present in pot plant soil.

Questions 2.2

1 What is a pathogen?
2 What is the difference between pathogenic and non-pathogenic bacteria?
3 How are bacteria classified?
4 How do bacteria reproduce themselves?
5 What is mitosis?
6 How quickly do bacteria reproduce?
7 List the six conditions necessary for bacteria to reproduce?
8 What are cocci?
9 What are staphylococci and what infectious diseases can they cause?
10 What are streptococci and what infectious diseases can they cause?
11 What are bacilli and what infectious diseases can they cause?
12 What are spiral-shaped bacteria known as and what disease can they cause?
13 What are comma-shaped bacteria called?
14 Can bacteria be seen with the naked eye?
15 How is blood poisoning caused?
16 How can bacteria survive adverse conditions?
17 What is the difference between aerobic and anaerobic bacteria?
18 What is the last to be killed during sterilisation?
19 Why should a hairdresser be vaccinated against tetanus?

2.3 Skin infections caused by bacteria

Most of these conditions are caused by staphylococci and streptococci and can be cleared with antibiotics.

(1) Furuncles and carbuncles

A furuncle, commonly known as a boil, is a deep abscess of a hair follicle due to infection by staphylococci. It starts as a slightly raised, tender red area of skin. This rapidly develops into a large and painful pustule, with a characteristic head. It discharges a greenish-yellow core and pus. Boils are most common in young men, usually on the back of the neck, buttocks, groin or armpits. They may be caused by poor hygiene, such as inadequate washing, or by stress or diabetes. Some people carry the bacteria that cause boils in their nose or groin. A doctor should be consulted, especially if you are prone to boils. Heat will help bring up the developing boil – use a clean flannel with hot water. After a boil has burst, magnesium sulphate paste on a dressing will help to draw out any remaining infection. Boils often leave scars. You will often see such scars on men's necks.

A carbuncle is a number of boils together, often described as being 'multi-headed'. It can be a serious condition if neglected, as it can cause blood poisoning (septicaemia). A doctor will often decide to lance carbuncles as part of the treatment. Abscesses in the armpits, sometimes brought on by aerosol sprays, can also cause blood poisoning so medical help should be sought.

Recurrent or severe cases of furuncles or carbuncles may need treatment with antibiotics.

(2)   Impetigo

Impetigo is a superficial skin infection that can be caused by both staphylococci and streptococci, often acting together. The usual sites for impetigo are the face and any area where the skin has been irritated; it can, for instance, be a secondary infection of lice, scabies and eczema (see Chapters 3 and 4). The infection starts as a raised red area of skin which quickly forms small blisters. Later these become covered with yellow crusts which can be removed to show an area of moist pink skin beneath. The disease is very contagious, especially in young children. It can be spread quickly where things such as make-up and towels are shared. A doctor should be consulted and great care should be taken not to spread the infection by direct or·indirect contact. Antibiotic creams are often enough to clear impetigo, which does not normally leave scars. A client with impetigo should not be given service in the salon in case the infection is spread.

(3)   Sycosis barbae

This is folliculitis of the beard area in men. It is a staphylococcal infection which typically is seen as an area of tender red skin. Common names for the condition include 'barber's itch' or 'rash'. It is often spread on infected shaving equipment, so razors and shaving brushes should be washed in boiling water or disinfectant. Treatment is with antibiotic creams or with a course of antibiotics if it persists. A doctor should be seen if the infection does not respond to improved hygiene. A picture of barber's itch is shown in Figure 2.3. Razors should never be shared and women should not shave their legs with a razor used by a man in case they develop the infection.

(4)   Acne vulgaris

Acne is so common during adolescence that it is abnormal not to suffer from it. The severity of the condition varies from a few pimples and blackheads to severe forms where most of the face is involved. It is possible for a pit-like scar to be left in some severe infections.

The skin first develops blackheads (comedones), and these are eventually followed by inflamed areas containing pustules. The face, chest and back are the three places that are mostly affected, as these correspond to the areas of sebaceous glands that become active at puberty. About 90% of teenagers develop acne to some extent.

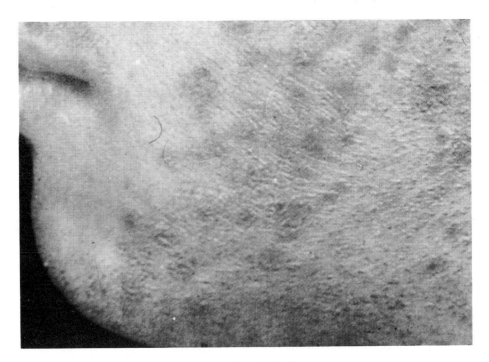

Fig. 2.3 Sycosis barbae.

The cause of acne has been debated for years. Older textbooks suggest that excess amounts of greasy foods, especially chips, are important. Some teenagers claim that eating a bar of chocolate is enough to bring on an attack of acne. The prevalence of acne decreases after adolescence, even if the chocolate eating doesn't. Activation of the sebaceous glands by androgenic stimulation is the main cause of acne, not diet.

There is a type of bacillus which breaks down sebum into fatty acids and it can be found on the follicle near the sebaceous gland. A blackhead or comedone is formed when the epidermal keratin is trapped with sebum to form a plug that eventually oxidises and darkens. This is rather like mixing some cooking oil with flour, which will begin to oxidise after some time in the air and form the equivalent of a 'blackhead'.

The mouth of the follicle in acne thus becomes blocked and staphylococci, which are already present in the follicle, begin to breed in the plug and cause the formation of a pustule. Some doctors will treat acne as a trivial condition which will be grown out of, but it does not seem trivial when you have it. Try the following to keep it in check:

● Wash frequently to remove sebum.
● Use skin peelers which are available over the counter. They help to unblock the follicles and also reduce the bacterial population of the skin. Examples include Clearasil and Pan Oxyl 5. They make the skin more sensitive to sunlight after use, so be extra careful of burning.
● Use antiseptics to help control bacteria.

- Cut out any foods you associate with acne attacks.
- Get as much sunlight as possible as this helps clear the skin. Sun tan lamps can be used in winter.
- Ask your doctor for antibiotics if you have long-term acne.
- Taking oral contraceptives will help reduce sebum flow if they are based on oestrogens. Those which contain progesterone may make acne worse.
- The 'pre-menstrual' flare of acne which happens each month in females is due to water retention obstructing follicles. Little can be done to prevent it.

If you suffer from blackheads, comedone extractors are available. There are two types: one is a metal implement which is pressed against the blackhead to force it out from the skin, while the other is a little like a hypodermic syringe without a needle. This extracts the blackhead by forming a vacuum into which the blackhead is sucked.

(5)   Folliculitis

Folliculitis is caused by a bacterial infection of a follicle, so it is similar to a furuncle except that there is a hair protruding from the follicle opening. Occasionally a hair 'pierces' the side of a hair follicle instead of growing out of the follicle opening. The body will then recognise it as foreign.

This 'ingrowing' hair will cause inflammation in the dermis because of irritation, but there is usually secondary infection by staphylococci to produce a raised area. Ingrowing hairs are termed 'pseudo-folliculitis'.

Folliculitis is very common in the beard area of black men and the legs of women after waxing. Shaving cuts the hair off at skin level and the curly hair ingrows. To prevent this many black men use chemical depilatory creams which simply dissolve their 'stubble'. Ingrowing hairs can be removed with tweezers. A service should not be given to a client with folliculitis of the scalp hairs as it can be infectious.

Questions 2.3

1   What type of bacteria cause the majority of bacterial skin conditions?
2   Can they be cleared up with antibiotics?
3   What is a furuncle commonly known as?
4   How does a furuncle develop?
5   What bacteria causes furuncles?
6   Where are furuncles usually found and how would you recognise one?
7   How should furuncles be looked after?
8   What is a carbuncle?
9   What is septicaemia?
10   Would medical treatment be necessary for furuncles or carbuncles?
11   What type of bacteria cause impetigo?
12   Where is impetigo usually found?
13   How would you recognise impetigo?
14   Why could impetigo develop as a secondary infection of some other conditions?
15   How can impetigo be spread?
16   How is impetigo usually treated?

17   Would you give a service to a client with impetigo?
18   What bacteria causes sycosis barbae?
19   What other common names is sycosis barbae known as?
20   How is sycosis barbae spread?
21   How can the infection be prevented?
22   At what age do most people suffer from acne vulgaris?
23   How does the severity of the condition vary?
24   Which areas of the skin are mainly affected?
25   What is the cause of acne?
26   How is a blackhead or commedone formed?
27   What can be done to prevent acne?
28   Why do many girls get acne immediately prior to a period?
29   What are commedone extractors?
30   What is folliculitis?
31   What condition is folliculitis similar to and how would you distinguish between the two conditions?
32   What is the connection between ingrowing hairs and folliculitis?
33   Would you offer a service to a client with folliculitis of the scalp?
34   Why is folliculitis common in the beard area of black men?
35   Where is folliculitis commonly found in women?

2.4 Fungi   *CAPITALS*

Fungi are plants which contain no chlorophyll (green colouring matter) so cannot make their own food. The majority of fungi are *nonpathogenic saprophytes* (a saprophyte lives on dead or decaying materials). There are two main types of fungi: *filamentous* and *yeast-like*. The filamentous ones do not have cells like most organisms; they grow as a tangled mass of thin threads of hyphae. The whole collection is called a *mycelium*. This spreads over the food material on which the fungi grows. Filamentous fungi are responsible for ringworm. The yeasts live as single cells, and are used in both brewing and baking. Some are parasitic and cause thrush and nappy rash.

Questions 2.4

1   What are fungi?
2   Why do the majority of fungi live on dead materials?
3   What is the difference between the two main types of fungi?
4   What type of fungi cause ringworm and thrush?

2.5 Skin infections caused by fungi   *Underline block. Write.*

Ringworm   *CAPITAL S*

All ringworm fungi are highly contagious and have two main actions on the skin. The first is an irritant action caused by their rapid growth and the toxic affect of the enzyme which results in inflammation. The second is a corrosive action on the epidermis, hair and nails due to the production of a keratin-splitting enzyme.

Most ringworm fungi are transmitted through direct or indirect contact. Examples of the latter include towels, floors, clothing, cutting tools, brushes, etc. These can be contaminated with skin or hair fragments. Ringworm is usually described according to the area of the body affected.

(1)   Ringworm of the feet — Tinea pedis

This is commonly known as *athlete's foot*, and is the most common fungal complaint in Britain. The commonest type involves the skin between the fourth and fifth toes, spreading to the other toes and occasionally involving the soles. The skin is sodden and white, often rubbing off to leave a raw area underneath. It is most common in summer because the feet sweat more. The fungus is usually spread indirectly, on changing room floors. It can be cleared by using fungicidal creams or dusting powders. The socks or tights of sufferers should be washed at the hottest cycle of a washing machine.

(2)   Ringworm of the beard — Tinea barbae

This condition is now rare and most likely to be seen in country areas. The infected area looks like the site of small boils, at the tip of which a broken hair projects. It is spread by contact with dirty towels or razors in the salon. Treatment is with anti-biotics such as griseofulvin.

This condition could be confused with two bacterial diseases – boils and sycosis barbae. Boils will usually be few and widely spaced, while with sycosis barbae the lesions are less raised and a wide area of skin is usually involved.

(3)   Ringworm of the body — Tinea corporis

This is usually seen on exposed parts of the body, such as the face, arms and shoulders. Pink circular patches, which are often scaly, are characteristic of this condition. It is usually caught by direct contact with an infected individual.

(4)   Ringworm of the groin — Tinea cruris

This is a condition associated with excessive heat and sweating. It is seen most often in Britain in people like laundry workers and bakers. This is found mainly in men, and is spread by indirect contact with infected towels and from a person's own fungal foot infection. The rash is often itchy, and has a well-defined edge which may be blistery and scaly. In hot climates such as India it may be known as the 'dhobi itch'.

(5)   Ringworm of the nails — Tinea unguium

This type of ringworm is very damaging because it can cause permanent nail damage. It is a difficult condition to clear quickly, and can last several months. The disease is highly infectious and must be covered with gloves to avoid spreading infection. The nails become yellow and powdery. People with weak nails are most likely to develop the condition, which is usually spread by direct contact.

(6) Ringworm of the scalp — Tinea capitis

This fungus attacks the newly formed keratin of a growing hair at the point where the shaft emerges from the scalp. By eating away at the keratin the hair becomes brittle and often breaks away leaving short stubs. The disease starts in one or more areas of the scalp as small patches which spread out at the edges. It can involve the whole scalp. It is usually caught by direct contact.

The patch itself is covered with white or grey scales and short broken hairs. The infected area is closely clipped and the antibiotic griseofulvin is taken orally. The disease is most common in children and transmitted by contact with infected scalps or animals, or indirectly by contact with infected objects. Children who ride horses often catch horse ringworm from them, and this must be treated urgently as it can cause more damage (such as scarring) than human ringworm. On the scalp, horse ringworm could cause permanent baldness.

There are, however, two other types of scalp ringworm, described below. No hairdressing service should be given to a client suffering from any type of scalp ringworm.

(7) Favus — Tinea favosa

This type of ringworm is caught by direct contact with infected people. The fungus affects individual follicles, and is usually seen in childhood. A yellow coloured mycelium grows down the follicles, penetrates the hair shafts and spreads across the scalp producing saucer-shaped crusts. Unlike Tinea capitis the hairs do not break off. The follicles are often destroyed, resulting in permanent baldness. Treatment is the same as for Tinea capitis.

(8) Black-dot ringworm

This is a rare form of scalp ringworm with a distinctive appearance. Bald, circular patches are present, but are not scaly. They appear to contain black dots which are actually due to broken hairs, the ends of which are just visible at the openings to the follicles. It is caught directly, and can cause permanent baldness.

Ringworm can be detected early by the use of a special lamp (Wood's light) which emits ultra-violet rays. An infected area will fluoresce with a greenish-blue light. All types of ringworm require medical attention and are often treated with antibiotics. If ever you have a 'rash' with a definite solid red edge see your doctor to check whether or not it is ringworm.

Questions 2.5

1 What are the two main actions that ringworm fungi have on the skin?
2 How can ringworm be spread?
3 What area of the body does tinea pedis affect?
4 What is the common name for tinea pedis?
5 How would you recognise tinea pedis?

6   How is tinea pedis usually spread?
7   How is tinea pedis treated?
8   What area of the body does tinea barbae affect?
9   How can tinea barbae be recognised?
10   How is tinea barbae spread?
11   What is the treatment for tinea barbae?
12   What other conditions could tinea barbae be mistaken for?
13   What area of the body is affected by tinea corporis?
14   How can tinea corporis be recognised?
15   How can tinea corporis be spread?
16   What is the correct term for ringworm of the groin?
17   Which groups of people suffer from groin ringworm and why?
18   How can ringworm of the groin be contracted?
19   How would you recognise ringworm of the groin?
20   What is the correct term for ringworm of the nails?
21   How would you recognise ringworm of the nails?
22   How would you prevent the spread of ringworm of the nails?
23   What is the correct term for ringworm of the scalp?
24   How does ringworm of the scalp affect the keratin of hair?
25   How is scalp ringworm caught?
26   How would you recognise ringworm of the scalp?
27   What is the treatment for scalp ringworm?
28   Why is horse ringworm more harmful to catch than normal scalp ringworm?
29   What is the other name for favus?
30   How can favus be recognised?
31   Why can favus cause permanent baldness?
32   How can black-dot ringworm be recognised?
33   What is the cause of the black dots?
34   Would you give a service to a client who had any form of scalp ringworm?
35   What age group of client is most likely to suffer from scalp ringworm?
36   How is a 'Woods light' used to detect ringworm?

2.6   Viruses

A virus consists of a protein shell which contains particles of genetic material, either DNA or RNA. The virus infects a cell and uses the host's genetic material to reproduce itself. Viruses can then leave this first host cell and invade other cells. Viruses, such as the one shown in Figure 2.4, often have shapes like crystals.

Most viruses enter the body through the mouth or the skin and then spread to cells throughout via the blood stream. Symptoms of a virus usually begin once the second wave of viruses has been produced in the host cells. Figure 2.5 shows how a virus develops in the cells and then infects further cells. Because they can multiply only in living cells viruses cannot live in the horny layer of the epidermis, but do stay a considerable time in the lower living layers of the epidermis.

Questions 2.6

1   What does a virus use to reproduce itself?
2   How do viruses enter the body?

Fig. 2.4 A virus.

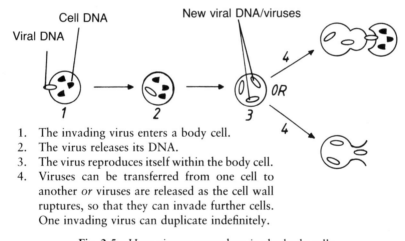

1. The invading virus enters a body cell.
2. The virus releases its DNA.
3. The virus reproduces itself within the body cell.
4. Viruses can be transferred from one cell to another *or* viruses are released as the cell wall ruptures, so that they can invade further cells. One invading virus can duplicate indefinitely.

Fig. 2.5 How viruses reproduce in the body cells.

3 When do the symptoms of a viral infection usually show?
4 Why can viruses not live in the horny layer of the epidermis?
5 Draw a diagram to describe how viruses reproduce.

2.7 *Skin infections caused by viruses*

Because these conditions cannot be cured with antibiotics they can last for long periods of time.

(1) Herpes simplex

This is commonly known as the cold sore and is usually seen on the lips as a red patch with blisters. This itches and later develops into a moist crusty patch. It was given the name 'cold sore' because it usually develops when the sufferer is run down, perhaps after a cold. It can arise from over-exposure to the wind or sun, or occur during menstruation or stress. The virus responsible for herpes is HSV1, which remains in the trigeminal root ganglion (this is a facial nerve) for life, sending virus particles down the nerve to the skin. The cold sore can affect the mucous membranes inside the nose and the eyes. Care should be taken not to touch the eyes and nose if you have been touching a cold sore. Attacks last for one to two weeks, recurring every few months in many people.

The virus can be spread only when there is an attack. It can then be caught either directly by kissing or indirectly on shared cups or towels.

Students often get upset when I identify the blister on their mouth as herpes. They do not think that I mean a cold sore but genital herpes! Although both conditions can be caught by direct contact and form similar blistery sores, they are caused by two different types of herpes simplex viruses, so are *not* the same. Genital herpes is caused by HSV2, and is also more painful.

Confusion arises because of stories of how you can catch the two types of herpes. HSV1 virus, the common cold sore, is usually found around the mouth. However, it can be transferred to the genitals if an infected person indulges in oral sex. It is *still* the common cold sore and *not* genital herpes. Similarly, if someone with genital herpes indulges in oral sex they can pass it on so that it infects the skin near the mouth. Although it is not the normal site of infection, it will be genital herpes that is near the mouth.

- There is no way that genital herpes can turn into common herpes simplex.
- With both types of herpes the disease can only be spread when sores are present.
- At the present time there is no cure for either type of herpes. Because, once caught, the virus is always in the body, the sores will develop whenever you are run down. Common cold sores are often seen after colds because of this, while genital herpes often develops in infected women when they have their periods.
- It is hoped that in the near future a vaccine will be developed for preventing both types of herpes.

(2) Herpes zoster

This is commonly called shingles. It is a painful blistering rash caused by the chicken-pox virus. The virus is usually caught originally in childhood as chicken-pox, lying dormant for years until it is triggered as shingles. If you have shingles a child may develop chicken-pox from you. A rash develops which resembles cold sores and this may be preceded by pain which may go on for months or even years. Shingles is most common in the middle-aged and elderly. Medical attention should be sought.

- People only get shingles if they have had chicken-pox, usually when they were children.

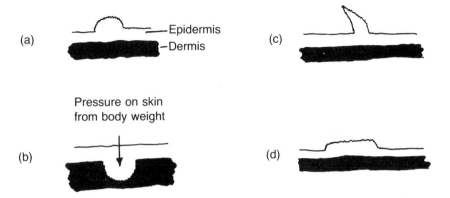

Fig. 2.6 Types of verrucae. (a) Common wart. (b) Plantar wart. (c) Filiform wart. (d) Plane wart.

- An adult with shingles can give a child or an adult chicken-pox if they have not had it before.
- Shingles usually develops in someone who is under stress, either emotionally or from overwork.
- The intense pain of shingles is due to the virus stimulating the nerve endings for pain.

(3) Verrucae

Verrucae are commonly called warts. They are most common on the hands and feet of children and there are four basic types: common, plantar, filiform and plane. These are illustrated in Figure 2.6.

Common warts are firm, roughened, raised areas of skin, which occur singly or in large masses (see Figure 2.7). The back of the hand is a common site. They are not painful and may vanish within two years. Many people paint their warts with proprietary wart paints which are acids and gradually remove keratin. If these do

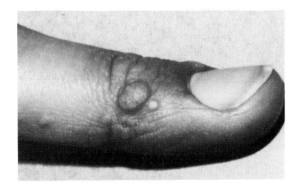

Fig. 2.7 A common wart.

not work you must be referred by your doctor to the hospital to have them frozen off. This can take several applications to work. Very stubborn warts are electrically cauterised.

Plantar warts occur on the soles of the feet and many people know this type of wart as the verruca, although that is the correct term for all warts. The weight of the body makes them grow inwards rather than outwards. They may be painful and are highly infectious. Swimming pools are one of the main places that they are caught. An acid is applied to the wart which is covered with a plaster for a few days. This softens the keratin and allows it to be pared away. Plantar warts can be cut out, frozen or burnt away by the doctor, but not charmed away!

Filiform warts are small filamentous warts which are often seen on the face and are usually burnt off.

Plane warts are flattened and often occur in groups. They are usually removed with wart paints.

Many people will tell you that a common wart can be 'charmed' away by a number of bizarre methods such as: buying the wart from the sufferer; rubbing a piece of meat on the wart and burying it; and rubbing the belly of a toad on to the wart. These methods have been shown to work apparently, although there is no scientific basis for any of them. If warts are old enough they have been known to vanish spontaneously without treatment. Perhaps this is the reason why such strange methods of 'charming' have appeared to be effective.

Great care should be taken not to cut warts as this can spread them. Have them removed if you keep cutting or scratching them.

(4) Molluscum contagiosum

This viral infection of the skin is commonly seen in children but does occur in adults as well. It is seen as raised areas of skin with a central depression. These usually have a 'pearly' colour but are often infected and red, and are commonly found in groups, on the trunk or on the face. On squeezing the larger nodules of the infection a thick white substance can be expressed. If left alone, the nodules usually vanish. They are often caught in swimming pools.

A doctor will remove the nodules by freezing or by spiking the depressed centre with an orange stick which has been dipped in 1% liquid phenol. The infection does not leave scars as it is superficial and only affects the epidermis.

Questions 2.7

1 Why do viral infections of the skin last a long time?
2 What is herpes simplex commonly known as?
3 How would you recognise herpes simplex?
4 When would the sufferer be most likely to get an attack of herpes simplex?
5 Which virus is responsible for herpes simplex?
6 How long does the sufferer have the virus for?
7 How long does an attack of herpes last?
8 When and how can herpes be spread?
9 What is the difference between the common cold sore and genital herpes?
10 What is the medical name for shingles?

11   How can shingles be recognised?
12   Where is shingles usually caught from originally?
13   In what age group is shingles most common?
14   What causes the intense pain of shingles?
15   What is the correct name for a wart?
16   What are the four basic types of wart?
17   Where are warts most commonly found?
18   How do wart paints work?
19   What other methods are there of removing warts?
20   What are plantar warts and how are they usually spread?
21   Why should care be taken not to cut warts?
22   Should hairdressers have warts removed from their fingers?
23   How would you recognise molluscum contagiosum?
24   What age group usually suffers from molluscum contagiosum?
25   How is the condition usually caught?
26   How would a doctor treat molluscum contagiosum?

2.8 AIDS

AIDS is the newest and most deadly virus condition known to man. It was first reported in 1981, and was given the name 'acquired immunodeficiency syndrome'. The virus responsible is HIV. It is thought that the virus originated from green monkeys in Central Africa. In North America the virus has spread rapidly among homosexual men. The virus has been found in human blood, semen and saliva. So far the virus has only been known to be spread by blood or semen.

Because people with AIDS had donated blood which was later used to make products for haemophiliacs, this group became the second largest grouping to develop AIDS. Some women developed AIDS through artificial insemination with infected semen. The third group to have a high risk of AIDS are intravenous drug users, through using unsterilised needles. The fourth high risk group are people from Central Africa. There is an AIDS belt which runs across Zaire, Ruanda and Burundi, where men and women have the disease in equal numbers. It has been spread through normal sexual intercourse, a worrying development in the future spread of the disease.

Not everyone who has been exposed to the AIDS virus has developed the disease. The test for the disease is to check the blood to see if it contains antibodies for the AIDS virus. If the test is positive it means that the person has been exposed to the virus, but it does not mean that he or she will develop the symptoms. Many people who have antibodies against the AIDS virus have not developed any symptoms. In fact more people have been exposed to the virus than have actually developed the AIDS syndrome. Many may develop no symptoms whatsoever (though it is not known whether these people are infectious or not). A proportion of those exposed to the AIDS virus have developed ARC (AIDS-related complex). They suffer a mild version of immune system depression which gives symptoms such as malaise, weight loss, fevers and swollen lymph nodes. It is feared that they might develop AIDS in the future.

Until a vaccine is developed to prevent AIDS, it will continue to kill sufferers

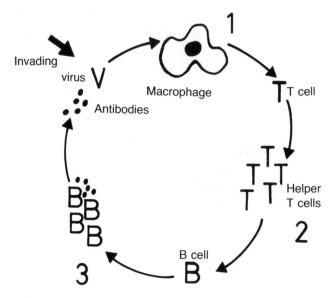

Fig. 2.8 How the immune system deals with invading viruses. (1) A virus enters a healthy body and is detected by a macrophage which identifies it for T cells. (2) The T cell is activated and multiplies to develop several types of helper T cells. Helper T cells stimulate the B cells. (3) The B cells multiply and produce antibodies that will attack and destroy the virus. Immunisation 'mimics' the invading virus so that a 'memory' of it is retained, enabling a quick immune reaction if the real virus invades. This is why having some viruses gives an immunity against further attacks.

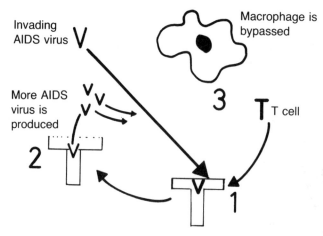

Fig. 2.9 How the AIDS virus attacks the immune system. (1) The AIDS virus infects the helper T cells. This blocks their ability to recognise foreign substances such as other viruses. (2) The T cells are then turned into 'factories' that make more AIDS virus. These are then released to invade more T cells. (3) The T cells no longer perform their function of fighting infection, so that other viruses which would not 'get a hold' in a healthy body develop. This is why victims of AIDS suffer from such a wide range of illnesses, which eventually kill them.

within about two years of developing the disease. Figure 2.8 shows how the immune system normally deals with a virus. Figure 2.9 shows how AIDS prevents this and leads to the development of numerous other infections. It is a build-up of other infections that eventually kills someone with AIDS.

There have been other deadly viruses in the past. In 1918 and 1919 Spanish flu killed twenty million people worldwide. People could, however, survive this virus. At present, once AIDS is diagnosed it is a death sentence.

What does all this mean to the hairdresser?

You are only at risk if blood is produced on cutting a client who has the AIDS virus. As more people develop the virus the risks will become greater. In salons, ear-piercing devices and electrolysis equipment present a possible route for transmitting the virus. You can protect yourself by always covering cuts. If the skin has eczema do not allow blood to come in contact with it at any time. If blood is spilt in the salon it should be cleaned with household bleach.

You can catch AIDS by:

- Having sex with someone who has AIDS. There is no such thing as 'safe' sex, although a condom would offer some protection.
- Allowing infected blood to enter a break in your skin. This could happen during ear piercing, *or* electrolysis *or* by infected blood touching skin with eczema.
- Sharing needles if you are a drug addict.

But,

- You *cannot* catch AIDS from sneezing or by sexual contact with someone who has *not* got the virus.
- You should protect both yourself and clients from AIDS by following the safety measures for ear piercing and electrolysis given in Section 8.5.
- Because it is so difficult to sterilise needles some acupuncturists now use new needles on every client.
- If you cut a client with a razor or scissors it is important that you sterilise these tools before using them on another client.
- Autoclaving will sterilise equipment adequately (see Figure 5.2(c)).

As more is known about the disease there will be more chance of fighting it and finding a cure. At the present time however, *prevention* is the most important thing.

Questions 2.8

1   What is the name of the virus responsible for AIDS?
2   Where is it thought that the virus originated from?
3   Through what groups of people has the virus spread?
4   How can the virus be spread?
5   How have haemophiliacs become infected with the virus?
6   How have some women become infected?

7   Why do drug users become infected with the virus?
8   Why are people from central Africa at risk?
9   How are people tested for AIDS?
10 If an AIDS test is positive, what does this mean?
11 What is ARC?
12 Approximately how long will an AIDS sufferer live?
13 How does the immune system usually deal with a virus?
14 How does the AIDS virus prevent the immune system from working properly?
15 How could the AIDS virus infect the hairdresser?
16 How can the hairdresser help to protect herself from AIDS?
17 What precautions should someone suffering from eczema take?
18 How should spilt blood be dealt with in the salon?
19 How should you deal with tools and equipment that come into contact with blood?

2.9 *Hepatitis*

Hepatitis simply means inflammation of the liver. This is usually caused by a virus and the skin and eyes often develop a yellow colour due to jaundice. Urine becomes darker in colour while faeces becomes lighter. Viral hepatitis can be classified in three ways:

(1) *Hepatitis A*
    This is caused by hepatitis A virus (HAV). It is also known as infective or short incubation hepatitis. The virus is present in infected faeces, and is caught from infected food or drink. It takes between 20 and 40 days to incubate.
(2) *Hepatitis B*
    This is caused by hepatitis B virus (HBV). It is also known as serum or long incubation hepatitis. It takes between 40 and 150 days to incubate. More is said about this virus below.
(3) *Hepatitis non-A non-B*
    This is caused by a virus that cannot be categorised as being caused by either HAV or HBV.

The hepatitis B virus is highly infectious and is commonly spread in blood. If the skin is cut even a tiny drop of blood should be thought of as potentially infectious. The virus is capable of surviving long periods (several years!) outside the body. Because of this it can be caught from dried blood. It is killed by heat and also by the majority of disinfectants if they are used correctly. Early symptoms of the disease include fever, loss of appetite and a feeling of sickness. The illness is usually curable after several months, although it can be fatal. Many people also develop fatal liver cancer in later life.

From this you can see that it is a disease that must be prevented in the salon. Interestingly enough, hairdressers are three or four times more likely to develop the disease than nurses. Every client must be treated as a potential source of infection. If you cut them, sterilise the tool involved and wear gloves if you are going to come into contact with blood. It is best to give the client cotton wool to stem any bleeding, and this can then be disposed of in a plastic bag. Spilt blood should be mopped up with household bleach. Immunisation is now possible against hepatitis; ask your doctor if you feel you are at risk.

Questions 2.9

1   What does the term hepatitis mean?
2   How would you know if a client had jaundice?
3   How is viral hepatitis classified?
4   Which type of hepatitis is the hairdresser or beauty therapist in danger of catching at work?
5   How is the virus spread?
6   Could dried blood still contain active virus?
7   How can the virus be killed in the salon?
8   What action would you take if you cut a client?

3

Non-infectious Conditions

The term 'non-infectious conditions' is used here rather than diseases, because we are referring to disorders of the body rather than diseases. Most of us think of a disease as 'catching', but these conditions are not. It is important that you are able to recognise some of the main conditions, as they can be confused with infectious ones. A client who is refused service for a non-infectious condition could easily be lost forever, whereas a client who is reassured by a knowledgeable hairdresser could become a valued client for life.

3.1 Psoriasis

This is a skin condition that affects 2% of the population. It tends to run in families (i.e. it is inherited) and can develop for the first time at any age. It can vanish as quickly as it started. The average age of onset is in the thirties, and it is uncommon in the first three years of life. The initial attack and subsequent further outbreaks may be provoked by a streptococcal infection, such as a sore throat. It is also linked with stress, but may occur for no apparent reason.

The characteristic appearance of psoriasis (you do not pronounce the 'p') is a number of well-demarcated, large red patches, which are covered by thick silvery-white scales. The most common sites to find these patches of psoriasis are on the knees and elbows. Psoriasis is seen on the scalp, and a patch on the edge of the hair line is shown in Figure 3.1. Many people assume that they have had dandruff when in fact they have psoriasis of the scalp, and dandruff shampoos will do little to help them. Unlike dandruff, the scaling occurs in thick patches that can be felt with the fingers. It may cause bald patches, but these will recover with treatment of the psoriasis.

It can affect any area of skin but is rare on the face. When the scales are lifted, there are often small areas of bleeding. Although many textbooks claim that psoriasis does not itch, many people who suffer from the condition (including myself!) would disagree. If the nails are affected, they will have characteristic pits called

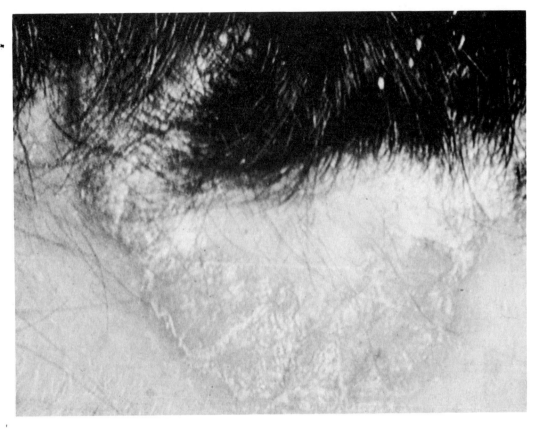

Fig. 3.1 Psoriasis scales on the front hair margin.

'thimble pitting'. This is shown in Figure 3.2 and derives its name from the appearance of the top of a thimble. The nail may thicken and separate from the nail bed below.

What causes psoriasis? Put simply, it is an over-production of epidermal cells. There is an increased amount of mitosis in the basal layer, so that more cells than usual are produced. Also, the epidermal transit time (see Section 1.2) is decreased from twenty-eight to only about five days. As a result of this the cells in the horny layer of the epidermis still retain their nuclei and stick together to form thick scales. The granular layer is reduced or absent. New cells are forming more quickly than dead cells are being shed. The capillaries in the upper dermis dilate, and there is also oedema (water retention). What causes these things to happen is still unknown. A diagram to show the changes that occur in the skin in psoriasis is shown in Figure 3.3.

If either you or a client suffers from psoriasis, it can be treated in a number of ways by a doctor:

- Application of steroid creams, usually twice daily. These will reduce scaling and redness, as well as itching if it is present.
- The use of tar shampoos for the scalp may help to clear the scaling. Polytar is the

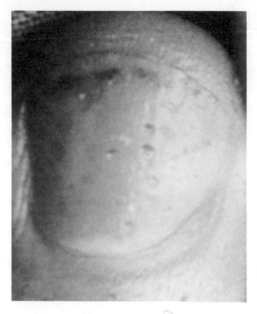

Fig. 3.2 Psoriasis of the finger nail. There are a number of small rounded depressions in the nail plate, termed 'thimble pitting'.

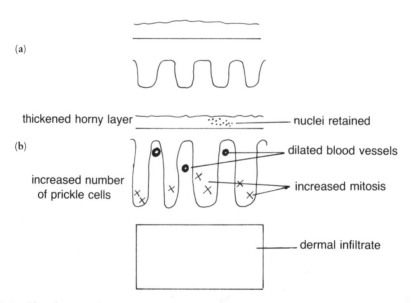

Fig. 3.3 The changes that occur in the skin in psoriasis. (a) Normal epidermis. (b) The epidermis in psoriasis.

most well known proprietary preparation. Pragmatar is another proprietary preparation that may be rubbed into the patches a few hours before shampooing, once or twice weekly. It is not known which one of the hundreds of ingredients contained in coal tar is responsible for helping to control psoriasis.

- Sunlight and artificial ultra-violet radiation have proved beneficial. In some hospitals patients are given a plant extract called a psoralen in tablet form. This makes their skin more sensitive to ultra-violet, and they are then exposed to UVA (a longer wavelength type of ultra-violet radiation). This is known as PUVA treatment.
- In severe cases treatment with anti-mitotic drugs is given. These reduce cell division but have harmful side-effects, such as loss of hair and poor healing of wounds.
- A number of people have benefited from swimming in the Dead Sea in Israel, where the salt concentration is very high.

Remember that psoriasis is not infectious and all the usual services can be offered, providing that there are no breaks in the skin. The client will often welcome a perm or tint as it helps clear the scaling!

Questions 3.1

1   What do you understand by the term 'non-infectious condition'?
2   Why is it just as important for you to be able to identify a non-infectious condition as an infectious one?
3   How many people are affected by psoriasis?
4   What is the average age that a person is likely to become affected by psoriasis?
5   What causes are there for attacks of psoriasis?
6   Describe the appearance of psoriasis?
7   Where are the most likely places that psoriasis would be seen?
8   What is the difference between psoriasis and dandruff?
9   What does the nail look like if psoriasis is present?
10   What is the cause of psoriasis?
11   What happens to the epidermal transit time in psoriasis?
12   What methods are available for treating psoriasis?
13   How can a perm or tint help a case of psoriasis?
14   Can a service be given to a client with psoriasis?

3.2 Eczema

The terms 'eczema' and 'dermatitis' are often used synonymously. In the past, the term eczema has been used to refer to inflamed skin caused by an internal factor, while dermatitis has been used to refer to inflamed skin caused by an external factor. This is why I am dealing with inflamed skin in the two traditional sections, as old names die hard. Eczema may be referred to as endogenous or constitutional, whereas dermatitis may be referred to as contact or exogenous. In some cases inflammation of the skin can be due to both internal and external factors in which case it is difficult to apply two names!

The main symptoms of eczema are itching and redness. The skin may become thickened with scaling and there may also be weeping and crusting. The redness gradually fades into the natural skin colour, and this distinguishes it from fungal infections which have clearly defined edges.

Eczema is never present at birth, but can appear a few weeks afterwards. It may continue into adult life. The face is the usual area involved when eczema first occurs. Later it is seen on the knees and elbows. Itching can be severe. About 10% of the population of Britain suffer from eczema, although over 90% of sufferers are clear by their mid-teens. Eczema, along with asthma and hay fever, runs in families and all three sometimes develop simultaneously in the same child. Exactly what causes eczema is unclear, although there is definitely some fault with the immune system. Diet can provoke eczema, as some food acts as the trigger or allergen. Cows' milk is well known but surprisingly, natural things like orange juice can also have this effect. Babies from families with a history of eczema should be breast-fed for three months as this reduces the risk of eczema occurring.

Eczema produces a dry flaky skin. The dryness makes the itching worse, so emollient creams should be used as these protect the skin from losing moisture. Having baths will make the skin drier as natural oils are lost, so shower instead.

Seborrhoeic eczema (often called dermatitis) is a type of eczema with a very inappropriate name. The condition probably has no relationship to the sebaceous glands, and many people with the condition have very dry skins! There is redness and scaling of the scalp which may be mild or severe. There may be red scaly patches in the eyebrows and at the sides of the nose; often there is also a rash behind the ears. If it occurs on the body it is usually seen as small red scaly patches on the sternum or on the back, between the shoulder blades. Perhaps this accounts for the naming of the condition, as these are areas with many sebaceous glands, often called 'seborrhoeic' areas. Stress will bring on an attack.

If you or a client have eczema, medical help should be sought. Usually a steroid cream is used to prevent inflammation. The following things should be kept in mind also:

- With weeping eczema, dilute potassium permanganate can be used to soak the skin. The dilution is 1:800, producing a pink rather than a purple colour. This will not only reduce weeping but will also help prevent secondary infection. Do not use once the skin begins to dry.
- Avoid the use of perfumed products such as soaps, face creams and cleansers. The 'Simple' range of products (or any other range of unperfumed products) should be tried instead.
- Avoid wearing woollens next to the skin as these can irritate. Try to wear loosely fitting cotton clothes.
- If you have a baby with eczema, mitts can be worn to avoid scratching and possible infection.

Questions 3.2

1   What is the difference between eczema and dermatitis?
2   What are the main symptoms of eczema?

3   How can you distinguish between eczema and a fungal infection?
4   At what age does eczema usually first appear?
5   How many of the population suffer from eczema?
6   What part of the body is usually first to develop eczema?
7   What things in the diet have been shown to provoke eczema?
8   Why should babies be breast-fed if there is a history of eczema in the family?
9   How would you advise a client to look after their skin if they have eczema?
10   What is seborrhoeic eczema?
11   How would you recognise seborrhoeic eczema?
12   What effect does potassium permanganate have on eczema?
13   What should an eczema sufferer avoid?
14   What precautions could you take to prevent a baby from scratching?

3.3 *Dermatitis (contact eczema)*

This section should be read in conjunction with the previous one on eczema. As has already been mentioned, dermatitis is regarded as skin inflammation caused by external factors.

Some substances, called *primary irritants*, will provoke dermatitis with a single exposure because they are so strong. The obvious examples are caustic chemicals such as acids or alkalis. A primary irritant will produce dermatitis in *anyone* if it is applied in a sufficiently strong concentration for a sufficiently long period of time. Relaxers are an example of primary irritants.

Children often get dermatitis from their nappies. This is due to prolonged contact with urine or faeces. In turn, this may be due to inadequate changing of nappies or cleaning of the buttocks, or the wearing of rubber or plastic pants. Unlike nappy rash due to a yeast, in dermatitis the skin folds are usually spared. This type of 'nappy rash' will respond to improved hygiene and the application of an emollient or a silicone protective cream.

The second type of dermatitis, the one seen in hairdressing, is the development of a delayed hypersensitivity to a chemical which is known as the *sensitiser* or *allergen*. These chemicals would not cause dermatitis, even in high concentration, in a normal person. Severe dermatitis, however, will be provoked by brief exposure to a very low concentration of the chemical in a person who has been sensitised to it. Hair dye dermatitis, caused by a severe allergic reaction to a hair tint, is shown in Figure 3.4.

There is a genetic link here, as the number of exposures to the sensitiser will vary from a few to infinity in different individuals. You could be using a particular substance for years and suddenly show an allergy to it, whereas someone else may develop the same allergy after a few days. This is often seen in hairdressing with shampoos. The soapless detergents in most shampoos are strong, and degrease the natural oils of the skin. Some hairdressers never suffer from dermatitis, while others have it in their first week. Virtually any chemical can cause sensitivity, but the following are well known:

• Metals such as chromium and nickel, used in the manufacture of cheap jewellery. If you have ever worn a bracelet or earrings which have resulted in redness,

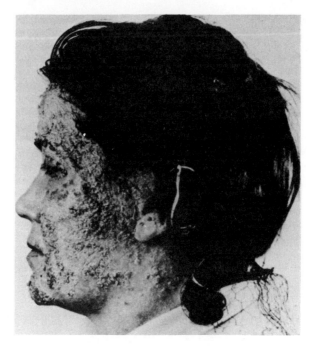

Fig. 3.4 A severe allergic reaction to a hair tint. (From *Practical Dermatology* (3rd Edition) by I.B. Sneddon and R.E. Church, published by Edward Arnold. Courtesy of authors and publishers.)

weeping and swelling, you have suffered from this, and will continue to for a number of years.

- Biological washing powders. Where these are used on jumpers and not rinsed properly, there is often a concentration of the remaining powder in the arms and neck if it is dried on a line. The resultant rash is normally around the wrists and neck.
- Oxidation tints, especially those containing paraphenylenediamine. Paraphenylenediamine may also be found as one of the ingredients in some semi-permanents. Check the packaging to see whether a skin test is needed.
- Preservatives and perfumes in cosmetics.
- Plastics and resins, present in nail varnish and spectacle frames.

Once a substance is suspected of being the cause of an allergy you can try to eliminate contact with it. To confirm that a substance does cause an allergy, a patch or skin test can be carried out. The substance is applied to an area of clean skin and covered with a piece of tape. After forty-eight hours the tape is removed and the patch is examined. It is possible that the person is so sensitive that the reaction may occur within minutes or hours. In case this happens, a warning must be given to wash it off if it irritates too much.

In hairdressing, we are supposed to perform this test before every tint. The procedure is to mix a little of the tint with peroxide (of the strength you are going to use on the client) and apply it to an area of skin behind the ear or in the crook of the elbow. This should have been cleaned with some alcohol first to remove sebum which might otherwise form a protective barrier between the dye and the skin. The area should then be covered with collodion (sold as 'Nuskin') or a plaster to protect the tint from being washed off, and also to make sure that nothing else comes into contact with that piece of skin. The client should be warned to wash it off if it irritates, and use something like calamine lotion to ease the irritation. Some hairdressing textbooks claim that a dark shade of tint should be used for a skin test because it contains more paraphenylenediamine. This should not be done. What if you are using a blonde tint on a client (which contains mostly paratoluenediamine)? If you told a doctor that you thought you were allergic to strawberries and he gave you a skin test for bananas, you would not be too impressed! The skin test should be checked after 24–48 hours. If a client is allergic (i.e. develops any irritation) the skin test is positive and a tint should *not be given* (see *Colouring – A Salon Handbook* or *Foundation Hairdressing*).

A hairdresser who gets an allergic response to chemicals in the salon must either avoid using them, avoid contact with them, or minimise the effects produced by them. It is impractical not to use them if you wish to remain a hairdresser, so you must avoid contact with them. This is done by wearing rubber or plastic gloves whenever you handle them. This is accepted practice for tints and perms, but clients often complain if their hair is shampooed by someone wearing gloves. In this case rinse all shampoo from your skin and dry the hands thoroughly. Use barrier creams and hand creams to protect the skin and, if the outbreak of dermatitis is bad enough, see your doctor for special steroid creams.

If you suffer from dermatitis, try to think what has possibly caused it. If your legs are affected, has it been caused by tights, shoes or the bottom of a skirt or dress? Jewellery is usually obvious, so try gold instead if you are affected. After a few years away from something that once provoked dermatitis you may suddenly be clear of it, so do try again every so often.

Questions 3.3

1 What is the other name for dermatitis?
2 What is dermatitis?
3 What is a primary irritant?
4 Give an example of a primary irritant used in hairdressing?
5 Why can a child get dermatitis from its nappy?
6 What can be done for nappy rash?
7 What is a sensitiser or allergen?
8 What happens if a person becomes 'sensitised' to a chemical?
9 List the well known chemicals that can cause dermatitis.
10 How can you confirm that a chemical causes an allergy?
11 Why should you carry out a skin test before a tint?
12 How would you carry out a skin test?
13 What shade of tint should be used to perform a skin test?
14 What strength hydrogen peroxide should be used for the skin test on a client?
15 What advice should be given to the client when a skin test is given?
16 When would the skin test be checked and how would you know if it was positive?

17   What action should be taken if the skin test is positive?
18   What should the hairdresser do if she gets an allergic reaction to a chemical?

3.4 Pityriasis

This is the generic name for conditions such as dandruff, the loss of small flakes of skin from an otherwise normal scalp. This can be seen on other areas of the body besides the scalp, so the name pityriasis capitis is given to dandruff of the scalp. Dandruff is uncommon in infancy and early childhood, but by puberty about half of all males and females become affected. It may persist throughout life but lessens with age (in the fifties and sixties) as the turnover of cells decreases.

Many textbooks have claimed that dandruff is caused by yeast and bacteria found on the scalp. Although it is true that the population of Pityrosporum ovale (a type of yeast) and staphylococci (round bacteria in bunches) increases, this is *because* of the dandruff, and not the cause of it. The actual dandruff is caused by an increased turnover rate of cells in the germinative layer of the epidermis. However, the reason for this increase is not understood.

The flakes of dandruff adhere to the hairs; in severe cases the dandruff is clearly seen on the shoulders. Dandruff may cause inflammation of the eyelid (blepharitis) or the mucous membrane which covers the eyeball (conjunctivitis).

The production of dandruff can be controlled with shampoos that contain either selenium sulphide or zinc pyrithione. The selenium sulphide shampoos have the side effect of increasing sebum production (unwanted if you have a greasy scalp or acne, but desirable if you are a sailor or anyone else with a dry scalp). Some people are allergic to sulphur, so this should be borne in mind. Both chemicals work by reducing the rate of cell division in the germinative layer. The scales appear again on the scalp in four to seven days.

In those people whose scalps become greasy at or after puberty, the scales may bind in a greasy paste so that they are no longer shed. This is referred to as pityriasis steatoides. Inflammation of the scalp is often associated with this, and itching develops, something that is not experienced with normal dandruff. If the yellow scales are lifted the scalp will be red and moist. Medical help should be sought if the condition is severe.

Questions 3.4

1   What is the generic name for dandruff?
2   Can you get dandruff anywhere else besides the scalp?
3   What age group does dandruff become common in?
4   By what age does dandruff start to vanish from sufferers?
5   Why was it thought that dandruff was caused by yeast and bacteria?
6   What is the cause of dandruff?
7   How do you recognise dandruff?
8   How can dandruff affect the eyes?
9   What are the names of the two chemicals that can be used to treat dandruff?
10   What effect do the two chemicals have on the scalp?

11   Why might a client with a dry scalp want to use a dandruff shampoo containing selenium sulphide?

12   What is pityriasis steatoides?

3.5   *Seborrhoea*

Put simply, seborrhoea is the production of too much sebum. It is difficult to quantify actually how much sebum has to be produced to be classified as seborrhoea, as an individual may consider that he has it when the scalp and hair are only slightly greasy. It is perhaps best to label seborrhoea as that production of sebum which makes the hair unmanageable.

Seborrhoea is caused by the secretion of male hormones, the androgens. Androgen levels begin to rise at about ten years of age, causing the sebaceous glands to enlarge and the production of sebum to begin. Between the ages of thirteen and sixteen the production of sebum is equal in males and females, thereafter rising rapidly in the male to reach a peak by the age of twenty. In males it will remain high into old age but there will be a marked decrease in females once the menopause is reached.

Many women wonder how they can produce male hormones since they do not have testicles. Male hormones are produced by the adrenal glands and the ovaries in a less potent form than the male testicles. If women did not have these male hormones they would not grow pubic or underarm hair, as the production of this hair is under the control of these hormones. Many women who suffer from seborrhoea also suffer from hirsutism; this is production of excessive facial and body hair (see Section 3.7) and acne (see Section 2.3). Males tend to suffer from acne as well. Bald men often think that they produce more sebum because of the characteristic shine of their bald scalp, but it is just that the sebum is more evident.

Just using a shampoo for greasy hair will do nothing to get rid of seborrhoea. In fact, many sufferers complain that shampooing increases the flow of sebum. If the seborrhoea is combined with hirsutism and acne, see a doctor who may be able to do something about the cause. The following points will help in the management of the condition:

- Avoid stimulating the scalp as this will also stimulate the sebaceous glands and make the hair more greasy (avoid vigorous brushing, massaging or washing in *hot* water).
- Try a coal tar shampoo such as Polytar.
- See your doctor if you also have bad acne or hirsutism.

Questions 3.5

1   What is seborrhoea?
2   What are androgens?
3   How are androgens linked to seborrhoea?
4   How does the production of sebum differ in males and females at different ages?
5   Where are male hormones produced in women?
6   What is hirsutism and how is it related to seborrhoea?
7   What advice would you give to a client who suffered from seborrhoea?

3.6 Alopecia

This is the general term for baldness, of which there are a number of different types. Some types are permanent whereas others are only temporary. You may be the first person to notice a thinning of hair in a client, so it will be useful for you to know what advice to give them.

(1) Alopecia areata

This is first noticed as a small bald patch on the scalp, or in the beard of men. Usually a number of patches in an area of the scalp develop and eventually join up to form larger patches. A patch can sometimes form overnight, so that the shed hairs are found on the pillow in the morning. The skin in the patch is usually pale and glossy, with no hairs present.

The sides of each patch have short protruding hairs with a frayed point, giving the appearance of an exclamation mark. This has given rise to the term 'exclamation mark' hair. These hairs are present where the area of baldness is still increasing. They can be plucked out and are about one-eighth of an inch (0.3 cm) long. They have a shrunken white bulb and a brush-like tip: the hair has broken off at scalp level and the remaining stump has then been pushed out.

What causes alopecia areata is not fully understood. Many people do have a family history suggesting some genetic link. Others have none, but there have been numerous documented cases of stress or shock causing the onset of the baldness. One client of mine actually had her new house fall down while she was in it just after returning from honeymoon! Stress and shock both cause the production of hormones but no link with these has been proven. Hair often regrows of its own accord within two to four months. Seeing a doctor or trichologist may be of help, as many people with this condition make it worse by worrying. There may be recurrent attacks throughout someone's lifetime, usually at times of stress.

In alopecia areata, the majority of falling hairs are in anagen; this leaves the scalp bald during the period corresponding to the catagen and telogen phases of the growth cycle. Hair will then regrow in the next anagen period. If the cause of the baldness goes in this bald period, the new hairs will be healthy (although regrowth is sometimes white, giving rise to a 'piebald' appearance). If, however, the cause is still present throughout the bald period, the regrowth of hair will be thin and stunted, falling out again during anagen. It is important that stress is removed if it is a factor in the hair loss. Alopecia areata may be an auto-immune disease, where the body has a faulty immune system which affects its own cells. Advise clients who have this baldness to seek medical help as quickly as possible or it may progress to cause permanent baldness, not only on the head but also the body.

(2) Alopecia totalis

This is the complete loss of scalp hair combined with the loss of eyebrows and eyelashes, as well as beard hair in men. Regrowth is rare once the condition is established, so medical help should be sought as quickly as possible.

(3) *Alopecia universalis*

This is the total loss of all body hair as well. Once this is established regrowth is rare. Again, medical help should be sought as quickly as possible.

(4) *Male pattern baldness (androgenic alopecia)*

This is the most common type of baldness and most men will have it to a greater or lesser severity at some time. It can start in the late teens, in middle or in old age. The hair line recedes and there is loss from the crown until the whole vertex is denuded of hair. This may develop over a few or many years. The progression of male pattern baldness is shown in Figure 3.5. Figure 3.6 shows a thirty-year-old man who began to lose hair in his late teens. There is a reduction in the length of time anagen lasts and the hairs become gradually shorter and finer. Eventually the hairs do not re-

Fig. 3.5 Progression of male pattern baldness.

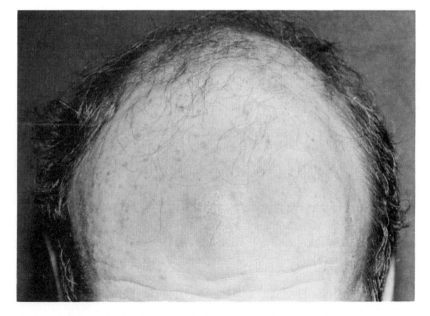

Fig. 3.6 Male pattern baldness in a thirty-year-old man.

grow, and the follicle either remains hairless or is taken over by a fine vellus hair. These give nothing like an adequate covering and the scalp is bald.

Male pattern baldness has a definite genetic link. Parents inflict both the severity and the age of onset of the baldness on their unfortunate male children. The only sure method of preventing baldness is to choose your own parents, making them as hairy as possible! If you have inherited this genetic tendency of baldness you need one other thing, male hormone. This is why young women are safe, because their androgen levels are generally too low. Eunuchs are males who have been castrated (had their testicles removed), and if this was done before puberty they do not go bald. Some eunuchs who have been given male hormone have developed baldness, although bald men given more male hormone have not had increased hair loss. This means that an adequate level of male hormone need only be present for male pattern baldness to occur in susceptible men, destroying the popular myth (with bald men at least!) that bald men are more virile, because it was assumed that they had more male hormone. The fact that many bald men have very hairy bodies may be put down to the fact that their hair patterns are very sensitive to male hormone.

Increasing age is a third factor. After the menopause, androgenic alopecia develops in many women. There are just as many bald women as men in the geriatric wards of hospitals.

If you want to know what can be done for baldness, see Section 3.8.

(5) Diffuse alopecia

Diffuse alopecia is a gradual loss of hair across the whole scalp without any itching or scaling being present. It occurs in females for a variety of reasons. Medical help should be sought in all cases because some of them may be serious. Here are some probable causes:

- Telogen effluvium (moulting) following childbirth, high fever or severe emotional stress. Many scalp follicles enter catagen simultaneously, causing thinning of the scalp hair. There should be regrowth within a few months. During pregnancy many women have a prolonged anagen period and as many as 95% of scalp hairs may be in anagen by the time they give birth. This is 10% more than normal. Within three or four months of giving birth this figure may drop back down to as low as 70%. Regrowth generally takes another three months. Not all pregnant women lose their hair so don't despair if you are ever pregnant!
- Under-activity of the thyroid or pituitary glands. This will decrease the rate at which the body uses energy (basal metabolic rate) and may be due to a tumour or, more rarely, a lack of iodine in the diet.
- Iron deficiency. You do not have to be anaemic. If you have increased hair loss monthly, it could be linked to the menstrual cycle. Tiredness is often a symptom. Try to eat liver or kidneys to replace lost iron (or take iron tablets if vegetarian).
- The side-effects of drugs. Ask your doctor if this is possible. Drugs to prevent cancer, for instance, are anti-mitotic and therefore slow down cell division in healthy cells such as the hair.
- Severe illness such as cancer, kidney or liver failure.

• Some women have experienced hair loss after they *stopped* taking the oral contraceptive pill, because it upsets hormone levels.

(6) Traction alopecia

Traction alopecia is baldness due to placing tension on the hair, causing it to loosen in the follicle. If a pony tail is too tight there may be hair loss at the frontal hair line. Tight plaiting can result in hair loss at the sides of the base of the plait. Attachment of hairpieces may cause hair loss at the point of attachment. Over-vigorous brushing may cause general hair loss. Wearing of rollers which are wound too tightly can result in dramatic loss of hair. The hair should grow back once the bad practice is discontinued, but can be permanent if the practice goes on too long.

(7) Cicatricial alopecia

This is baldness due to scarring. The follicles are absent in scar tissue. Scarring may be due to wounds, burns or infection. Boils can cause scar tissue, as you may have seen on the necks of many men. Great care must be taken with strong hair straighteners, as these highly alkaline chemicals can burn the skin. I have seen a number of cases where girls thought they had dermatitis due to a straightener, when in fact they were permanently scarred. Nothing can be done once scarring has occurred. An example of cicatricial alopecia, due to scars following an infection, is shown in Figure 3.7.

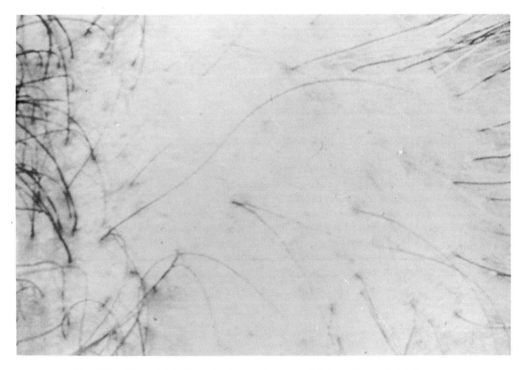

Fig. 3.7 Cicatricial alopecia due to the scars left by a bacterial infection.

(8)   Alopecia senilis (or senile alopecia)

Alopecia senilis is baldness due to old age. In most people the metabolism slows down with increasing age, and nutrients fail to reach the follicles. A similar thing happens to the bones in old age, where although enough calcium is taken in the diet, the bones lose it and become brittle. This occurs in the majority of old people. There is usually a general thinning on the head for which nothing can be done.

(9)   Trichotillomania

This form of hair loss is caused by pulling out one's own hair, usually without realising it. In young children it often occurs after the birth of a new child, to get the attention of the parents. If a child is right-handed the baldness will tend to be greater on the right side of the scalp. It usually stops with the knowledge that one is pulling out one's own hair, but nervous 'twiddling' of hair carries on throughout life in some individuals. In older people, this habit can persist throughout the rest of their life, even though large areas of baldness result. In such cases psychiatric care may be required.

Questions 3.6

1   What is the general term for baldness?
2   Why is it useful for the hairdresser to know something about the different types of baldness?
3   How can alopecia areata be recognised?
4   What does the term 'exclamation mark' hair mean?
5   What can cause alopecia areata?
6   How long does hair take to regrow in alopecia areata?
7   What stage of the hair growth cycle are most hairs at in alopecia areata?
8   What is the reason for a 'piebald' appearance in alopecia areata?
9   What is an auto-immune disease?
10   Why should medical help be sought in the case of alopecia areata?
11   How would you describe alopecia totalis?
12   Should medical help be sought for alopecia totalis?
13   What is alopecia universalis?
14   What is another name for male pattern baldness?
15   At what age can male pattern baldness start?
16   How long does the condition take to develop?
17   What two things together cause male pattern baldness?
18   At what time of life are women likely to suffer from male pattern baldness?
19   Describe diffuse alopecia.
20   Why is medical help necessary for diffuse alopecia?
21   How can pregnancy cause hair loss?
22   What other reasons are there for diffuse hair loss?
23   What is traction alopecia?
24   List some possible causes of traction alopecia.
25   What advice would you give to a client who was suffering from this condition?
26   What is cicatricial alopecia?
27   List some causes of cicatricial alopecia.
28   Why is there never recovery of hair growth with this condition?

29   What is alopecia senilis and what age group would you see the condition in?
30   What is trichotillomania?

3.7 Hirsutism and hypertrichosis

These are the terms used to describe two different types of abnormal hair growth. Hirsutism refers to a male pattern of hair growth in a female (terminal hairs in the beard area, chest and back, with a pubic hairline extending up to the navel). This is induced by an extreme sensitivity to androgens. Hypertrichosis is the growth of terminal hair in an area which is not normally hairy in either sex, such as the forehead.

Hirsutism varies from race to race. Girls from India and some Mediterranean countries are often more hairy than British girls, whereas the Japanese are often almost hairless. Some girls develop hirsutism because their androgens have been converted from a weak to a strong variety (testosterone into dihydrotestosterone) by enzymes. Such girls usually have trouble also with acne, seborrhoea and male pattern baldness. Hirsutism can also be caused by an adrenal gland malfunction, usually due to a tumour, or ovarian cysts. It is important always to seek medical advice if hirsutism suddenly develops. A number of things can be done, however, to make hair less noticeable:

- Depilatory creams may be used (but these may irritate the skin).
- Dark hairs can be bleached with peroxide. Special paste bleaches are available for this.
- Electrolysis. (Have this done professionally, not by using a home electrolysis kit; mistakes mean scars.)
- Waxing. This is generally painful because it is a mass form of plucking. Many women develop ingrowing hairs from waxing which can result in painful infection.
- Shaving. This is thought by many women, however, to be too masculine. It does *not* make the hair grow any quicker or coarser. Although many girls have assured me that their leg hair has grown faster, darker and coarser as a result of shaving their legs, careful scientific experiments have not shown any change in the hair. It may just feel coarser when short. (Compare a man with a 'stiff' beard stubble to a man with a soft full beard.)
- Anti-androgens may be given by a doctor to inhibit the effect of the androgens.

Hypertrichosis can be caused by a number of different factors, including trial drugs which are intended to produce hair growth on bald scalps. Anorexia nervosa, the slimming disease, is a form of malnutrition that can result in this condition. Repeated rubbing of the skin in one area, skin inflammation and steroid creams can all produce this type of hair growth.

Questions 3.7

1   What is hirsutism?
2   What is hypertrichosis?

3   How does hisutism vary with race?
4   If a girl is hirsute, what other related problems might she have?
5   Why should medical advice be sought if hirsutism suddenly develops?
6   In what ways can unwanted hair be removed or made less noticeable?
7   List some causes of hypertrichosis.

3.8   Treatments for baldness

There have been miracle hair growth restorers for years. If you see a preparation advertised in the newspapers or sold from a stall for treating male pattern baldness you can generally be sure that it does not work. People claim bizarre cures like miracle well water, liquid plant food or being licked by a cow. Whenever tests have been carried out, however, they have proved negative. Currently there has been some success with a drug that was originally used for treating high blood pressure, but had the side effect of producing hair growth. This is minoxidil, which may be able to arrest the loss of hair or produce new hair in some individuals.

Scalp reduction surgery involves the removal of a bald area of the skin. The skin stretches so the operation must be repeated a number of times which can be expensive and can also give you an undesired facelift! It is only suitable for removing a small bald area.

Flap grafting involves lifting an area of hairy skin and replacing it into a bald area. Again, this works only for small patches. The established surgical technique is punch grafting, which has proved successful over a number of years. Small circular plugs of skin containing hair follicles are transplanted from the back of the head into prepared holes in the bald area. They do not fall out as did the original hair, because the hairs from the nape are not affected by the androgens. The hairs must be carefully positioned so that the hair growth matches the original pattern of hair or the result will look unnatural. Also, it is important to realise that only so much hair can be taken from the nape without it going bald. If more hair is lost from the transplanted area the transplants can look unnatural, as they appear like small tufts. Transplants to the front hairline are difficult to make look natural, but individual hairs can be transplanted to fill in the gaps between the plugs of hair. Hope for the future lies in being able to culture hair follicles for transplant in the laboratory, so that there would be unlimited supply.

Wigs can be a good answer if they are made of real hair and properly colour-matched. A well-fitted hand-made wig will pass unnoticed. The wigs that we all spot on people are usually the wrong colour for the individual and are not tailor-made for the bald area. Hair weaves involve sewing a wig in place for several weeks. About every six weeks the client returns for it to be washed and refitted. This method cuts out the risk of the wig coming off but such tension is necessary that traction alopecia results. The only way to avoid the traction alopecia is to not have a hair weave.

There is hope for the development of anti-androgen drugs without side effects, which would prevent male pattern baldness. Currently such side effects include complete loss of sex-drive. Better to save money and stick to the story of bald men being more virile!

Questions 3.8

1 Do hair growth restorers work?
2 What is scalp reduction?
3 When would it be a suitable treatment?
4 What is flap grafting?
5 What is punch grafting?
6 Why are punch grafts not affected when they are placed in the crown area?
7 When does punch grafting look unnatural?
8 How can bald areas be covered up without surgery or drugs?

3.9 Defects of the hair

(1) Monilethrix

This is a condition in which the hair shaft is beaded due to uneven hair growth rates in individual follicles. This results in alternate constrictions and swellings, with no medulla present where the hair constricts. The hair breaks off within 2 cm (less than 1 in) of the scalp. This is an inherited condition that runs in families (see Figure 3.8).

(2) Pili torti

The hair is twisted and flattened at intervals along its length, giving it a 'spangled' appearance when observed in light. It usually breaks off short near the scalp. This condition is genetic and runs in families.

(3) Trichonodosis

This is an abnormal growth of the hair where the hair becomes knotted (see Figure 3.9). There may be one or more knots just above skin level. The most common cause of this condition is rough handling of the hair. It is almost always found in people with curly hair and will be found in only a few hairs. It has been found in pubic hair of individuals with pubic lice, caused by their continual scratching!

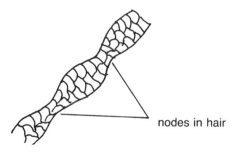

nodes in hair

Fig. 3.8 Monilethrix.

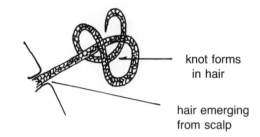

knot forms
in hair

hair emerging
from scalp

Fig. 3.9   Trichonodosis.

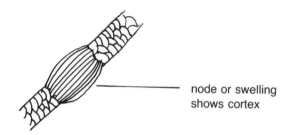

node or swelling
shows cortex

Fig. 3.10   Trichorrhexis nodosa.

(4)   Trichorrhexis nodosa

Nodes which look like rough swellings develop along the hair shaft. These are formed in response to either physical or chemical injury. It is the commonest defect of the hair shaft. The cells of the cuticle are disrupted, allowing the cortical cells beneath to splay out. The hair can easily break at these nodes in response to chemical processing or physical handling. Causes include chemical processing, shampooing, brushing, bathing and sunlight. The condition will improve with the avoidance of all possible causes of injury. It is illustrated in Figure 3.10 and resembles two paintbrushes pushed into each other with bristles interlocked.

(5)   Fragilitis crinium

Fragilitis crinium (see Figure 3.11) is also known as split ends. The ends of the hair are dry and brittle and splits occur along their length. This is caused by processing the hair or handling the hair roughly, including drying. Use the low heat setting of your drier and less damage will be caused. Some conditioners claim to mend split ends but this can only be a temporary clinging together of the damaged cortex. Cutting off the damaged end is still the only 'cure', but avoid processing and rough handling.

(6)   Green hair

This is included out of interest. It is possible for some people with fair hair to acquire a green hair coloration from dissolved copper in the water supply. The copper

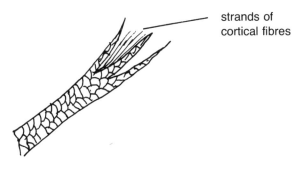

strands of
cortical fibres

Fig. 3.11   Fragilitis crinium.

is dissolved from water pipes and is trapped in the cuticle. It must be grown out of the hair. Some blondes who swim regularly complain of green hair, especially in open air swimming pools. This is due to the addition of chemicals called algicides to water (these are designed to stop green algae growing in the water). Algicides often contain copper compounds that react with the chlorine in the swimming pool to produce a green deposit on the hair. This can be avoided by wearing a swimming cap. Other colours are due to fashion!

Questions 3.9

1   What is monilethrix?
2   How is it caused?
3   How would you recognise pili torti?
4   What is trichonodosis?
5   How can trichonodosis be caused?
6   What is trichorrhexis nodosa?
7   What are the causes of trichorrhexis nodosa?
8   How can it be prevented?
9   What is fragilitis crinium more well known as?
10   What are the causes of this condition?
11   How should the hairdresser look after hair with fragilitis crinium?
12   What are the causes of green hair?

3.10   Sebaceous cysts

A sebaceous cyst may be recognised as a smooth mobile lump, often on the scalp, which is hairless. The lump varies in size from that of a pea to that of an egg. These lumps are harmless, but are removed under local anaesthetic if they are large or unsightly. Sebaceous cysts are also called wens. The cyst is derived from keratinising epidermis, but may contain sebaceous material. It is important that the hairdresser can recognise these cysts during the consultation stage of a service, so that they are not discovered with a shriek of horror during the service itself.

Questions 3.10

1 How would you recognise a sebaceous cyst?
2 What are sebaceous cysts also known as?
3 When do people have sebaceous cysts removed?

4

Infestations

The idea of having something else living on your body is very hard for most people to accept. We think that we are too clean for this to happen, but many of us will harbour some kind of parasite in our lifetime. This section will help you know what to look for, and what to do if you find them.

A parasite is a living creature that lives in, or on, another living creature, causing it harm. The amount of 'harm' varies because the most successful parasites cause such little harm to their hosts that they are not noticed.

4.1   Head lice – the hair invaders

Head lice have been with us for a long time; they have even been found on American Indian mummies that are several thousand years old. Many hairdressers think that head lice are rare, and that it is unlikely that they will ever see them on their clients. The facts, however, make it a most likely occurrence. It is estimated that each year *over one million people in Britain have lice*. They are most common in children, of whom one in every fifteen is infested. September and October are the peak months of the year for head lice, as children get back together after their summer holidays.

What kind of people get head lice?

Anyone with hair can get head lice. It is most common in children, particularly girls. If you have a child who has head lice, he or she will take them to school and infest other children, and in turn the children bring the infestation home to spread to the family. They are less common on negroid hair, because the claws of British lice cannot grip the flatter-shaped hair properly.

Head lice do not only infest dirty people – head lice love clean hair. Short hair is no protection either, they prefer it to long hair.

How do I recognise a head lice infestation?

In general the lice and their eggs, called nits, are found in the nape region of the head. Head lice can also infest the eyebrows. Most nits are found on girls in the area just over or behind the ears; on boys they are nearer the top of the head.

Whenever you are about to start on a client, you should always check the condition of the scalp before the service is started. It is most likely that you will see the nits within 1.25 cm (½ in) of the scalp. They are small, white, oval-shaped 'beads' which are attached to the hair by sticky cement. If you try to move these with a comb, they will stay in place. This is important to be sure you have not confused the nits with flakes of skin. It is unlikely that you will spot the lice without very careful examination. Figure 4.1 shows a heavy infestation of head lice; the nits can be clearly seen on the hair. This may be on a small section of the hair only, so it may not be as obvious as it appears in the picture. If you ever see scratch marks on the scalp, or general redness, always examine for nits. They are most difficult to spot on people with white or blonde hair, because of the light colour of the nits.

What should I do if a client has lice?

Don't panic! Your client is very unlikely to know that he or she has lice, and may not accept the fact too easily as most of us think that only dirty people have them. Quietly, ask a colleague, senior if possible, to check the scalp to confirm your diagnosis. The client should *not* be offered a service, and you should *not* treat them for lice in the salon. If other clients caught lice, it could ruin the reputation of the salon. Tell the client that you cannot offer them a service because they have lice, explaining at the same time that anyone can have them, regardless of cleanliness or class. Have they been in contact with young children? Advise them to get a lotion from a chem-

Fig. 4.1 A heavy infestation of lice showing the attachment of nits to the hair.

ist and to treat the *whole* family. Tell them that you will welcome them back once the infestation is cleared; make another appointment to check their scalp.

Try to do this away from other clients. They may be too embarrassed ever to come back if they are not reassured.

How can I be sure that the lice are not spread?

Take towels and gowns which have been near the infested client and boil them. You should also wash your own clothes or have them dry-cleaned – there is no need to throw them away! Soak your tools in disinfectant for an hour. If you have been in close contact with the client treat yourself with an insecticide lotion from the chemist. To be thorough, you can dust the client's chair with lindane powder. Try not to draw the attention of other clients to what is going on.

What should I do if lice are only spotted after starting the service to a client?

Again, don't panic! Once hair is wet or you have started cutting you must finish the service as quickly as possible. Do as above, but collect all cut hair from the floor and put it in a rubbish sack. Tie the open end firmly, and put the sack into another one for safety. Alternatively, this hair could be burnt. However, the fumes make this difficult in most salons.

As you should inspect the scalp before starting a service, this problem should not arise!

Lice facts

Lice are insects with six legs. They are between 2 and 3 mm in length so can be easily seen with the naked eye. To breed and lay eggs that will hatch, there must be a male and a female louse. Females outnumber males by four to one to maximise egg laying. A female will lay about eight eggs per night; mating of male and female occurs between the laying of each egg. Eggs require a temperature of 30°C to hatch in seven days, and because eggs are laid so near the scalp they get this. The live egg (nit), is plump and pale white, about the size of a pinhead (1 mm in diameter). Figure 4.2 shows a nit attached to a hair shaft. These will be found within 1.25 cm (½ in) of the scalp. Older, darker eggs are malformed, so do not hatch. The nits will hatch out within ten days and as soon as this happens the young louse will feed five times a day on blood. It has a mouth part like a needle that pierces the skin. Its saliva contains an anticoagulant to prevent the blood from clotting while the louse is feeding. After a few months the build-up of bites on the scalp causes the infested person to become sensitive, and they itch. The scratching is often the first indication that someone has lice. Young lice become mature adults within ten days of hatching, and will then begin laying their own eggs. As they live about one month, there will be two or three weeks of active egg laying.

The louse can adapt its colour to suit the particular host. Thus lice on blondes are paler than those on brunettes. Some people with an infestation will have small red spots, and hardly any itching. Others who are more sensitive will have severe itching

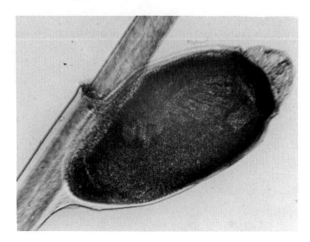

Fig. 4.2   An enlarged photograph of a nit showing its attachment to a scalp hair.

and redness, with swollen glands. Infections, such as impetigo (see Section 2.3), can result from this. Impetigo contracted this way is referred to as a secondary infection. There have been cases of over one thousand lice on an individual's head.

Lice are spread by direct contact – by simply walking from one head to another. (This is very easy when children play games or huddle together.) Lice can move at a speed of 30 cm (1 ft) per minute. Because long hair impedes the journey from scalp to scalp, they prefer short hair. At night, they may be attracted to body warmth.

Here are some more facts about lice:

- They cannot fly or jump.
- They spread mostly by direct contact from head to head.
- Normal shampooing will not stop you from getting lice. It will only guarantee clean lice!
- Lice have no defence against injury; a scratching finger or a comb moving through the hair will often result in their death.
- Although some lice are resistant to insecticides such as DDT, there are still other insecticides that will kill them.
- A louse does not stick to one head, it can pass to as many as five heads in one day!
- They do not prefer dirty heads.

What is the correct treatment?

Special lotions and shampoos are available, but I urge you to use a lotion as it will work in one application, and will kill both lice and nits. Shampoos may need to be used several times, and the infestation may be spread in the time it takes for a series of applications. The dose of insecticide can be one thousand times stronger from a lotion that it is from a shampoo!

A lotion containing either 0.5% malathion or 0.5% carbaryl will kill lice and eggs in one two-hour application. If left on the hair for twelve hours (overnight) a residual effect will help prevent reinfestation. Lotions are either alcohol- or water-based. The alcohol may sting broken skin and irritate eczema-prone skin. As it is flammable, do not smoke or use it near a naked flame. If it dries out the scalp, apply a little vegetable oil to the scalp afterwards. Water-based lotions should be used on sore or broken skin, and for asthmatic children who may develop an attack from alcohol fumes. They do not give the residual effect of lotions based on alcohol, so are less effective in preventing further infestations.

Keep lotions away from the eyes!

When I treat someone with lice I usually put some lotion on my hairy arms as a precaution. If you saw the lice running through the hair to escape the lotion you would understand why!

Other points:

- Use up all the lotion over the entire scalp.
- Do not store lotions in direct sunlight or above a radiator as a temperature of above 25°C will make them unstable.
- Treat all members of a household where one person has been infested or the infestation may reoccur.
- Use a fine-toothed comb to comb the hair. This will help to dislodge lice.
- Regular combing of hair will help to discourage lice, especially at night as this dislodges any that have been picked up during the day.
- So-called 'super lice' do exist. They have built up a resistance to some insecticides. This could happen if an incorrect, sub-lethal dose of insecticide were given, such as a shampoo or too small a dose of a lotion. Some of the chemicals used after the Second World War, such as DDT, can be broken down and made harmless by the lice. Malathion and carbaryl in lotion form, however, will destroy any lice.
- Lotions applied within two days of hair being bleached or coloured could cause the colour to become 'patchy'.
- If a lasting residual effect is required from the lotion, so that reinfestation does

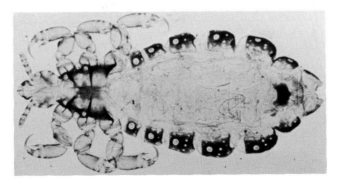

Fig. 4.3 A human head louse.

Fig. 4.4   The life cycle of the louse. (Courtesy Napp Laboratories Ltd.)

(1) Transfer

The head louse spends its day wandering around from head to head, feeding where it wants to.

(2) Lays eggs

The female lays eggs. It's an intricate task, glueing an egg to a hair, very near to or touching the scalp to keep warm. She usually does it at night, when her host is still. She tries to make it blend with the surroundings, and will lay 7 or 8 each night.

(3) Mating

The female usually mates between laying each egg. As females outnumber males about 4 to 1, father louse's night work is at least as demanding!

(4) Hatching

Each egg takes 7–10 days to hatch. When the louse is ready to hatch, the plug at the end of the egg is too small, when removed, for the louse to get out. So it gulps in air, passes it through the body until the louse, under pressure, 'pops' out of the egg. The empty egg shell (the nit) is left on the hair and is now gleaming white.

(5) First drink
The newly hatched, colourless, louse has its first feed and its body can be seen filling up with blood. It pierces the skin with its mouthparts and couples up to a capillary, meanwhile pumping in a local anaesthetic and anti-coagulant. The louse feeds five times a day.

(6) Moulting
The young louse moults three times before becoming adult (and will then be just under match-head size).

(7) Opportunity
Now an adult all the louse wants to do is travel (from head to head) and have a good time with the opposite sex, never missing a chance to change heads or partners, and doing its bit for the louse population.

(8) Old age
If it lives that long, it will die of old age at about forty days.

not take place, do not swim in a chlorinated swimming pool. The residual effect will also be lost if perming, bleaching or colouring are carried out within two days of lotion application.

● The head louse shown in Figure 4.3 is greatly enlarged. On the scalp it would be the size of a pinhead and hidden amongst the hair. Be on your guard and remember what to do.

The Latin name for the head louse is Pediculus capitis. The correct medical term for an infestation of head lice is pediculosis capitis. Figure 4.4 represents the life-cycle of the head louse.

Questions 4.1

1   What is a parasite?
2   How long have head lice been known on humans?
3   How many people get head lice each year in Britain?
4   Who is most likely to have head lice?
5   In what months are they most common?
6   Do lice prefer clean or dirty hair?
7   Do lice prefer long or short hair?
8   How would you recognise an infestation of head lice?
9   Where are nits found on males and females?
10   What can nits be confused with?
11   Why are nits difficult to spot on blonde hair?
12   What should you do if a client has lice?
13   Should the client be offered a service?
14   How can you try and ensure that the client returns to the salon?
15   What should you do to prevent the lice spreading in the salon?
16   What should you do if you have already started the service? .
17   Using Figure 4.4, briefly describe the life cycle of the head louse.
18   If nit cases were found two inches from the scalp, roughly how old would they be (check back to Chapter 1 if you cannot remember how fast hair grows)?
19   How do lice get from head to head?
20   What do they feed on?
21   Why does combing or brushing the hair help prevent lice?
22   Would you use a lotion or shampoo to treat head lice?
23   What is the reason for your choice?
24   What do the lotions and shampoos contain?
25   Are there any safety precautions to be observed when using lotions?
26   When would you use a water-based lotion?
27   How can the residual effect of alcoholic lotions be lost?
28   What is the latin name for a head louse?
29   What is the medical term for an infestation of head lice?
30   What secondary infection is often associated with head lice?

4.2   Body lice

These are very similar to head lice but they are larger. As the name implies, the body louse feeds on blood from the body and not the head. Although it is called a body louse it is in fact found in the seams of clothing, and goes on to the body only to feed. The eggs will be found in the seams along with the lice. Body lice have been responsible for many deaths in the past because they transmitted the disease called typhus when they bit people. They have also been known to spread relapsing and trench fevers. Unlike head lice, body lice are associated with poverty and poor living conditions.

Treatment is still with DDT powder, dusted on to the clothes. The host should be bathed while the clothes are treated. In Britain body lice are more likely to be found on vagrants (those who 'sleep rough'). The correct name for a body louse is Pediculus corporis.

Body lice cause intense irritation and restlessness. The subsequent scratching may cause impetigo and swollen glands. The general feeling of ill-health has led to the everyday term of 'feeling lousy'. Figure 4.5 shows a body louse alongside both head and pubic lice to give an idea of relative size. It is thought that the body louse developed from the head louse when man began to wear clothing. Lice are well adapted to the human body, so much so that they cannot live for long in cool conditions, or in very dry heat. If you were to die, any lice on you would leave quickly in search of another warm body!

Questions 4.2

1 What do body lice feed on?
2 What would be found in the seams of clothing of someone who had body lice?
3 Who is likely to have body lice in Britain?
4 Where does the term 'feeling lousy' originate from?
5 Can lice live for long away from a human body?

4.3 Pubic lice

Very few things are as upsetting as finding out that you have pubic lice. They are quite common, and it is thought that several hundred thousand people have them in

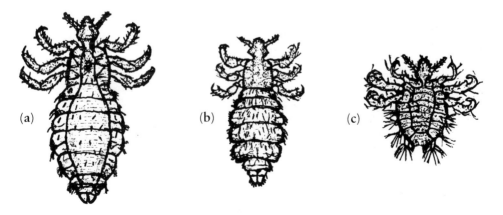

Fig. 4.5 The three types of lice that live on man. (a) The body louse. (b) The head louse. (c) The pubic louse.

Britain. In the past 'crabs', as they are commonly known, were associated only with prostitutes and those with low moral values. This is no longer the case, and I have had past students come to me for advice. One student had a child of two with pubic lice in his eyelashes and she could not understand how it was possible for him to be infested at that age.

The pubic louse belongs to a different grouping from head and body lice. It is correctly called Phthirus pubis, although the infestation is still referred to as pediculosis pubis.

How and where would I get pubic lice?

The louse is usually transmitted by sexual contact. It can also be spread on shed hairs present in borrowed clothing, towels or bedding. Some young babies have caught it on their eyelashes from the breast hairs of their mothers while feeding. Medical help should always be sought if the eyelashes are infested.

Although, as its name implies, it is most commonly found in the pubic hairs, it is also found frequently under the arms, in beards and on the eyelashes. It is even possible for it to be found on the thinning hair of bald men!

There are usually less than a dozen adult lice on an individual if the infestation is confined to the pubic area, but as many as one hundred have been found on eyelashes! The louse is smaller than head lice, usually 1.5–2 mm long and about as broad. It can be clearly seen from the photograph in Figure 4.6 why pubic lice are called 'crabs'. The front claws are large and designed for gripping coarse hairs. The female attaches her eggs to these coarse hairs and they hatch in about seven days. Maturity is reached in just over two weeks. Eggs are laid at a rate of about five a day, limiting the number of eggs to about two dozen, as the life cycle of a pubic louse is some twenty-five days. The lice are very difficult to spot, and can hide under the hairs. They tend to stay in one place, feeding up to twelve times a day. They will

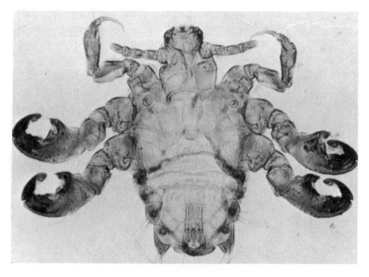

Fig. 4.6 The pubic louse.

move up on to the trunk of a hairy body to lay their eggs. If you have pubic lice the symptoms depend on how sensitive you are, ranging from mild irritation to swollen glands. Scratching can result in bacterial infections.

How would I get rid of pubic lice?

There are a number of lotions and shampoos on the market. There is no need to shave off all your pubic and body hair! If you go to the chemist and get a shampoo, try to use it all over the hairy parts of your body (excluding the eyes), repeating the process a few days afterwards. Lotions are available with 0.1% malathion. Lice on eyelashes or eyebrows should be removed manually.

- Crab lice can be caught directly or indirectly.
- They can be found on any hairy area of the body but not usually on the scalp.
- They can only live for one day without blood.

Questions 4.3

1   What is the common name for pubic lice?
2   How can pubic lice be caught?
3   Where on the body can pubic lice be found?
4   What symptoms do sufferers of pubic lice show?
5   What is the treatment for pubic lice?

4.4   Scabies

This is the name of the infestation caused by the itch mite, whose proper name is Sarcoptes scabiei. The mite is a tiny eight-legged creature (because it has eight legs, rather than six, it is not an insect). It is about 0.4 mm long and is just visible to the naked eye. The female mite burrows into the epidermis where she lays her eggs. The burrows are about 3 mm long, and are seen as thread-like lines. Male mites are rarely seen, since mating with the female results in their untimely death!

People are usually aware that there is something wrong because of the severe itching that the presence of the mite eventually produces. This is particularly noticeable at night in bed. The burrows may be few and far between, but usually a characteristic rash and scratch marks can be seen. The burrows are most likely to be observed between the fingers or under the wrists (over 60% of all cases are found here), but they may also be under the breasts or around the groin. Women and children get them on the palms of the hands. The itch mite never goes above the neckline.

Many people wonder how it can burrow into the skin. It usually starts at a natural wrinkle, and uses its jaws and front two pairs of legs for digging. These have suckers and a cutting edge. The backward-facing spines on its back give it a hold as it pushes into the tunnel. Figure 4.7 shows an itch mite; the pairs of legs can be clearly seen. It burrows at a rate of 2 mm per day. The female lays two or three oval eggs each day, leaving between ten and twenty eggs along the length of a burrow. After laying her eggs the female dies at the end of her burrow, usually having lived for about two

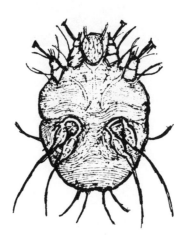

Fig. 4.7 The itch mite.

months. The eggs hatch within four days. The male goes through two stages of development: the egg first hatches to give a six-legged larva, which later moults to give an eight-legged nymph which grows into the adult. The female goes through three stages of development (it has one other nymph stage). From hatching, it takes just over two weeks to become an adult.

It takes between six and eight weeks to get the itching associated with scabies. Continual scratching actually keeps the numbers of the mite down, as many are scratched out. If an individual is not sensitive to the itching, it is possible to develop what has been termed 'Norwegian scabies'. In this a huge population develops in the skin and the skin thickens. The skin, riddled with mite burrows, flakes off. Such people are usually of low mental development and have a defective immune system that gives them an unnatural tolerance of the infestation so that they do not seek help. They can have an infestation where over a million mites are present. They are highly infectious and will cause many cases of scabies in people with whom they come into contact.

- Scabies is caught almost exclusively from direct contact with another person, usually by sleeping in close contact.
- As many as 2% of the British population will have scabies some time in their lifetime.
- In two European countries the incidence has been as high as 10% of the population.
- Animal scabies, in cats and dogs, is called mange. It can be caught by humans.
- Scabies is often not diagnosed, usually being confused with eczema.
- It can sweep through institutions. At Long Kesh, the internment camp in Northern Ireland, there were over three hundred cases.
- Once treated, a second attack produces itching almost immediately. The mite is then usually scratched out so that the second infestation does not get started.
- Treatment is carried out on two consecutive nights. After soaking in a warm bath for ten minutes to soften the skin, the body is briskly towelled. Then a 1%

gamma benzene hexachloride (or 25% benzyl benzoate) cream is applied to the whole body from the neck down. This treatment can cause eczema, however, and itching may take several days to clear up.

- *All* members of a household should be treated, after which all bed linen, towels and clothes should be washed.

Questions 4.4

1 What causes scabies?
2 How many legs has an itch mite?
3 Where are the mites found?
4 How do most people know there is something wrong with their skin when they have scabies?
5 Where are mite burrows most likely to be seen?
6 Describe the life cycle of an itch mite.
7 How is scabies caught?
8 What is animal scabies commonly called?
9 How is scabies treated?
10 Who should be treated?

4.5 Bedbugs

Many of us are familiar with the expression 'don't let the bedbugs bite'. They live in cracks in walls and skirting boards, or in the seams of mattresses where they lay their eggs. Bedbugs feed on any warm-blooded animal and can live up to eighteen months.

They come to feed on their hosts at night, feeding on the throat or face. There are two types: Cimex lectularius which is found in temperate climates (Europe and

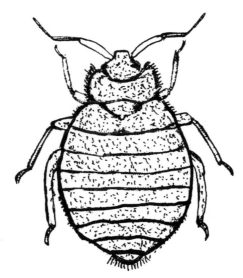

Fig. 4.8 The bedbug.

North America) and Cimex hemipterus which is found in the tropics. The adult bedbug is about 6 mm long and reddish-brown in colour with the appearance of a flattened beetle. One is shown in Figure 4.8. Bedbugs feed every night in warm temperatures (25°C), and about every sixth day at 15°C. However, bedbugs can survive by feeding once a year if the temperature is low enough. At freezing point they can last several months without feeding at all. A bedbug lays about three eggs per night and about one hundred in her lifetime. Some people suffer little reaction to their bites while others get a blister-like swelling. Bedbugs are now comparatively rare in Britain but in the 1930s they were found in one in ten houses. There is usually a peculiar sickly smell in houses infested with bedbugs. Although they do not do so in Britain, in West Africa they have been shown to transmit the hepatitis B virus.

Questions 4.5

1   Where do bedbugs live?
2   When and what do bedbugs feed on?
3   How does temperature affect the feeding of bedbugs?
4   Are bedbugs common in Britain?

4.6   Fleas

The human flea is correctly called Pulex irritans. It is a small brown insect renowned for its jumping power because of its long and powerful hind-legs. If a flea were the size of a man it could jump over St. Paul's cathedral or complete a long jump of 400 metres (¼ mile). A flea is shown in Figure 4.9.

The flea lives on blood, and has mouthparts adapted for biting and sucking. It is

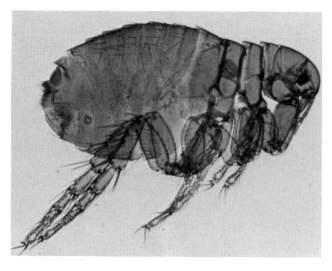

Fig. 4.9   A cat flea.

usually cat and dog fleas that bite people in Britain, as the human flea is becoming rare. The bites cause small red spots surrounded by a pink patch. They will produce intense irritation, and the bites and subsequent scratches are often seen around the ankles.

The reason for the human flea becoming rarer is that housing conditions have become drier and cleaner. Indeed, it is the vacuum cleaner that has picked up most of the eggs and hatched out larvae.

Cat fleas like dry conditions, and although the flea must feed on the host (whether cat or human) it lays its eggs in carpets and on chairs. Even with a vacuum cleaner, the carpet next to the skirting board and near radiators is usually missed. A cat may carry as many as one hundred fleas with it at any one time, but as it moves between several spots where it lies within the house, the total flea population may approach two thousand. Female fleas can lay between six and eight eggs per second, so it is possible for a room to have thousands of eggs, which hatch to form maggot-like larvae which live in dust and dirt. The adults will require two meals a day.

The reason cats are not so bothered by their fleas is that the bites cause them little irritation. If you are bitten repeatedly for five years you will also become desensitised and not get any more bite marks – cat lovers please note!

If you are troubled by fleas, use insecticide powders everywhere the cat goes, and treat the cat as well.

Questions 4.6

1   What do fleas feed on?
2   What type of flea is most likely to bite you in Britain?
3   Where would bite marks usually be found?
4   Where are flea eggs likely to be found?
5   How many fleas might be found in a house?
6   How would you get rid of them?

4.7   Face mites

The face mite, Demodex folliculorum, feeds on sebum and inhabits the follicles of the eyelashes and the nose. It may also be found on the chin and forehead, particularly in adolescents with acne. It has also been found in the majority of nipples. All these areas have large sebaceous glands in common. The mites are tiny, about 0.3 mm long, have four pairs of short legs and their bodies have a worm-like shape. They are probably present on almost everyone, and do not appear to cause any harm to humans.

If you have a microscope, see if you can find some on an eyelash follicle (pluck one out and examine the root end). This can be placed on a slide with a little olive oil to keep the mite alive. They will spend several happy hours gorging themselves on the oil. There can be as many as twenty-five mites on an eyelash root. Each lives for about two weeks. A heavy infestation of mites can lead to 'soggy' eyelashes which can be easily removed. Face mites are best kept under control by washing with soap and water and avoiding face creams.

Questions 4.7

1   Where would face mites be found?
2   What do they feed on?
3   Are face mites harmful?
4   What can a heavy infestation of face mites cause?
5   How can they be controlled?

4.8   Dust mites

The dust mite, Dermatophagoides pteronissinus, is about 0.3 mm long and is found in most houses. It feeds off our shed skin which has accumulated in the seams and buttons of mattresses. Dust mites are more common in damp rooms and are therefore discouraged by central heating or by airing beds. They cause no harm to most people, but when beds are made their faeces and the mites themselves are thrown into the air. On being inhaled this can lead to sneezing fits – caused by an allergy to the mites.

If you are allergic, try to eliminate the mite. Mattresses should be covered with plastic and all bedding, floor coverings and curtains should be frequently cleaned. As many as 40% of people who show allergy symptoms are allergic to dust mites.

Questions 4.8

1   What do dust mites feed on?
2   Where are they most likely to be found?
3   How can somebody who is allergic to dust mites avoid contact with them?

4.9   Threadworms

This is the most common intestinal worm in Britain, properly called Enterobius vermicularis. The common term for having threadworms is 'itchy arse' and if you have had it you will know why. It is children who are mostly affected. The worms inhabit the lower part of the intestine (caecum and rectum) and may sometimes be seen in the faeces as fine white threads. At night the female worm comes out of the anus and lays eggs on the skin. There is intense irritation and the host itches. It can cause restlessness and loss of sleep. Because of the itching, children get eggs under their finger nails from which they are reinfected. When the bed is made the air becomes full of eggs which can then be breathed in by adults. The worms may be found on clothing or even lavatory seats. The initial infestation may have been from eating food or drinking water containing the eggs.

To treat the child it is best to cut the finger nails short and frequently boil their flannel and towels. As it is almost certain that several people will be infested in the household, everyone should be treated. A product called Pripsen is available, consisting of granules which are dissolved in water to make a drink. One nasty thing about this particular medicine is the smell; it makes many children feel like being sick. My own childhood memories are of my mother holding my nose as she forced me to swallow the medicine.

The majority of parasites dealt with in this chapter are *Ectoparasites* – that is, they live on the outside of the body. Parasites like tapeworms and threadworms are *Endoparasites*, because they live inside the body.

Questions 4.9

1 Who is most likely to have threadworms?
2 Where are threadworms found?
3 How would you know if you had threadworms?
4 How are threadworms caught?
5 How would you get rid of threadworms?
6 Why is a threadworm referred to as an endoparasite?

4.10 Parasites on holiday

As air travel has become cheaper and more people go abroad on holiday, the incidence of parasitic infection while abroad has risen. These unwelcome holiday 'experiences' can be very serious, and also very difficult to cure. Before you go on holiday ask the travel agent if there are any preventative medicines that should be taken. This section will examine some of the better known parasites that could be encountered; medical help would be important in all these cases.

Hookworms

There are two varieties, Ankylostoma duodenale and Necator americanus. These are found mostly in the tropics but can also be found in North America and the Mediterranean. The adult worms attach themselves by their hooks to the walls of the small intestine. Their eggs are passed out in faeces and develop in warm humid soil to form larvae, which can infect those who walk barefoot. Hookworm larvae can also be ingested with food, but this is uncommon. The hookworm bites the intestine and blood may be seen in the faeces. Weight loss and anaemia result. Chemicals are available for treatment. Prevention includes the sanitary disposal of waste, wearing shoes and general hygiene of food and drink, which otherwise might become infected.

Roundworms

The species of roundworm parasitic in man is called Ascaris lumbricoides. They can be up to 30 cm in length (1 ft) and live for up to a year in the intestine. If there is a heavy infection of worms the intestine can be obstructed. The eggs are passed out in faeces and can live for up to five years in damp soil. The eggs are often eaten on salads and raw vegetables. Chemicals are available for treatment but prevention includes sanitary disposal of waste and general hygiene of food and drink. They are found in many areas of the world including North America and Europe.

Tapeworms

These parasites get their name from their flattened, ribbon-like appearance. In Britain it is still possible, though very rare, to get pork and beef tapeworms, but there are many different varieties throughout the world including some that spend part of their life cycles in fish, dogs and cats. Taeniasis is the name given to an infestation by the worms. The beef tapeworm can grow to a length of twelve metres (40 ft) and can have a body made up of as many as two thousand segments. Each segment contains eggs which can be released in faeces. If the eggs are eaten by cattle they form embryos which infest the muscles of cattle and form small cysts. If beef is eaten undercooked any cysts present will survive and later hatch to form new worms in the intestine. If there is a heavy infection with worms they do not absorb as much food from the intestine, and the worms remain small so that they do not cause an intestinal blockage. To prevent tapeworms, always eat meat or fish which has been properly cooked. Meat inspection has reduced their prevalence in Britain but tapeworms are still common in many parts of the world. (In Victorian England illegal but very effective slimming tablets were sold which contained the tapeworm cysts!) Chemicals are available for treatment.

Elephantiasis

Elephantiasis is one of the most obvious diseases of the tropics because the worms cause parts of the body to increase in size. Ankles may become as big as a person's waist; fingers become as big as wrists and the scrotum of the male genital organs may become so enlarged that a man cannot walk. These symptoms are caused by the small worms invading the lymph spaces and obstructing the flow of lymph. The swelling is followed by a growth of connective tissue which makes it permanent. The worm causing this condition is Wuchereria bancrofti. It is spread by the larvae in the bloodstream being picked up by the bite of a mosquito (such as Culex). The larvae develop further in the body of the mosquito and within a few days infect another person when the mosquito bites again. The disease takes a year to develop and can be killed with drugs before parts of the body enlarge. The disease is found in many Pacific Islands, Australia, China, Korea, Japan, the West Indies, North and South America, India and S.E. Asia. Prevention is by eradication of the mosquito and avoidance of being bitten.

Guinea worm

People in Asia and Africa may acquire this disease by drinking water contaminated with the larvae of the worm Dranunculus medinensis, which are contained in water fleas which can be taken in as one drinks. The larvae migrate through the intestinal wall and travel to the skin of the lower leg. The adult female worm causes an area of red raised skin to develop which blisters. On contact with water a milky fluid is discharged, and this releases larvae into the water so that they can again enter the water fleas and the cycle starts again.

Malaria

Malaria is caused by the protozoan Plasmodium. It is carried to man by the bite of a certain species of the female mosquito Anopheles. The disease is widespread in

Asia, Africa, Central and South America and a number of Pacific Islands. A feeling of ill-health is followed by a shaking chill, which eventually develops into a fever with profuse sweating. These attacks occur at one to three day intervals. Preventive treatment is available in the form of tablets which should be taken the day before entering the malarious area, daily therein, and for two weeks after leaving. A number of people develop malaria each year in Britain because they do not take preventive medicine. Malaria is a disease that cannot be permanently cured, and there will be relapses. The main hope for eradicating malaria is in controlling the mosquito that spreads the disease. Swamps are therefore drained and areas near villages are sprayed with insecticide.

Always check before you travel to see if you need to take precautions.

Questions 4.10

1   Why are parasites becoming more common in Britain?
2   In what countries are hookworms found?
3   How could you become infected with hookworms?
4   How could you become infected with roundworms?
5   Where does the tapeworm get its name from?
6   What meats could tapeworms be caught from?
7   How can this be prevented?
8   How is elephantiasis spread?
9   What can be done to prevent elephantiasis?
10 How are guinea worms caught?
11 Where can malaria be caught?
12 How can malaria be prevented?
13 What should you do before you go abroad?

5

General Salon Hygiene

Anyone who deals closely with people has a duty to make sure that the spread of infection is prevented. The hairdresser is in close contact with the public, and it is possible to spread infection on infected tools or in the warm, moist atmosphere that a salon provides.

This chapter examines how the hairdresser can prevent this, by the use of sterilisation and disinfectants, and by regulating the salon environment.

5.1 Methods of sterilisation

Sterilisation is the complete destruction of all living organisms on an object. Although this is the ideal you should aim for in the salon it is difficult to achieve in practice. The three main methods of sterilisation used are heat, chemical vapours and radiation. *Tools should be washed before sterilisation.*

(1) Heat

Dry heat refers to either the use of an oven, naked flame, burning or glass bead steriliser. These methods are not really suitable in salons for a number of reasons.

(1) *Oven*
   For an oven to sterilise it is necessary to leave an object in it for an hour at 160°C. This will kill even resistant bacterial spores. Dry heat can only be used where the item to be sterilised will not suffer physical damage through heating, so this would exclude most pieces of hairdressing equipment.
(2) *Naked flame*
   A naked flame can be used to sterilise metal. If a needle is heated until red hot it will be sterilised. A flame can blunt sharp edges so it would be unwise to treat your scissors like this – their costly blades could be ruined if they were repeatedly sterilised in this way.

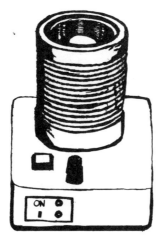

Fig. 5.1 A glass bead steriliser

(3) *Burning*

Burning of salon refuse, particularly hair, is a very effective way of sterilising salon rubbish. The drawback is that when hair is burnt it smells strongly of sulphur, which is present in the keratin of which hair is made. Neighbouring shops or houses would not appreciate this. Also, your area may be a smokeless one, where it is illegal to burn such refuse.

(4) *Glass bead sterilisers*

Glass bead sterilisers are often used in beauty establishments. They are small electrically-heated boxes with an insulated round cylinder full of small glass beads. One is illustrated in Figure 5.1. Because of their small size they cannot be used for much more than a few needles or the blades of scissors. They must be turned on for between 15 and 60 minutes to heat up before use. The metal to be sterilised is plunged into the beads as deeply as possible. The temperature reached varies with different models from 190° to 300°C. It takes from 1 to 10 minutes to sterilise, depending on the temperature reached, so you must check manufacturers' instructions. For electrolysis needles, it is recommended that a fresh sterile needle is used for every client.

Moist heat refers either to boiling at the normal boiling point of water or to boiling at an even higher temperature using pressure. Moist heat kills germs more quickly than dry heat, as it penetrates more quickly.

Placing an object into boiling water will kill most germs within fifteen minutes. However, the spores formed by bacteria may take longer to be killed. Water boils at 100°C, and this is suitable for sterilising towels. In the salon this may not be possible, but if you are washing towels in an automatic washing machine do so on the hottest wash cycle. If you use either wash cycle 1 or 9 this will produce a temperature of 95°C. Boiling should not be used on most plastics as the heat will distort them. Some metals might rust, so do not boil metals either, except for stainless steel.

To increase the temperature at which water boils it must be put under pressure.

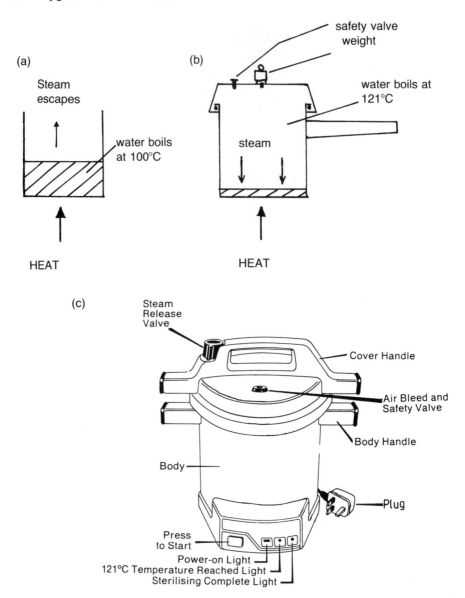

Fig. 5.2 Water boiling (a) in an open container (b) in a pressure cooker and (c) in an automatic autoclave.

Have you ever wondered why things cook faster in a pressure cooker? It is because the food is cooked at a higher temperature than it would be if it were just boiled normally. How do we put the water under extra pressure? Look at Figure 5.2(a). This is an open container of water that is being heated. When steam is being given off and the water is bubbling the temperature is 100°C. The steam is escaping into the atmosphere. In Figure 5.2(b), there is a tightly fitting, sealed lid on the container. Once the water boils the steam is given off but has nowhere to go as it is trapped within the container. This eventually leads to a build-up of pressure within the container, and with this increased pressure there is also an increase in the boiling point of the water.

In most pressure cookers used in homes, the pressure is maintained at 15 pounds per square inch by means of a small weight on a hole in the lid of the pressure cooker. At this pressure, the temperature at which water boils is increased to 121°C. Once the steam inside the container reaches this pressure, the weight is pushed out of the hole by the steam, allowing steam to escape. If there were no hole to allow the steam to escape the pressure would build up until the pressure cooker exploded. As a safety precaution, in case this hole gets blocked, there is a safety valve which should prevent such an explosion. *Never open the lid of a pressure cooker until all steam has been allowed to escape or you could be badly scalded.*

In hospitals and laboratories, autoclaves are used for sterilising. These work in the same way as pressure cookers but take much bigger loads, and have pressure gauges instead of weights to maintain pressure correctly. Fifteen minutes' exposure will kill even the most resistant spores.

Cheaper automatic autoclaves which cost a few hundred pounds are available for use in salons. One is illustrated in Figure 5.2(c). Tools are loaded into an internal tray and a small amount of water is placed in the autoclave. Once the autoclave is turned on the full cycle will take about 30 minutes. Although sterilisation is relatively quick, in a busy salon a hairdresser would need at least two pairs of scissors so that one could be used while the other was being sterilised.

(2) Chemical vapours

When some chemicals are heated they give off vapours. When the liquid called formalin (you may have seen this at school – it is the liquid most biological specimens are 'pickled' in to preserve them) is heated up, it gives off formaldehyde vapour. Because the fumes are irritating to the nose and throat, the vapour can only be released to sterilise tools if it is done in an enclosed cabinet. Such a cabinet is shown in Figure 5.3. A piece of cotton wool or foam is first soaked in 5% formalin (it is available up to 40% strength) and placed in a holder in the steriliser. There is a heating element just below this, and when the electricity is turned on this element

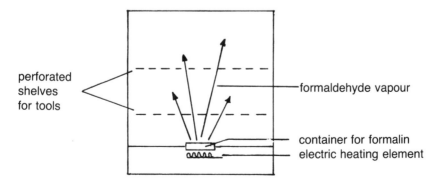

Fig. 5.3 Formaldehyde cabinet.

heats up to cause the formalin to give off formaldehyde vapour. The steriliser has shelves with holes to allow the vapour to circulate. The door should be kept closed so that fumes do not enter the salon. *Before placing tools in the steriliser, wash them with soap and hot water to remove grease, otherwise some germs may not be killed.* Tools must be kept in the cabinet for twenty minutes.

The formaldehyde cabinet is a suitable method for sterilising rollers, brushes, combs, nets, and most other non-metal tools. If it is used to sterilise metal tools it tends to spoil the surface, by producing minute pits. It will blunt the cutting edge of scissors or a razor, so do not sterilise metal tools using this method. Do not sterilise vibro applicators or highlighting caps as the rubber hardens and perishes (use disinfectant instead).

(3) Radiation

In the majority of salons sterilisation is carried out using small ultra-violet cabinets which are relatively inexpensive. They are often used incorrectly so that the tools placed inside them are not sterilised.

Figure 5.4 shows a diagram of an ultra-violet cabinet. It has a door which usually pulls down or up, and a wire grid shelf for placing the objects to be sterilised. The tools must be thoroughly washed in hot soapy water to remove all traces of sebum. Any grease remaining on the tools will form a protective barrier for germs, as the radiation will be absorbed by the grease and will not pass through. Also, because radiation, like light, only travels in straight lines, the tools must be turned. This means that if you have tools in the cabinet for ten minutes on one side, they must be turned for another ten minutes to complete sterilisation.

The cabinet should also be cleaned regularly so that there is no dirt on the ultra-violet tube which could reduce the efficiency of the steriliser. As ultra-violet radiation can cause eye damage (conjunctivitis) the opening of the cabinet door usually acts as a switch to turn off the mercury vapour lamp.

Ultra-violet cabinets cannot be considered efficient enough sterilisers to be used with tools if blood has been drawn. Then autoclaves or disinfectants should be used. However, the ultra-violet cabinets should not just be thrown away as they make a good area for the storage of your tools. Clients will at least think that you are hygienic and looking after their welfare so make sure you use them effectively. I have known salons where plugs were not fitted to the cabinets, yet people were using them, thinking that they were working!

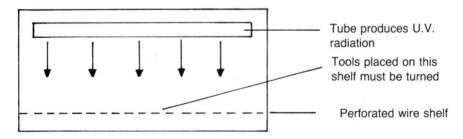

Tube produces U.V. radiation

Tools placed on this shelf must be turned

Perforated wire shelf

Fig. 5.4 Ultra-violet sterilising cabinet.

Questions 5.1

1 Why should you be hygienic in the salon?
2 What is sterilisation?
3 What methods of sterilisation are used in salons?
4 Why are ovens not used in salons?
5 Why are naked flames not used to sterilise scissors?
6 When might burning be used in the salon?
7 What drawbacks usually prevent it being used?
8 What is a glass bead steriliser?
9 Should it be used to sterilise electrolysis needles?
10 Why is moist heat a better sterilising agent than dry heat?
11 What items would you sterilise by boiling?
12 How can the boiling point of water be increased above 100°C?
13 What is an autoclave?
14 How are chemical vapours used to sterilise tools?
15 What would you sterilise using this method?
16 How would you use an ultra-violet cabinet?
17 What are the drawbacks of these cabinets?

5.2 Disinfectants

A disinfectant is a chemical that will kill germs (including viruses) if used long enough and if strong enough. If you place your tools in some very dilute disinfectant for hours it will not kill many germs, nor will it if you put your tools into some very strong disinfectant for a few seconds.

Disinfectants can be used for a number of things in the salon. As baths, they can be used to disinfect tools. They can also be used for cleaning and disinfecting surfaces in the salon. How many times do you put your comb down on the work surface? When is the last time it was washed down properly?

Several different types of disinfectant are available for use in the salon:

- *Coal tar derivatives* These include phenol and cresols. The best known of these is Dettol. They are best used for washing down salon surfaces, diluted according to manufacturers' instructions. They can also be used as a bath for tools.
- *Quats* These are quaternary ammonium compounds, the best known of which is cetrimide. This is available as Savlon. They are *cationic* detergents – that is, they have a positive charge. Most detergents and soaps are *anionic* and have a negative charge. This leads to one complication: quats are not compatible with anionic detergents and their qualities as a disinfectant can be cancelled by shampoos or soaps. This happens because the opposite charges cancel each other out. Cetrimide can be used as a 1–2% solution as a bath for tools. It is suitable for metal tools and ten minutes should be long enough to disinfect. It works best in alkaline conditions.
- *Hypochlorite* This is a form of chlorine, used by most manufacturers of baby sterilising fluids, Milton being the most well-known. It is very effective against all germs including viruses and spores. At a neutral pH it may corrode metal so

Fig. 5.5 Barbicide disinfecting jars being used on a variety of tools. (Courtesy of Renscene Ltd, Surrey.)

should be alkaline when used for metal tools. Ten minutes' exposure in a bath will be sufficient for sterilising tools.

- *Bleach*   This term is used here for household bleach which contains chlorine. I recommend this for cleaning work surfaces, sinks and toilets. If, however, you are cleaning the toilet *never allow bleach to come into contact with another lavatory cleaner – many react to give off poisonous fumes.*
- *Glutaraldehyde*   This is available as a liquid, the best known being Cidex. As a 2% solution it is effective as a bath for tools; immerse for about ten minutes.
- *Alcohol*   This is available in a number of forms, methylated spirits and iso-propanol being easily available. They can be used to wipe over tools as they dry quickly. In the skin test they can be used to clean skin, and are good for removing dried hairspray and setting lotion from salon surfaces such as mirrors.
- *Disinfectant kits*   The increasing use of disinfectants in salons has led to the introduction of special kits to make the process of disinfection more easy. One company manufactures a glass container with a pull-up holder for tools. The disinfectant has a rust inhibitor so it can be used safely on metal tools. This is illustrated in Figure 5.5.
- Try not to put wet tools into disinfectant or the solution will be diluted.
- If disinfectants are contaminated with debris they will 'go off'. Discard solutions which change colour.

Figure 5.6 sets out a table of commonly used disinfectants and antiseptics.

Questions 5.2

1   What is a disinfectant?
2   How can disinfectants be used in the salon?
3   What disinfectants are in use in your salon?
4   Find out from the manufacturers' instructions how they should be used and note this down.
5   What would you use as a bath for tools?
6   What would you use to wipe down work surfaces?
7   Why should washed tools be dried before being put in disinfectants?
8   What should you do if a bath of disinfectant changes colour?

5.3   Antiseptics

Antiseptics are substances that will inhibit the growth of germs; this does not mean that they will kill them. An antiseptic must be suitable for applying to skin, as its main use is to stop any kind of wound from becoming septic.

It is often said that weak disinfectants can be used as antiseptics, but this is not true in all cases. Stick to the ones you know such as cetrimide (a disinfectant which *can* be used as an antiseptic if diluted). In the salon, hydrogen peroxide can also be used as an antiseptic if its strength is kept below 10 volume strength 3%. The ideal strength is 5 vol. Higher strengths not only can burn the skin, as peroxide is acid, but can also cause cells to mutate (cause cancer). It should not be used as a mouth wash because of this, although some people think it brings their teeth up beautifully

Name	Forms available	Recommended strengths	Recommended uses in salon
Disinfectants			
Quaternary ammonium compounds (quats)	Liquid or tablet	1:1000 solution	Immerse implements into solution for 1–5 minutes.
Formalin	Liquid	25% solution	Immerse implements into solution for 10 minutes.
Formalin	Liquid	10% solution	Immerse implements into solution for 20 minutes.
Ethyl alcohol	Liquid	70% solution	Immerse implements into solution for 20 minutes.
Cresol (Lysol)	Liquid	10% soap solution	Cleanse floors, sinks, and toilets.
Antiseptics			
Tincture of iodine	Liquid	2% solution	Cleanse cuts and wounds.
Hydrogen peroxide	Liquid	1½–3% solution	Cleanse skin and minor cuts.
Ethyl alcohol	Liquid	60% solution	Cleanse hands, skin and minute cuts. Not to be used if irritation is present.
Formalin	Liquid	5% solution	Cleanse hand bowl, cabinet etc.
Chloramine-T (Chlorazene ; Chlorozol)	White crystals	1½% solution	Cleanse skin and hands and for general use.
Sodium hypochlorite (Javelle water ; Zonite)	White liquid	½% solution	Rinse the hands.

Fig. 5.6 Antiseptics and disinfectants commonly used in hair and beauty salons.

white! When peroxide comes into contact with blood it releases bubbles of oxygen, so it is suitable to help clean a dirty cut as the oxygen bubbles can dislodge dirt. (See Figure 5.6.)

Questions 5.3

1 What is an antiseptic?
2 What is the main use of an antiseptic?
3 How can a disinfectant be used as an antiseptic?
4 Can all disinfectants be used in this way?
5 At what strength should hydrogen peroxide be used as an antiseptic?

5.4 Keeping the salon clean

The salon should be cleaned regularly to prevent the spread of infection. The various salon surfaces must be kept free from dust and dirt which would otherwise provide a breeding ground for germs. This can be accomplished by regular cleaning, and having the surfaces made of easily cleanable materials.

People often wonder where all the dust in a salon comes from. It is mainly small pieces of hair, flakes of dead skin, fluff from towels and clothing, ash from cigarettes, and particles of hairspray. A vacuum cleaner will remove dust quickly from most places; failing this, use a dustpan and brush or duster. Good ventilation (see Section 5.6) will remove a lot of dust before its settles. If dust mixes with grease, or even moisture, dirt is formed. This must be removed with detergent and hot water. Do not use a scouring powder on any smooth surface or it will leave tiny scratch marks where bacteria can breed.

Floors should be made of non-slip vinyl as this can easily be washed. Walls must be easy to clean. Gloss or vinyl paints, and tiles near sinks are all good decorative finishes which can simply be wiped over. Ceilings are often artexed and dirt can easily become trapped on the uneven surface. They do not have to be cleaned in the same way as walls and floors, but should not be allowed to look grubby. Plain plastered ceilings are suitable as they will collect less dust.

Chairs should be made of a washable vinyl rather than fabric which cannot be wiped clean. Trolleys are available with lift-out plastic containers which can easily be washed.

Hair should be regularly swept up and placed in covered bins. If these are pedal-bins it will not be necessary to touch them with the hands. Empty bins throughout the day and do not let them overflow. Keeping bins covered will discourage smells and vermin, such as rats and mice.

Questions 5.4

1   Why must the salon be cleaned regularly?
2   Where does the dust in a salon come from?
3   How is dirt formed?
4   Why should scouring powders not be used in the salon?
5   What should floors be made from?
6   What kind of finishes should walls and ceilings have?
7   Why is vinyl a suitable chair covering?
8   Why should bins be kept covered in the salon?

5.5   Toilets and washbasins

All washbasins and toilets are connected to the main drains and sewers where germs flourish and breed. To prevent pathogens and odours from entering the salon or home, traps are formed in the waste pipes underneath the washbasin or lavatory pan. The water that you see in the sink plughole and lavatory pan is held in these traps. They form water seals which act as a barrier to the drains. Figure 5.7 shows the S-trap and bottle trap which will be found beneath most sinks. Every time the sink is emptied the water is replaced in the trap, keeping the water fresh. The traps can be unscrewed to make it possible to clean them if they should become blocked (usually with hair in salons). The bottle trap has the advantage of only one screw joint to open, so it is preferred beneath shampoo basins for easy removal of hair. *When you do unscrew the trap remember to have a bucket ready to let the water in the trap drain into it.*

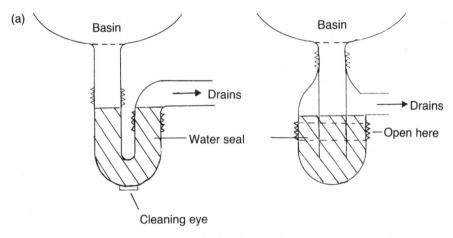

Fig. 5.7 An S-trap (a) and a bottle trap (b) under a shampoo basin.

- If you drop something down the sink, like a ring or contact lens, turn off the taps immediately and then open the trap to retrieve it. If it is a plastic contact lens, it should float for a few seconds. It will be lost if you do not turn the water off.
- If it is difficult to open the trap and it becomes blocked with hair, it may be cleared with caustic soda (sodium hydroxide). (Caustic soda is dangerously corrosive to skin and eyes so follow the manufacturer's instructions carefully.) This dissolves the hair which can be flushed clear with running water. It also removes grease – a useful tip for kitchen sinks.

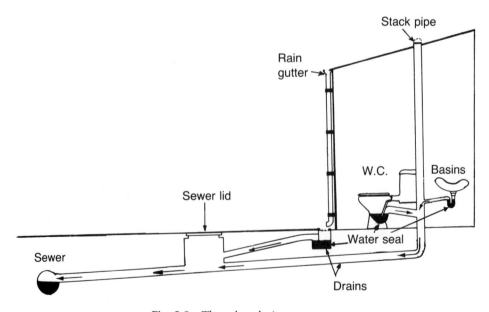

Fig. 5.8 The salon drainage system.

- Many salons use hair filters in the plug hold to stop the hair going down the sink. These should be cleaned as soon as the flow of water slows down.
- A little bleach put down sinks and toilets will help kill germs. In summer they are more likely to smell, so run the water more in the sink.
- Clean lavatories regularly and provide a covered bin for sanitary towels in the ladies' toilet. Insoluble ones could block the drains.

Salons will sometimes have problems with the outside drains. Basic drainage is illustrated in Figure 5.8. It is common for leaves to block gullies in autumn and winter, so this is the first thing that should be looked for if rainwater is not flowing away. The wash basins from some salons may go to these outside gullies directly, rather than straight into soil pipes. Soil pipes which take away sewage and waste water may become blocked if insoluble sanitary towels or nappies are flushed down toilets. If the metal inspection lid for your salon is opened up and someone flushes the toilet, you will see water rush down the open pipe if there is no blockage. If soil pipes become blocked you may need to call in professional help (check the telephone directory and seek help from your local council). In summer use disinfectant on smelly gullies or run some fresh water down them from a bucket or hose. Smells are more likely in summer if there is little rain to freshen the water in the gullies, and there are more micro-organisms present in water in warm weather.

Questions 5.5

1 What is the function of a trap?
2 Why are bottle traps found under most shampoo basins?
3 What should be done if something is accidentally dropped down a sink?
4 How can a hair blockage be cleaned from a sink trap?
5 What is the purpose of a hair filter on a sink?
6 Why should sanitary bins be provided in ladies' toilets?
7 What often causes blockage of outside gulley drains?
8 How can the inspection chamber be used to tell where a blockage is?
9 Why are drains more likely to smell in warm weather?

5.6 Ventilation

Ventilation is the process by which stale air is replaced by fresh air. It is not simply opening a window to let in a blast of cold fresh air, as correct ventilation should avoid too great a rise or fall in temperature.

Human beings alter the composition of the air in the salon by respiration (breathing) and perspiration (sweating). The level of oxygen is reduced, while the levels of carbon dioxide, water vapour and bacteria are increased. The salon could therefore offer ideal conditions for the spread of infection, if it is allowed to become warm and humid. A high humidity can also cause set hair to drop.

To ensure correct ventilation, the following points should be kept in mind:

- The air in the salon should be changed three or four times an hour.
- Cool air should not enter the room at floor level as this is draughty to the legs.

- Air which enters the room above head height should be directed upwards so that it is slightly warmed before it moves downwards on to the clients.
- Clients with wet hair feel a cooling effect as moisture evaporates from their heads, and further cooling by a draught could make it unpleasantly cold.
- Air outlets should be smaller than air inlets, so that air does not circulate too quickly. This would result in both draughts and a fall in temperature.

If air movements occur by natural processes this is known as *natural* ventilation. If the movement of air is assisted by fans, it is known as *artificial* ventilation.

Natural ventilation occurs by two processes, diffusion and convection. Diffusion occurs because the molecules of a gas are always moving, so that gases distribute themselves evenly throughout the space they occupy. If someone spills a bottle of perfume, the smell is very strong where it is spilt and gradually spreads to the rest of the room, where the smell was weaker at first. The molecules of perfume have distributed themselves evenly throughout the room. Water vapour produced when hair is washed and dried eventually spreads throughout the salon by this process. Convection is the movement of air caused by heat. If air is warmed, the molecules in the warm air move further apart, making the air less dense. This lighter, warm air then rises. Once the warm air has risen it will become cooler, and the molecules of air will move closer together again, making the air more dense. The denser, cooler air then falls again. By this process convection currents of warm air are set up. You can see this when someone smokes near a fire, the smoke quickly rising when it is caught up in a convection current. This is why the warmest air in a room is near the ceiling.

Figures 5.9 and 5.10 show two types of window which can be used to direct air entering a salon upwards, where it can be warmed. Hopper windows are often placed above doors. Louvre windows became very popular during the 1960s and 1970s in Britain. Because the strips of glass can be moved the windows may be used as air inlets or outlets, and the entry of air can be controlled. Keep one thing in mind, however: place the windows high up and never next to door locks or large

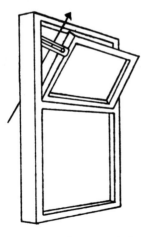

Fig. 5.9   A hopper window.

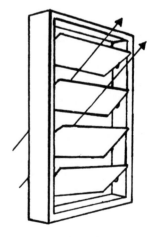

Fig. 5.10   A louvre window.

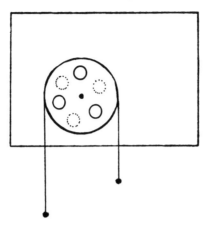

Fig. 5.11 Cooper's disc.

window catches, as it is extremely easy to remove the strips of glass and break into the premises. Figure 5.11 shows a Cooper's disc, a device which can be rotated to let in a limited amount of fresh air by lining up the holes in two discs.

Artificial ventilation using electric extractor fans is more efficient and controllable than natural ventilation. These should be fitted to an outside window or wall, although it is cheaper to fix them into windows. Many can be switched to intake as well as extract. This is useful to cool the salon on a hot summer day. They should be situated away from fresh air intakes such as doors or windows, or fresh, rather than stale, air will be extracted.

The number of fans needed for a particular size of salon, or room, should be calculated by multiplying the volume of the salon by the number of complete air changes required per hour.

Example

A salon is 10 m × 5 m × 3 m (length × breadth × height) = 150. The volume is therefore 150 cubic metres.

If we require four changes of air per hour, the amount of air to be moved per hour is 4 × 150 = 600 cubic metres.

If one fan is fitted it must be able to extract this amount of air per hour. You could use two smaller fans. If you have one small fan which was designed for a bathroom or toilet, it will not be powerful enough to work properly in a larger room.

Questions 5.6

1   What is ventilation?
2   Why is the opening of a window not a good method of ventilation?
3   How do people alter the composition of air in a salon?
4   How often should the air in a salon be changed?
5   How should air enter a room?
6   Why should air outlets be smaller than air inlets?
7   What is the difference between natural and artificial ventilation?

8   Describe diffusion and convection.
9   Where is the warmest air in a room?
10   Why are hopper and louvre windows used?
11   What advantage has artificial ventilation over natural ventilation?
12   Where should extractor fans be sited in a salon?
13   How would you know what size of extractor fan should be fitted in your salon?

6

General Salon Safety

Like the home, the salon is a place where accidents occur. If you read and do the tasks in this section, the number of such accidents should be reduced. Accidents often result from not understanding how equipment works, or simply because of a lack of common sense.

6.1 Electrical safety

A number of different types of electrical apparatus are used in the salon, on even the smallest premises. Electricity can be a killer, so treat it with respect at all times. If you are ever in doubt, don't take risks – consult an electrician. The following are simple rules that you should follow:

- Wire plugs correctly. If, for instance, you were to connect the earth wire of some equipment to the live pin of a plug, the equipment itself would become live and the user could be electrocuted (see Figure 6.1).
- Fit the correct fuse – not everything is designed to work on a 13 amp fuse. The fuse will protect the appliance if something goes wrong. If, for instance, the fan of a hairdrier jams, instead of it catching fire the fuse will blow, costing little to replace and saving you the cost of a new hairdrier (see Section 6.2).
- If an earth wire is present on a piece of equipment it must be used because it will protect the user from electrocution. It works by carrying electric current away if the piece of equipment becomes live. If the earth wire is not connected properly to the plug it cannot work. A lot of modern electrical equipment, however, has only two wires and is double insulated so that it cannot become live if a wire becomes loose inside the equipment. Check for the double insulation sign on the equipment – one square inside another (see Figure 6.2).
- Never use broken plugs or sockets – you could be electrocuted if your fingers touch something live.
- If a lead or flex becomes worn, don't wait for bare wires to show – replace it to

1

Carefully cut away about 5 cm (2 in) of flex of outer sheath. Use an old pair of scissors to do this and not your hairdressing pair! Take care not to cut through the other wires.

2

Remove the fuse from its holder as this will make it easier to wire the plug. Check that you know the correct size of fuse to use when you come to use the appliance.

3

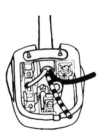

Loosen the flex clamps so that you can pass the wires through as shown. You will not need to do this if the plug has a 'V' cord holder. Fasten the cord firmly under the clamp so that the wires reach about 1.25 cm (½ in) beyond the terminals.

4

Use wire strippers or scissors to remove 0.6 cm (¼ in) of insulation if the plug has screwhole terminals. Remove twice as much if they are clamp type terminals.

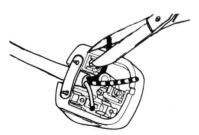

5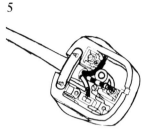

Position the wires next to the correct terminals:
brown to live
blue to neutral
green/yellow to earth
(If an appliance has only two wires make sure that it is double insulated by checking for the mark.)

6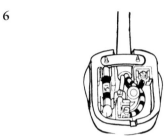

Insert the wires into the correct terminals, having twisted the wires so no loose strands show. Tighten the screw terminals and check again that you have wired the plug correctly before replacing the fuse.

7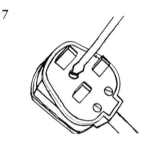

Finally, close the plug by replacing the tightening the main holding screw. This should fit firmly so that no gaps show around the plug. Do not use cracked or broken plugs as these could allow you to come into contact with a live current.

Fig. 6.1 Wiring an electric plug.

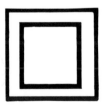

Fig. 6.2 The sign for double insulation.

prevent electrocution and fires. This can happen if a flex is twisted a lot, or put down near a source of heat.

- Do not run too many appliances from one socket as shown in Figure 6.3. It can cause overloading and a possible fire. If you cannot have more sockets installed (the best solution), get adaptors which are protected by fuses.
- If you have to make a lead longer do so with insulated jointing blocks, not by twisting wires together and covering with insulating tape. If they were to be

Fig. 6.3   An overloaded electric socket.

pulled, a live wire might become exposed and could be a potential electrocution hazard.

- *Never examine an appliance without first disconnecting it from the mains* or it could be the last thing you ever do.
- Never put wires directly into an electric socket without a plug; you could be electrocuted as you attempt to do this.
- Never trail leads where people walk or they may trip. This may not only hurt them but could damage equipment. Imagine the damage that could occur if a steamer were knocked over.
- Never run a lead under a carpet where people might walk over it. In time the lead could twist and pull out of the appliance. If this were in a staff room with a fridge, for instance, it could cause the metal cabinet to become live.
- Do not make holes or knock nails into walls where electric cables could be buried. This could cause fires or electrocution. Cables are most likely to be located above light switches.
- *Finally, never use electrical equipment with wet hands – you could be killed by electrocution.*

Electrical equipment can be guaranteed safely made if it complies with British Standards specifications. If it does it will have the kite mark and a B.S. number (see Figure 6.4).

Miniature circuit-breakers are sometimes fitted instead of mains fuses. Instead of the fuse blowing and having to be replaced before the electricity can flow again, a switch simply turns itself off. This disconnects the circuit from the mains supply,

Fig. 6.4   The British Standards kite mark.

until the switch is turned back on. The mains will cut out if the circuit becomes overloaded or an appliance develops a fault.

Special earth leakage circuit breakers for protection against electrocution from cut, frayed or wet cables have been developed. These plug into existing sockets and give added protection when using electrical equipment. They are similar to miniature circuit breakers.

Questions 6.1

1   How do accidents occur?
2   Why must great care be taken with electricity?
3   How could the incorrect wiring of a plug make an appliance become live?
4   Why should the correct size of fuse be fitted to a plug?
5   What does the earth wire do?
6   Wire a plug using the instructions in Figure 6.1.
7   What is double insulation?
8   How would you know that an appliance was double insulated?
9   Why should you not use a broken plug or socket?
10 Why should electrical flexes be replaced if they become worn?
11 How should electrical leads be joined?
12 List, with reasons, eight electrical safety precautions that you would follow.
13 How would you know if a piece of equipment met British Standards?
14 What is a miniature circuit-breaker?

6.2   Calculating fuse sizes

This is important because the fuse protects the appliance from damage. It is the weakest part of the circuit when the current is switched on, so it will blow and cut off the power supply as soon as something goes wrong. (Actually, the fuse melts if the current is excessive.) If the fan of a hairdrier jammed, for instance, the fuse would blow and stop the current instead of a fire resulting from overheating. Instead of ruining an expensive piece of equipment, you would only need to replace the fuse.

The size of fuse depends on the power of the appliance and the current it uses. The more powerful a piece of equipment, the larger the fuse required.

Fuse size is calculated according to the following:

$$\text{Current (amps)} = \frac{\text{power(watts)}}{\text{voltage(volts)}}$$

Whatever number you get for the current determines the size of fuse to be used. If the fuse is smaller or the same as this number it will fail because the fuse blows when more current than it is designed to take passes through it. The fuse you choose must be bigger than the current that the appliance will draw, but only slightly. This will enable it to blow quickly if something goes wrong.

Example

If the voltage in a salon is 240 volts, what fuse would the following appliances use if the following sizes of fuse were available: 3 amps; 5 amps; 10 amps; 13 amps?

(1)   A 70 watt steriliser.
(2)   A 500 watt pair of crimping irons.
(3)   A 1000 watt hairdrier.
(4)   A 1500 watt steamer.
(5)   A 3000 watt fire.

To help you, here is an example:

What is the correct size of fuse for a 750 watt drier on a 240 volt supply?

$$amps = watts \div volts$$
$$= 750 \div 240$$
$$= above\ 3\ amps\ (this\ is\ exact\ enough)$$

The fuse that would best protect this appliance, therefore, is a 5 amp one; 3 amps would blow, whereas a 10 or 13 amp fuse would not blow quickly enough.

Remember   Most plugs come complete with a 13 amp fuse. Check that this is not too big to protect the appliance safely.

Questions 6.2

1   How does a fuse protect an appliance?
2   What size of fuse do most plugs come fitted with?
3   Work out questions (1) to (5), then check your answers: (1) 3 amps (2) 3 amps (3) 5 amps (4) 10 amps (5) 13 amps.

6.3   The modern 13 amp plug

Don't buy a plug just because it is cheap – it may be dangerous to use and could break easily if it is made of a poor quality plastic. All plugs should at least have a British Standards number and the kite mark, to show they have passed minimum safety standards. A modern 13 amp plug such as the one shown in Figure 6.5 should have the following safety features:

- It should be fitted with a cartridge fuse of the correct size to protect the appliance.
- The earth pin should be longer than the live and neutral pins. This opens up small plastic lugs in the wall socket which stop children putting pieces of metal straight into the socket holes.
- The brass of the neutral and live pins should be covered at the top with an insulated material, to stop small fingers from coming in contact with pins if a plug has been pulled out slightly from a socket.
- A cord grip should be fitted to prevent the wires from being pulled from the plug. This often happens if people remove plugs from sockets by pulling the cable. The best type of cord grip is two pieces of tough plastic in a 'V' shape which grip the cable more tightly as it is pulled. The type with two screws wears easily and makes it more difficult to wire a plug.

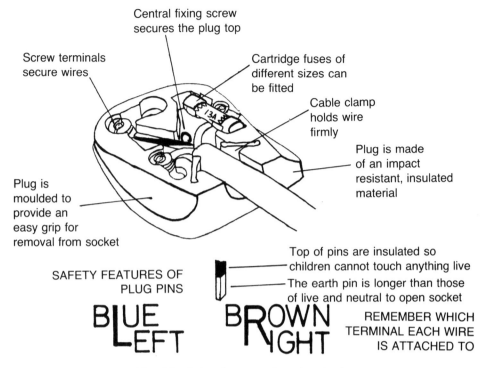

Central fixing screw secures the plug top

Screw terminals secure wires

Cartridge fuses of different sizes can be fitted

Cable clamp holds wire firmly

Plug is made of an impact resistant, insulated material

Plug is moulded to provide an easy grip for removal from socket

SAFETY FEATURES OF PLUG PINS

Top of pins are insulated so children cannot touch anything live

The earth pin is longer than those of live and neutral to open socket

B**L**UE
LEFT

B**R**OWN
RIGHT

REMEMBER WHICH TERMINAL EACH WIRE IS ATTACHED TO

Fig. 6.5 Safety features of an electric plug.

- The inside of the plug should be firmly covered by a screw-down plug top once the plug has been reassembled. On some cheaper plugs it is possible to pull off the back of the plug.
- Some plugs have a small hole near the live pin, so the colour code of the fuse fitted can be seen, without having to take the plug apart.
- The plug should be made of an impact-resistant, insulating plastic so that it does not break too easily. Once a plug is cracked it becomes dangerous to use.

Questions 6.3

1 What does a kite mark on a plug tell you?
2 Why is the earth pin longer than the neutral and live pins?
3 Why are the bases of the live and neutral pins covered with insulation?
4 What is the function of a cord grip?
5 How can you tell the fuse size fitted in some plugs without unscrewing them?

6.4 Chemical hazards in the salon

We use a number of chemicals in the salon to bring about changes in hair. If used correctly they should be safe. The following safety guidelines should help to prevent accidents.

- Chemicals should always be kept in their correct bottles. Never take home chemicals in food or drink containers. If you put peroxide into a lemonade bottle there would be no way of telling the difference until someone drank it.
- If a chemical is put into a different container it should be *clearly labelled*. Don't leave it till later, as we all too often forget.
- Never pour chemicals into other containers unless they have been washed out. If peroxide is put into an old perm lotion bottle, the alkalinity of any remaining lotion could cause the peroxide to decompose. The release of oxygen from the peroxide could cause an explosion.
- Always measure the amounts of chemicals that you use, as once a chemical has been poured it must not be returned to the original container (otherwise it could become contaminated and decompose). This will also mean that you know how much of a chemical you have used if you want to repeat the same procedure (as when adding peroxide to tint).
- Wipe up any spilt chemicals immediately. Some will irritate skin, damage clothes or simply cause accidents by being slipped on. It is also good practice to wipe the outside of bottles so that they do not become slippery to hold and therefore easier to drop.
- Avoid getting any chemical on to clients' skin as they may react to it. Never allow chemicals to get into the eyes: use cotton wool strips to protect them, and use back basins when rinsing them from the hair, as opposed to front washes.
- Keep cleaning materials separate from hairdressing chemicals. If two things are in similar bottles you could pick up the wrong one.
- Many chemicals are highly flammable. Hairspray should never be used near a flame, even a lit cigarette. If you tried lighting a small sample of hairspray you

Fig. 6.6 Hairspray being ignited by a lighter.

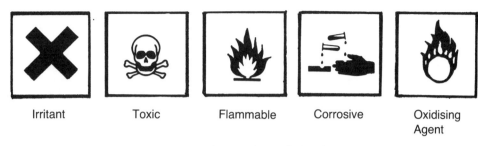

| Irritant | Toxic | Flammable | Corrosive | Oxidising Agent |

Fig. 6.7 Chemical safety symbols which advise caution.

would see just how dangerous it is (see Figure 6.6). Many styling and aftercare products are also flammable, and the ones that stay on the hair could be set alight by a flame or lit cigarette. How often have you leaned down in front of the fire? Your hair could easily catch fire from too much heat.

- Never mix chemicals which are not intended to be used with anything else. The mixture could give off heat or dangerous fumes.
- *Always read the instructions supplied with the product, especially if you have not used it before. If a chemical causes the client severe discomfort, rinse it off at once.*
- Always give a skin test if it is recommended by the manufacturer.
- Many chemicals will have symbols on their containers indicating something about their use. The five symbols shown in Figure 6.7 are the ones most likely to be seen on salon chemicals.

Questions 6.4

1 Why should chemicals be kept in their correct bottles?
2 How can it be unsafe to put chemicals into different containers?
3 Why should the amounts of chemicals be measured?
4 Why should chemical spillages be wiped up immediately?
5 How can you avoid chemicals getting into clients' eyes?
6 What safety points should be followed when using flammable chemicals?
7 What should you always do before using a chemical for the first time?
8 What should you do if a client complains of scalp irritation during a service?
9 When should a skin test be given?
10 List the safety signs found on chemical bottles.

6.5 Physical salon hazards

The average salon has a number of hazards which could be classified as physical, such as the furniture, flooring, lighting and equipment. The following are common faults, given alongside their possible remedies:

- Worksurfaces could have sharp edges and square corners. They could cause damage to clients or staff if they are knocked. The remedy is to have rounded corners on all surfaces.
- Handles which protrude can be caught by people as they walk by. The remedy is to have recessed handles.

- Cupboard doors which open outwards can be left open or can open by themselves if they do not have strong catches. To avoid this either fit strong catches or fit sliding doors.
- Floor surfaces are often slippery. This could be because of the type of flooring used, or because it has been polished. Avoid this by having non-slip flooring, preferably 'sheet-type' which is likely to wear better than tiles. Vinyl flooring is one of the best available. Do not polish floors, simply wash them with detergent instead. If liquids are spilt they must be dried up immediately or someone could slip.
- Carpet is used in most reception areas. It should be fixed so that people cannot trip on the edges. If a staircase is part of the salon, any carpet must be very firmly fixed.
- Any salon should be well-lit. The lighting should be diffused to prevent glare which can cause headaches, eye-strain and possible accidents. Fluorescent lighting can be very similar to daylight if the correct tubes are fitted, such as warm white. This type of light casts very little shadow, and it is easy to fit plastic diffusers to 'soften' the light more. Because it uses less power, fluorescent lighting is cheaper to run than light bulbs or spot lights. If the salon ceiling is in very bad condition it might be worth considering having a suspended 'light' ceiling fitted.
- Many salons have hairdriers and steamers on wheels, which may not only be left where people walk, but could also have trailing leads for people to trip over. Where possible, have wall-mounted driers and steamers, or drier banks. Trolleys for rollers, etc. should as much as possible be kept out of the areas where people walk.
- When using scissors, always be specially careful when cutting near the ears.
- When cutting, wear closed shoes to avoid hair entering the skin and causing infection. When sweeping up hair, sweep away from your feet for the same reason.
- Many hand hairdriers have a filter fitted over the air inlet at the back of the drier. Clean this filter regularly, with the drier turned off *and disconnected from the mains*. Do not use the drier without this filter; it will prevent your hair being drawn into the fan of the drier. For the same reason, keep your hair tied back if it is long.
- Keep the jet of air from a hairdrier constantly moving. Do not allow it to play too long on metal hair clips – they may heat up and burn the scalp.
- Never put bent hairpins into hair to secure rollers when setting. If they stick up and you are using a hood drier with an overhead fan, there is a danger that the pins could catch in the fan, and be driven into the client's scalp.

Questions 6.5

1   How can worksurfaces present a physical hazard?
2   Why should drawers have recessed handles?
3   How can cupboard doors be made safe?
4   What safety rules should be followed for floor surfaces in a salon?
5   How can lighting cause accidents?
6   How can accidents involving tripping be prevented in the salon?

7   What danger does cut hair present and how can this be avoided?
8   What problems can occur when drying hair?

6.6   Heating and fire safety in the salon

The salon must be kept warm for the comfort of both the staff and the clients. An ideal salon temperature would be about 20°C (70°F). The temperature should not be allowed to vary too much, and the heating used should not present any danger to people in the salon.

Central heating can be either by circulation of hot water in pipes, by ducted warm air or by floor warming. Hot water circulation is the most common method and is also the most economical to install and run. It also provides hot water for shampooing. The system operates by pumping heated water through pipes into fixed radiators on walls. The radiators can be placed near areas where clients require heat, and thermostats ensure that individual radiators give out the right amount of heat. Take expert advice if you are planning to have central heating installed, so that your system provides the correct amount of hot water as well as heating.

Portable heaters should not be used because of the risk of accidents by people falling over leads or burning themselves on hot surfaces. Heaters with a flame or radiant electric bar could also start fires if touched by anything flammable. A smaller salon where there is no central heating can be heated safely and well by using fixed heating appliances. These could be electric storage radiators or gas convector heaters (but the gas fire requires an external wall if it is to be fitted).

The poisonous gas carbon monoxide can be produced when a gas fire has inadequate ventilation or a paraffin fire has an incorrectly burning wick. Carbon monoxide is odourless and colourless and can kill. Have fires installed by professionals and read the instructions supplied with the fire.

Condensation

Condensation is caused by warm moist air (which is found in salons, bathrooms and kitchens) meeting a cold surface such as a mirror or window. The water vapour in the air is cooled and turns into water on the cold surface, this change of state from gas to liquid being termed condensation. Condensation can cause electric shock from damp sockets, cause the mains fuse to blow if moisture enters sockets, cause wooden window frames to rot, provide breeding grounds for germs and fungi, and prevent potential clients from looking into the salon through the steamed up windows!

Condensation can be prevented, or at least reduced, in two ways. One is to cut down the amount of water vapour in the air by ensuring adequate ventilation (see Section 5.6). The other is to heat the areas where condensation occurs. Radiators, or fixed electric heaters, would be positioned below windows to prevent the glass becoming too cold. Double glazed windows also help to reduce condensation.

What should I do if a fire breaks out?

- Try not to panic.
- Get the clients out of the salon *immediately*. You cannot be sure that a small fire won't become worse.

- If possible, close windows and doors. This will contain the fire and stop it spreading quickly, because it will reduce the supply of oxygen that the fire needs to burn.
- If possible, tackle the fire with the salon extinguisher, but do not put yourself at risk.
- Phone for the fire brigade, from a phone outside the salon if necessary (see Figure 10.17). If the salon is near any well-known store or landmark tell the operator this as it may help the fire brigade get there faster.
- If you are trapped in a smoke-filled room, try to put a wet cloth over your mouth and nose, then crawl along the floor towards an exit (you are less likely to be overcome by the smoke if you are near the floor).

What type of fire extinguisher should a salon have?

As a salon is likely to have only one type of extinguisher it should be one that can safely be used on all fires. It should also be a type of extinguisher that can be easily checked to ensure that it has not been previously used or is partially empty.

An extinguisher that utilises water cannot be safely used where there is electricity, as an electric shock can result. For this reason water or foam extinguishers are not recommended for this risk. Water extinguishers should never be used on fires involving oil either, as they could cause the fire to spread. The most suitable extinguishers for a risk involving electricity are carbon dioxide, Halon 1211 (BCF) or dry powder. Carbon dioxide gas smothers flames by excluding air; the end of the nozzle or horn can become very cold during use so do not hold the horn. BCF extinguishers give off a vapour that interferes with the chain reaction of fire and also has a cooling effect on the fire. Although BCF vapour is not poisonous, the fumes and smoke from a fire can be, so windows must be opened as soon as the fire is extinguished. The dry powder extinguisher can be used on all types of fire and puts out the fire very quickly.

The BCF and dry powder types of fire extinguisher are available fitted with a pressure gauge so that the content can be seen at a glance; in addition those currently manufactured feature a 'USED' indicator. This 'USED' indicator cannot be reset other than at the time of refilling. This helps prevent only an empty extinguisher being available when there actually is a fire.

Everyone in the salon should know where the extinguisher is and how to use it. Modern extinguishers carry instructions showing how they should be used, as shown in Figure 6.8. Manufacturers also make extinguishers in a range of sizes which means that you could have some smaller extinguishers strategically placed around the salon. The extinguishers also have wall brackets so that they can easily be seen and removed. Figure 6.9 shows a range of powder extinguishers.

How are fires caused in salons?

Fires are caused:

- By lighted cigarette butts being put in litter bins.
- By flammable liquids igniting because they are placed near a flame.

Fig. 6.8 A carbon dioxide fire extinguisher. Note the handle on the horn. (Courtesy of Chubb Fire Security Ltd.)

Fig. 6.9 Powder extinguishers are available in a range of sizes and can be mounted on walls. (Courtesy of Chubb Fire Security Ltd.)

- By towels and gowns being placed over the air vents of heaters, causing them to overheat.
- By using flammable liquids when smoking – such as methylated spirit for cleaning mirrors.
- By placing aerosol cans near heat. This is dangerous even when the can is empty as they are pressurised and can explode.

How can I put out a fire?

- If a bin catches fire, closing the lid will starve it of oxygen and it will go out. Water could be poured in if an extinguisher is not available.
- If someone's hair catches fire, smother the flames with a towel – damp if possible (see first aid for burns, Section 10.2).
- If someone's clothes catch fire, smother the flames with towels or coats.
- If your own clothing catches fire, roll on the ground.
- For other fires, use the fire extinguishers already mentioned and/or call the fire brigade.
- At home, if a pan of oil or fat catches fire, try to put the lid or a *damp* cloth over the flames and turn off the heat. *Never use water* – the oil would overflow and spit, spreading the fire and burning anyone nearby. *Leave the pan to cool for an hour before removing the pan cover, or the fire may re-ignite.* These fires are usually caused by people overfilling pans with oil or by having the heat too high.
- *Aim extinguishers at the sides of the base of the fire. Aiming at the centre could spread the flames.*

Questions 6.6

1   What is the ideal salon temperature?
2   What advantages has central heating over other systems?
3   Why are portable heaters not recommended for salon use?
4   What gas can be given off by a gas fire if there is inadequate ventilation?
5   What is condensation?
6   What problems can be caused by condensation?
7   How can condensation be prevented?
8   What would you do in the event of a fire?
9   How would you phone for the fire brigade?
10 What kinds of fire extinguisher are there in your salon?
11 When should water extinguishers not be used?
12 What extinguishers can be used on electrical fires?
13 How are fires caused in salons?
14 Describe how you would put out different types of fire that might occur in the salon.
15 Where should extinguishers be aimed when fighting a fire?

6.7   Salon lighting

Daylight will not be enough in most salons to see the client's hair comfortably. It is necessary to have some form of artificial lighting.

If the lighting is inadequate, eye-strain may result. If the lighting is too strong there could be glare, but this can be overcome by using diffusers which scatter the light to make it 'softer'. A room that is about 100 square feet or 9 square metres requires 500 watts of power if normal tungsten filament light bulbs are used.

Fluorescent tubes give out more light than normal light bulbs for the amount of power used. For example, a 40 watt fluorescent tube gives out the same amount of light as a 150 watt bulb. In general, it is cheaper to run fluorescent lights, because although they cost five times more than most light bulbs they last six times longer. Also, as they do not have to be changed as often, there is less chance of accidents when changing tubes. The life of the tube is shortened by switching light switches on and off. They can be easily fitted with plastic diffusers and 'warm white' tubes give a light that is similar to daylight.

All parts of the salon should be adequately lit, especially staircases and other areas where people might fall. Adequate lighting will also reduce the likelihood of salon accidents such as cutting the client's skin or overlapping chemicals on the hair. Light switches located near sources of water or condensation should be the pull-cord type and not surface-mounted, to prevent electric shock.

Questions 6.7

1   What does inadequate lighting cause?
2   How much lighting does each 100 square feet of room require?
3   How can glare be prevented?
4   What advantage have flourescent tubes for lighting?
5   How can lighting levels help prevent accidents?
6   What type of light switch should be used near water?

6.8   Health and Safety at Work Act, 1974.

This Act of Parliament covers *all* people at work with the exception of domestic workers in private employment. It includes employers, employees and the self-employed.

It covers all the people on work premises. The Act protects not only people at work but also the health and safety of the general public who may be involved in these work activities. It also covers the emission of any noxious fumes or substances. The main provisions of the Act are:

● Employers must set out written statements of their safety policy and its provisions. These statements must be made available to all employees (usually by having a copy in the staff room).
● Information about health and safety at work must be included in all directors' reports. This applies to salons which are limited companies and therefore have directors.
● Employees must be involved in the making and monitoring of arrangements for health and safety at their place of work.
● An obligation is placed on the employer to consult with employees on matters concerned with health and safety. Usually one person in the salon would be made the health and safety representative.

- Existing Acts such as the Factories Act and Offices, Shops and Railway Premises Act remain in force (but it is expected that they will gradually be phased out).
- The scope of the Act extends to employers, employees, self-employed and manufacturers where their acts or omissions could endanger workers or the public.
- Any person who designs, manufactures, imports or supplies any article for use at work is responsible for ensuring that the article is safe from hazard. (You should report dangerous products or equipment to the local environmental health officer so that they can be withdrawn from use.)
- Manufacturers are responsible for carrying out research and testing articles for safety.
- Inspectors can enforce Improvement or Prohibition Notices, with any appeals being heard by an Industrial Tribunal.

Employers have a duty to ensure the following:

- The place of work must be properly maintained, safe and without risk to health. It should have adequate fire fighting and first aid equipment.
- There must be no risk to safety in connection with the use, handling or storage of chemicals or equipment.
- Employees must be instructed, trained and supervised to ensure their health and safety. (An employee should not be asked to carry out a chemical process on a client that he or she has not been trained to do.)
- There must be both an entrance and exit from the place of work and it must be safely maintained.
- There must be a statement of safety policy. It must consist of a written statement of general safety policy and arrangements must be made to carry it out. It is the duty of employers to make sure that employees are aware of the safety policy and that they have a part to play in preparing and carrying it out.

General duties of employees

The Act places a duty on all employees to take reasonable care of themselves and other persons who may be affected by their acts. They should co-operate with their employer to ensure this.

Powers of inspectors

- Health and Safety inspectors can enter any premises if they believe it is necessary.
- They can examine the whole of the premises.
- They can remove any equipment or material for examination.
- If samples of anything are removed, part of any sample must be left with a responsible person (ensuring that you could have the sample checked yourself).

If you put someone in danger you can be prosecuted even if your actions were not done on purpose. For some offences limitless fines can be imposed, and even imprisonment.

Questions 6.8

1   What are the main duties of an employer under the Health and Safety at Work Act?
2   What are the main duties of an employee under the Act?
3   If you think a product or a piece of equipment is dangerous, who should you tell about it?

6.9   Gas safety

Many salons have a supply of gas for heating the premises and/or the water. It is important that all installation of equipment using gas should be carried out by properly qualified gas fitters. Adequate ventilation must be available in the premises or carbon monoxide (a poisonous gas) can be produced. In the event of a possible gas leak (the smell of gas is the first thing to alert most people), follow the following safety routine:

- Don't smoke or use naked flames.
- Don't touch electric switches (turning a switch on *or* off can cause a spark which could ignite escaping gas).
- Open windows and doors to get rid of gas.
- Check to see if there are any gas appliances on without a flame or pilot light. Turn them off if this is the cause of the gas leak.
- If you have not found an appliance which has been left on, turn off gas at the mains, which should be by your gas meter. This is the only safe way to turn off gas if a pipe is leaking.
- Look in the phone book under gas or seek assistance from the operator and phone the gas emergency service for help.
- If ever you smell gas in the street phone the same number, as there could be a leaking gas main.

Questions 6.9

1   What would you do in the event of a gas leak?
2   Why should a light switch not be turned off?

6.10   Salon Health and Safety exercises

Figure 6.10 is a plan of a small high street salon. The staff consists of two stylists (Mario and Vanessa), one junior (George) and a mature woman (Mrs Stephens) working part-time as a laundry lady. The salon is not as busy as it could be so, as the new owner, you decide to call a staff meeting to find out the reasons for this.

The staff voice many complaints and suggestions, and you listen carefully. As the owner, you are at liberty to make alterations to the salon layout, install new equipment, make staff changes (or change the duties of staff by negotiation) and introduce new safety procedures. Remember, as an employer, you *must* comply with

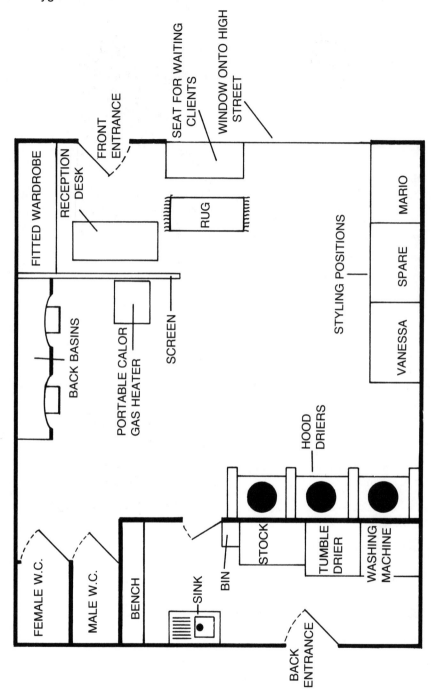

Fig. 6.10 A salon plan.

Figure 6.11 shows two pictures of the same girl dressed for her day's work in the salon.

She has chosen an overall made of cotton. Why?

Why is her posture on the left better for work than that on the right?

Are there any dangers from the way her hair is worn on the right? What about the jewellery?

Why has the girl on the left not got any clips in her pockets?

Should you wear shoes with high heels in the salon?

Why is it unhygienic to put your fingers in your mouth?

How would wearing a tight belt make you feel uncomfortable in hot weather?

Fig. 6.11   Personal health and safety exercise.

the Health and Safety regulations as stipulated by the 1974 Act of Parliament. The following points were raised by staff:

(1) George (the junior) complained that he was constantly running to and from the dispensary/staff room to give Mrs Stephens the towels. He asked if he could leave them in a pile on the floor for her to collect. He also said that clients had complained of being too hot at the basins because of the portable Calor gas heater.

(2) Mrs Stephens (the laundry lady) complained that staff were always sitting on the bench when she needed to use it to fold the towels. She added that the heat given off from the washer and drier was making her tired. A bottle of peroxide had exploded because of the heat, and when the rubbish bin caught fire, from a cigarette, there was no fire extinguisher.

(3) Mario (a stylist) said that several clients had tripped on the rug at reception. One client had cut her head on the corner of the reception desk when she fell. He also said he was fed up with having to leave a client to answer the telephone and see to waiting clients. He added that the drier bank kept fusing because one socket supplied the power for all three hood-driers.

(4) Vanessa (a stylist) also complained that she had to leave clients she was attending because there was no receptionist. She said her clients complained about draughts each time the salon door opened, and that the window always has condensation running down it. She found it a problem when using a hand-drier at the same time as Mario because there was only one socket supplying power to the styling position, so she has to use an extension cable which often trails across the floor. She added that no plasters were available when staff accidentally cut themselves.

Study the comments of the staff and the salon plan. How would you solve these problems?

7

Caution in the Hairdressing Salon

The word 'caution' is defined in the dictionary as 'the avoidance of rashness' or 'attention to safety'. This chapter of the book has been written specifically for the hairdresser and deals primarily with aspects of safety that should be observed when working with hairdressing chemicals. If you read it and make sure you use what you learn in the salon, you will be able to look forward to years of trouble-free working. Remember that hairdressing chemicals should not present a risk to hairdressers or their clients, if used sensibly. Manufacturers spend large sums on developing new products which must be thoroughly tested before being released for general use by the industry, so don't assume that you know how to use a product without having read the manufacturer's instructions. Once you have read them, FOLLOW THEM!

All chemicals used in the hairdressing salon should be handled carefully; they may be toxic, irritant, flammable or a mixture of all three. Even the water that we use in the salon should be treated with care, as it is often hot and could scald the skin. If misused, hairdressing chemicals can cause serious skin burns and hair breakage. This should never happen if the hairdresser has been properly trained. If such damage should occur, the hairdresser would have to pay compensation to the client or be taken to court. If you work in a salon you should wear a protective overall so that your clothes do not get damaged. Similarly, if you are working on a client, they should be properly protected with towels, gowns and capes as appropriate. Make sure that you know the correct gowning procedure for each service in your salon. Each group of hairdressing chemicals that we shall look at will be discussed in terms of general use, storage and disposal.

7.1 Essential first aid for hairdressing chemicals

First aid for hairdressing chemicals is discussed fully in Chapter 10, but a few essentials are appropriate to mention here. Hopefully they will never have to be used!

(1) On the skin

If a chemical irritates or burns either your own or the client's skin, hold the affected area under running cold water to dilute and remove it. This means that a chemical on the hair should be rinsed off to stop its action if it should start to irritate. Medical advice should be sought if irritation persists after this first aid.

(2) In the eye

If a chemical enters a client's eye, cover the unaffected eye (this will prevent any chemical being splashed on to this eye) and flood the affected eye with cold water to dilute and flush out the chemical. If irritation persists, seek immediate medical advice. Some salons will have special wash bottles, usually fixed to the wall, which can be used. The shampoo hand-set or a jug from which water can be poured are also appropriate. Never use an eye cup to remove chemicals from the eye. Because it is only using a small amount of water which is held in contact with the eye, it dilutes but does not remove the chemical.

(3) If inhaled

Remove the casualty to fresh air immediately. If the casulaty is a known asthmatic, they may have an inhaler which would give them relief. Medical advice should be sought if coughing, choking, wheeziness or breathlessness persists for longer than 10 minutes.

(4) Ingestion (swallowing)

In the majority of cases where hairdressing chemicals are eaten or drunk by accident, the appropriate first aid is to drink two or three glasses of water to dilute the chemical and then seek immediate medical advice. Do not induce vomiting as corrosive poisons such as bleaches will burn the oesophagus and mouth as they are brought up. Take the chemical container and any instructions for the product with you if a casualty requires further medical treatment or advice. They may give important information to help determine the correct treatment.

Questions 7.1

1   What is the first aid for a chemical which irritates or burns the skin?
2   When is it necessary to seek medical advice?
3   If a client with a perm processing complains of scalp irritation what should you do?
4   What is the first aid for a chemical entering the eye of a client?
5   Why should the unaffected eye be covered?
6   Why is an eye cup not suitable for such first aid?
7   Have you an eye wash bottle in your salon?
8   When would further medical treatment be needed?
9   What is the first aid for someone who has inhaled a chemical?
10   How would you know further medical treatment was necessary?
11   If the casualty was asthmatic, what extra treatment is there?
12   What is the general first aid treatment to be given when a chemical is swallowed?
13   Would you induce vomiting?

14   What would you take with you if accompanying a casualty to the hospital or doctor as
a result of an accident with a hairdressing chemical?

Note *The hairdressing tests referred to in the next sections of this chapter are fully
described in* FOUNDATION HAIRDRESSING. You should be able to carry them
all out as required.

7.2 Dressing and styling products

These are hairdressing products which are used to control the hair of the client. They
include hairsprays, creams, gels, mousses, waxes and setting lotions. Some will come
in pressurised aerosol containers (hairspray and mousse) which must be treated with
caution. The following safety points should always be observed when using pressurised containers:

- Store in a cool place as the contents may explode if overheated. This means that
  they should be kept away from heaters and radiators, and out of direct sunlight
  in hot weather. Remember this if you are building a display of products in your
  salon window, or if you have a retail stand near a window.
- Even aerosol cans which to all intents and purposes are regarded as 'empty' will
  explode if placed in a fire. Dispose of them in normal salon rubbish bins.
- Never puncture an aerosol can, even if you think it is empty. The contents would
  be forced out under considerable pressure which could damage the eyes or ignite
  and catch fire.
- In case of a fire evacuate everyone to safety and tell fire-fighters of the presence
  of aerosol containers.
- If the nozzle becomes blocked do not try to unblock it with a needle, but try
  soaking in hot soapy water or alcohol. If an aerosol container still contains
  product and you cannot get it to work, return it to your supplier who should
  replace it free of charge.
- Use aerosol sprays in well-ventilated conditions so that the spray is removed
  from the air quickly, and ask the client to close their eyes. Face guards are
  available in many salons to protect the client from hairspray. The hairdresser
  should try not to breathe in too much hairspray.

Many of the styling products used in the modern salon are flammable. They contain
alcohol and could be ignited by an incandescent object such as a lit cigarette
(incandescent means to glow with heat). There have been a number of cases of hair
catching alight in salons and also in schools. Indeed, some schools have banned the
use of gels because of such accidents. Such problems can be avoided in the salon by
not allowing smoking when styling products are in use (see Figure 6.6. to see hairspray being ignited); this rule applies to both the client and the hairdresser. Salons
should not have heaters with naked flames near clients (portable gas and paraffin
fires). Care should also be taken not to use aerosol products near infra-red lamps,
such as would be found in lamp dryers and accelerators.

   If ever the hair should catch alight, wrap the head immediately in a towel; this will starve the flames of oxygen and put them out. Alternatively, use the shampoo hand-set to douse the flames with cold water. If the scalp is burned, run cold water over it for 20 minutes or until pain has gone. Seek medical attention if burn is severe. (See Chapter 10.)

All styling products should be kept away from the eyes and off skin which is scratched or damaged, as they could cause irritation. If spilt they should be mopped or wiped up immediately; if a greasy surface is left it may be necessary to clean up with detergent in case someone slips over. Products should be disposed of in normal rubbish in their original containers. If setting lotion is spilt down a sink the taps should be run for a few minutes to dilute it, as it is flammable. This will prevent possible fire in the drains.

Questions 7.2

1   What are dressing and styling products used for in the salon?
2   List the dressing and styling products in use in your salon.
3   What are the main safety points that should be observed when using aerosols in the salon?
4   Are any of these points not observed in your salon?
5   If so, what are the potential dangers?
6   How would you try to unblock an aerosol nozzle?
7   What should you do with an aerosol that has stopped working but which still contains product?
8   How can the client be protected from hairspray?
9   How could a styling product catch fire in the salon?
10   What action should be taken if the hair of a client caught alight?
11   What should be done if a styling product is spilt on the floor?
12   If setting lotion is spilt down a sink, what should you do?

7.3   Bleaching

Bleaching is carried out in the salon to remove natural colour, using a variety of chemicals which are strong oxidising agents. When the natural pigments of hair are oxidised they become colourless. The dark brown pigment melanin is oxidised to colourless oxy-melanin for example. Bleaching chemicals can burn the skin and cause hair breakage. A head of hair is in considerably worse condition after bleaching; it will be more porous and have less tensile strength (it will break more easily when stretched).

Bleaching products are usually mixed with hydrogen peroxide immediately before use. Powder bleaches contain various persulphates (ammonium, sodium and potassium) which give off oxygen, and inert fillers to give bulk to the mixture, such as magnesium silicate. The former chemicals give extra bleaching power while the latter form a paste with the hydrogen peroxide. The following are important guidelines for the safe salon use of bleaching products:

● Powder bleaches should only be used in a well-ventilated area as inhalation can irritate the respiratory system, particularly in those who are prone to asthma. Face masks are available to stop accidental inhalation.

- Bleaching products, including hydrogen peroxide, should not be allowed to stay in contact with combustible materials such as paper, as fire can result. Dispose of bleaching materials by flushing down the sink into the drains with plenty of cold water.
- Hydrogen peroxide can react with some chemicals to form explosive materials, so only use hydrogen peroxide according to manufacturers' instructions.
- Keep lids of bleaching products firmly on, resealing as soon as you have taken your chemical from the storage container. Hydrogen peroxide will decompose if dust gets into it. If ever a container of hydrogen peroxide is swollen, open it with a cloth over the lid as some peroxide may be discharged in an aerosol effect.
- Store bleaching products away from sources of heat, out of direct sunlight in a cool dry place such as a cupboard. Keep away from flammable salon products such as hairsprays and setting lotions, as these will burn more fiercely in a fire with bleaching products, which would support combustion.
- Peroxide strengths above 40 volume (12%) strength should not be used. They could severely damage the skin. Remember that if you do not follow manufacturers' instructions and there is an accident you are legally liable.
- Unless the hair is covered in lacquer or is excessively dirty, it should not be shampooed prior to bleaching. The natural oil of the scalp, sebum, forms a protective barrier between the bleach and scalp. If hair has to be washed, use a mild shampoo (for normal hair, without additives) and thoroughly dry the hair. Wet hair would dilute the bleaching chemicals.
- Carry out all necessary precautionary hairdressing tests (see *Foundation Hairdressing*). Porosity and elasticity tests will indicate the state of the cuticle and cortex. A strand test will give an accurate indication of final bleaching results and possible damage on a sample of hair, rather than risk ruining a whole head. An incompatibility test should be carried out if you suspect the presence of metallic salts on the hair of the client. These would be present in hair colour restorers and some glitter hairsprays. They would react violently with bleaching products causing scalp and hair damage (they would also react violently with perm neutralisers and tint mixtures).
- Apply bleach mixture last to the hair nearest the scalp, as body heat from the scalp will accelerate bleaching.
- Use an anti-oxidant rinse following bleaching as this will reduce oxidation damage. Remember that even after you have washed a bleaching product from the hair, some will be left in the cortex and there will be 'creeping' oxidation damage.
- Protect your hands when bleaching by wearing gloves.
- If you are unsure of the strength of liquid hydrogen peroxide check it with a peroxometer (this is a special type of hydrometer available in both volume and percentage strengths).

Questions 7.3

1   What does bleaching do to the natural pigment of the hair?
2   What are bleaches chemically?
3   What adverse effect can bleaching chemicals have on the skin and hair?

4   How is the condition of hair altered by bleaching?
5   What chemicals do powder bleaches contain and what is their action?
6   How can you reduce the problems associated with inhaling powder bleaches?
7   Why should bleaching chemicals not be allowed to come into contact with paper?
8   How should bleaching chemicals be disposed of?
9   Why should hydrogen peroxide only be used according to manufacturers' instructions?
10 Why should lids be kept on bleaching chemicals?
11 What precaution should be taken when opening a swollen container of hydrogen peroxide?
12 How should bleaching products be stored?
13 What is the maximum strength of peroxide that should be used in bleaching?
14 Why should hair not be shampooed before bleaching?
15 Are there any exceptions to this?
16 Why is it best to carry out bleaching on dry hair?
17 What parts of the hair can be checked with porosity and elasticity tests?
18 When would you perform a strand test?
19 Why is an incompatibility test carried out?
20 Why is bleach applied last to the hair close to the scalp?
21 What is an anti-oxidant rinse and when is it used?
22 How should the hands be protected when bleaching?
23 What is a peroxometer?

7.4   Hair dyes and removers

The majority of dyes used in the salon can be divided into three main groups: temporary, semi-permanent and permanent.

Temporary colours have large molecules and their effect is on the cuticle of the hair. Semi-permanents have small molecules which penetrate the cortex of the hair. These two groups of colourants are direct dyestuffs in a shampoo base, available as liquids, creams, gels or mousses. Direct dyes do not have to be mixed with anything because they are in their final coloured form. The following are general rules for their safe use:

- Wear gloves when handling dyes to prevent staining and possible irritation.
- Do not use on broken skin.
- Store in a cool place away from direct sunlight.
- Avoid contact with the eyes.
- Mop up spillages immediately with plenty of water.
- Carry out a skin test if recommended when using semi-permanents; this is explained in Section 3.3.

Permanent dyes are also referred to as oxidation dyes or tints because they are mixed with hydrogen peroxide immediately before use. This hydrogen peroxide can be as strong as 60 volume or 18%. Precautions outlined for hydrogen peroxide in Section 7.3 should be observed. Skin tests should be given prior to application of tints as some people will suffer severe allergic reactions; refer back to Section 3.3. and look at Figure 3.4 which shows such a reaction. The following are safety points that should be observed when using tints:

- As with bleaching, it is best not to shampoo the hair before tinting as the natural oils of the scalp help form a protective barrier between the tint and the scalp.
- Perform skin tests prior to application of tint.
- Perform an incompatibility test if you suspect the presence of metallic salts (hair colour restorers) on the hair.
- If you are unsure of final colour results or whether the hair is suitable for tinting, perform a strand test first.
- Use an anti-oxidant rinse immediately after shampooing tint from the hair, to prevent creeping oxidation. These rinses are acidic (so close the cuticle) reducing agents which form water with any remaining oxidising agent.
- Mix chemicals using measured quantities in a non-metallic bowl (hydrogen peroxide reacts with metals).
- Replace lids on chemicals immediately, and squeeze tint tubes from the bottom to exclude air which would otherwise cause the tint to go off.
- Wear gloves.
- Liquid tints contain alcohol so should be treated as flammable and appropriate safety measures observed (see Section 7.2).
- Do not use on damaged skin.
- Keep chemicals away from the eyes, face and skin.
- Wipe up spillages immediately with plenty of water.
- Dispose of unwanted chemical with plenty of running cold water down a sink.

Tip If tint is spilt on to clothing, spray immediately with plenty of hairspray as this will help stop the stain from becoming fast and ruining clothing. The alcohol in the hairspray helps stop it from 'fixing' on the clothing. If the client has stains on the skin after shampooing, take a rather disgusting tip from some of the top colourists. Wet your finger or a piece of damp cotton wool, dip it into some cigarette ash (the smokers put their ash into a container without the butts!) and rub on the stained skin. It works!

Hair dye removers are used to remove unwanted permanent dyes or tints from the hair. They are based on either oxidising or reducing chemicals. If the system you are using requires the mixing of two chemicals it is usually the reducing type. Powders usually contain oxidising agents such as persulphates and are mixed with hydrogen peroxide. If you are unsure which system you are using treat as directed in Section 7.3 for oxidising agents. The following general safety points should be observed:

- Wear gloves and protective clothing such as an apron; colour removers will work on clothing as well as hair!
- Avoid contact of chemicals with the eyes and skin.
- Wipe up spillages immediately with plenty of water.
- If dye remover is a powder form, use in well-ventilated area and wear protective mask if available.
- Store chemicals in a cool dry place away from direct sunlight, resealing containers immediately.

- Dispose of unwanted chemical down a sink with plenty of running cold water.
- Remember that dye removers will also remove colour from clothes so protect yourself with a plastic apron.

Questions 7.4

1   What are the main types of dye used in the salon?
2   What part of the hair is affected by a temporary colour?
3   What part of the hair is affected by semi-permanent colour?
4   In what forms are they available?
5   What does the term direct dye mean?
6   How would you protect yourself when using these dyes?
7   How would you protect the client when using these dyes?
8   Why is a skin test sometimes necessary when using a semipermanent?
9   What are the other names for a permanent dye?
10   What is the maximum strength of hydrogen peroxide used with tints?
11   Why are skin tests given to clients before tinting?
12   Should hair be shampooed before tinting?
13   Why?
14   When would an incompatibility test be performed?
15   Why would a strand test be performed?
16   What is an anti-oxidant rinse and why is it used?
17   Why should metallic bowls not be used?
18   How would you stop unused tint going off?
19   How would you deal with spillages and dispose of unwanted tint?
20   What are hair dye removers used for?
21   What are they chemically?
22   How would you know which type you were using?
23   List three points for the safe use of hair dye removers.
24   Why is it advisable for the hairdresser to wear a plastic apron when using dye remover?

7.5   Perm lotions

Perming is a two-stage process to give 'permanent' curls to straight hair. During the first stage the disulphide bonds of the hair are broken down by a reduction process using the perm lotion. Hairdressers often refer to this as softening the hair. These lotions are of two main types, cold wave or acid. The acid perm is less damaging to the hair and has become very popular. Less common today is a third perm system referred to as a tepid perm, where heated clamps are used.

Hair is wound on to a mould such as a perm rod, which determines the shape the softened hair will take on. After rinsing, the neutraliser is applied to fix the curl, referred to by many hairdressers as hardening the hair. This second stage of perming is an oxidation process, so keep in mind some of the safety points from Section 7.4 for bleaching chemicals.

In Afro hairdressing curly perms are carried out on clients. These use similar chemical systems so the safety points below should be observed. One of the major differences between a curly perm and a conventional perm is that Afro hair has a tight curl which must be straightened so that the hair can take on a larger curl. The first lotion used is a perm lotion, which removes some of the curl so that the hair can be wound on to large rods. A curl booster is then applied, which is a weak perm lotion, so that the hair takes on the shape of the rods. A neutraliser is then applied as for conventional perms, to fix the curl. For more information see *Afro Hair – A Salon Handbook*.

The following are some of the main safety points that you should observe when perming:

- Carry out all precautionary tests on the hair that are appropriate to assess the condition of the hair (porosity, elasticity).
- Carry out an incompatibility test if you are unsure if the hair has metallic salts on it (hair colour restorers), as these would react with the oxidising agent in the neutraliser.
- Wash the hair with a pre-perm shampoo. If the salon does not have one use a shampoo which does not have any added ingredients, as these could form a barrier on the hair. Do not use a shampoo for greasy hair as this will contain more detergent and is therefore more likely to irritate the hair. Many hairdressers say the hair should be washed with a soapless shampoo before perming, but all shampoos in salons today are soapless.
- Avoid stimulating the scalp with vigorous rubbing during the shampoo, as this could make the scalp more sensitive to the perm lotion.
- Do not use if the scalp is damaged. Avoid dripping the chemical on to the face.
- If you are unsure which perm lotion to use, or whether the perm will take, carry out test curls first. Most lotions are available in three strengths, the ones for resistant hair containing almost twice the amount of active ingredient as those for tinted hair. Using too strong a lotion could cause serious damage. You cannot perm relaxed hair, while very often you will not get a satisfactory result on bleached hair or hair which has regularly had henna applied to it. The hair of women who are pregnant, or who have just given birth, may not take a perm. Testing before processing a whole head will cause less damage and save your time. You cannot expect to charge a client for a service if there is no result!
- Wind hair with an even amount of tension but do not stretch the hair. Remember that hair with perm lotion on it will easily overstretch and be damaged. Therefore if you pre-damp with lotion take care when winding.
- Wear gloves when perming.
- Use pre-perm treatments to even out porosity on damaged hair and ensure an even rate of processing and reduced chemical damage.
- Mix the activator with an acid perm immediately prior to application. Do not use external sources of heat unless recommended by the manufacturer's instructions.
- Use cotton wool strips dampened with water around the hairline to stop lotion from dripping. The water will slow down absorption of perm lotion and will also dilute the lotion. Change strips regularly. (See Figure 7.1.)
- Check that towels around the neck do not become damp with perm lotion as this will burn the skin.
- Use plastic strips to keep pressure off the hair, which can be caused by the

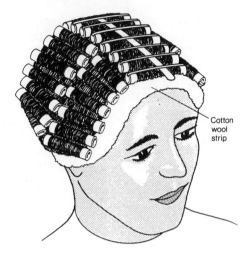

Cotton
wool
strip

Fig. 7.1   Use of cotton wool strips to protect a client's skin during perming. The plastic strip
along the top layer of rods will stop the rubber bands marking the hair.

rubber bands of perm rods. Pressure can cause hair breakage. A strip is shown
along the top row of rods in Figure 7.1.
- Be careful not to mix up sponges used to apply perm lotion and neutraliser. If a
  sponge that is contaminated with perm lotion were to be used to apply neutraliser, there would be a risk of under-neutralising the perm and there would be
  no result from the perm: the perm lotion would react with the neutraliser so that
  the neutraliser would not be making bonds rejoin.
- Remember that it is possible to over-neutralise someone's hair. This means that
  the oxidising agent is damaging the bonds of the hair rather than rejoining the
  ones broken down by the perm lotion. Check timings for neutralising given by
  the manufacturer.
- Use an anti-oxidant rinse following neutralising to restrict creeping oxidation
  and reduce damage.
- Store perming chemicals in a cool place away from direct sunlight. Replace
  bottle tops as soon as possible after opening, to keep products fresh.
- Dispose of excess product down the sink with plenty of running cold water.
- Mop up spillages immediately with plenty of water.

If you are straightening hair with the type of chemicals based on perm lotions,
follow the same safety precautions as above, being careful to use wide-toothed
combs and not to apply too much tension when manipulating the hair.

Questions 7.5

1   Briefly describe the perming process.
2   Which type of perm is least damaging to hair?
3   What is a curly perm and how is it different from the normal perming process?
4   What precautionary tests would you carry out before perming?

5   Why are perm lotions available in different strengths?
6   What type of shampoo would you use before a perm?
7   How can you check that you are using the correct perm lotion on your client?
8   List the types of hair that may not take a perm well.
9   How should you wind a perm?
10   Why is a pre-perm treatment used?
11   How and why are cotton wool strips used?
12   Why should the protective towels around the neck be checked?
13   Why should perming and neutralising sponges be kept separately?
14   What happens to the bonds of the hair in over-neutralising?
15   Why is an anti-oxidant rinse used after neutralising?
16   What process can be performed in the salon that uses the same chemicals as in perming?

7.6   Hair relaxers

The majority of hair relaxers used on Afro hair and European hair with tight curl formations are strongly alkaline chemicals. These open the cuticle and damage the internal structure of the hair. Because of this, incorrect use can cause serious hair and scalp damage. In this country the 1989 Cosmetic Products (Safety) Regulations limit the maximum amount of metallic hydroxide (sodium, potassium or lithium) to 4.5% in professional products. Be warned that some American products contain more than this. You may see the word 'lye' as an ingredient on American products; this refers to sodium hydroxide (commonly called caustic soda in this country). American products are sometimes marked 'contains no lye', to give the impression that they are weaker products. Do not be fooled by this because potassium or lithium hydroxides are equally strong chemicals.

Hair relaxers break the bonds of the hair so that it can be straightened by gentle manipulation. The neutraliser used with a relaxer is an acidic shampoo which counteracts the alkalinity of the relaxer used. It does not rebuild bonds like perming neutralisers because the relaxing process is continuous; broken bonds rejoin as a new type of bond of their own accord. The following are essential safety points to be followed when relaxing hair:

- Check the client's scalp for cuts and broken skin, only proceeding if the scalp is in good condition.
- Carry out precautionary tests on the hair to assess whether the hair could be relaxed (porosity and elasticity). Use the appropriate strength of relaxer. Prior to relaxing the whole head, carry out a test on a strand of hair to check for result and possible damage.
- Do not shampoo the hair prior to relaxing as sebum helps protect the scalp, and you should also avoid stimulating the scalp.
- 'Base' the scalp before proceeding with the application of the relaxer, unless you are using a no-base relaxer. The base cream is a neutral substance which helps protect the scalp. Care must be taken not to get it on to the hair.
- Application must be quick because of the relatively short processing times involved. Do not allow to over-process.

- When doing a re-growth application, do not overlap on to previously relaxed hair as it could cause breakage at the point of the overlapping.
- Wear gloves at all times.
- Manipulate hair gently with gloved hands or a wide-toothed comb, as this will cause less damage.
- Use a back-wash basin as this is safer when rinsing than a front-wash. Relaxer in the eye could cause blindness.
- Relaxer should be rinsed from the hair using the force of the water, with little or no massage action from the hands, as the hair is very delicate at this stage and could be easily damaged.
- Store products in a cool place away from direct sunlight and reseal containers immediately.
- Condition hair after treatment.
- Wipe up spillages immediately with paper towel or disposable cloth. A detergent may be necessary to prevent the area from becoming slippery.
- Dispose of excess product down the sink with plenty of running water.

If you would like to know more about relaxing, see *Afro Hair – A Salon Handbook*.

Questions 7.6

1 Why can relaxers cause serious hair and scalp damage?
2 What regulations determine the amount of active ingredient in relaxers?
3 What does the word 'lye' refer to?
4 If a product is marked 'contains no lye', is it necessarily a weaker product?
5 Describe the relaxing process.
6 What precautionary tests are necessary before relaxing the hair?
7 Should hair be shampooed prior to relaxing?
8 What does the term 'basing the scalp' mean?
9 Why should overlapping be avoided when relaxing re-growth?
10 How should the hair be manipulated during relaxing?
11 Why should a back-wash be used when relaxing hair?
12 How should relaxer be rinsed from the hair?
13 How should relaxing products be stored?
14 Describe how you would deal with spilt relaxer?

8

Caution in the Beauty Therapy Salon

Anywhere that the therapist works on members of the public is an area where safe working practices are essential. Although this is the only part of the book specifically devoted to beauty therapy, you must be able to recognise skin conditions, know about hair and skin, be able to give basic first aid and know all about general salon health and safety. All these areas are covered elsewhere in the book.

Beauty therapy is different from hairdressing in that the therapist deals with clients in a more intimate fashion. Clients place their bodies into the care of the therapist, believing that the therapist will act in a professional manner. Some of the treatments offered in beauty therapy could, if performed incorrectly, give rise to significant dangers such as scarring. There are many specific problems of hygiene because so many treatments involve physical contact between the therapist and the client, or the intimate contact of therapy apparatus which is then used on other clients. If you are cautious in your work, the service you give will be professional and your clients will know that they are in safe hands.

8.1 Skin hygiene and the prevention of infection

A number of beauty therapy treatments are performed using the hands directly on the skin. Techniques such as face and body massage cannot be performed wearing gloves, so attention must be given to the prevention of cross-infection between the therapist and client or clients. The following points should be observed:

- Cuts or abrasions on the hands of the therapist should be covered with plasters.
- If there are any cuts on the skin of the client, these should also be covered with plasters. If this is not practical, however, *do not* proceed with the service.

- If the therapist has problems such as eczema on the hands so that skin is damaged, gloves should be worn if the service permits this. Disposable surgical gloves are available which are thin but protect the hands. Care should be taken when removing gloves as cross-infection could result from their outer surface. Pull them off from the wrist in one movement and then wash the hands. Dispose of used gloves in a plastic bag.
- Hands should be washed regularly between treatments and clients, using a bactericidal washing cream. These are available in hygienic wall dispensers or bottles with a pump mechanism fitted. This means that the therapist uses fresh uncontaminated cream each time the hands are washed, much more preferable than a shared bar of soap. Hands should be dried with disposable paper towels; other towels, such as roller towels, may be the source of infective organisms.
- Jewellery (rings and bracelets) should not be worn as it can harbour germs and could be dangerous in some electrical treatments. Either leave jewellery at home or have a safe place to put it at work.
- Skin conditions such as warts on the hands of the therapist should be treated in case they get damaged and become infective. They do not, anyway, give the therapist a professional appearance.
- Barrier creams are available to protect the hands of the therapist; many are in a light non-greasy mousse form. They create a barrier over tiny skin crevices such as breaks in the nail cuticle, giving extra protection.

The feet are another area of skin where infection can occur. The therapist should wear low heeled comfortable leather shoes which are closed in (See Section 9.4). This helps prevent accidents from falling sharp objects or spillages of hot wax. Clients should wear shoes at all times except when on the couch or sunbed or in the shower, sauna or steam bath. If the client has infectious conditions on the feet such as plantar warts (verrucae) or athlete's foot, treatments that might involve a risk of cross-infection should not be given.

Questions 8.1

1 Why is the hygiene of the skin so important in beauty therapy?
2 What is cross-infection?
3 What should be done to cuts on the therapist or the client before a service is given?
4 When should the therapist wear gloves?
5 Can the therapist wear gloves for all treatments?
6 How should gloves be taken off and disposed of?
7 When should hands be washed?
8 How should they then be dried?
9 Why is a bar of soap not as hygienic as liquids for washing the hands?
10 Should hand jewellery be worn by the therapist?
11 Why should warts be removed from the therapist's hands?
12 Why are barrier creams a useful protection for the hands?
13 Why are closed-in toes preferable to open toes for shoes worn by the therapist?
14 When should clients not wear shoes?
15 When should clients not be allowed treatment because of foot conditions?

8.2   *Contra-indications to beauty treatments*

'Contra-indication' is a medical term for conditions that act as an indication against the use of a particular treatment. Sometimes a contra-indication is obvious: if the client has an infected area of skin containing pus you will automatically know not to touch that area or apply any treatments because of the possibility of spreading infection. However, if a client has something wrong with them that does not show externally, mistakes can easily be made. Once I was demonstrating scalp massage to a group of students and talking them through the contra-indications to the service. At the mention of high blood pressure the client chipped in with 'I suffer from that'! My scalp massage could easily have caused the client to pass out, possibly being injured by a fall.

A client should have a record card that lists their medical history, so time should be spent with new clients to establish this history. Below is a list of general contra-indications to beauty treatments, where you will have to apply your knowledge to judge whether they preclude a particular service for your client:

- Infectious conditions.
- Skin abrasions, eczema (client discomfort, cross-infection).
- Dermatitis (contact eczema).
- Circulatory disorders (high or low blood pressure) and oedema (water retention causing swelling).
- Heart pacemakers.
- Later stages of pregnancy.
- High body temperature.
- Taking of prescribed drugs.
- Epilepsy or spastic conditions.
- Diabetes (poor skin healing).
- Asthmatics.
- Scar tissue or keloids.
- Recent operations.
- Areas where there have been recent fractures and sprains.
- Metal plates or pins in bones.
- Sensitive skin (from sunburn, over-exposure to ultra-violet rays, etc.).
- Varicose veins.
- Warts, protruding moles, skin tags.
- A large quantity of metallic fillings or metal bridge work (specific to facial faradic muscle contraction).
- Nervous, highly-strung clients.
- Highly-coloured, vascular complexions.
- Sinus congestion.
- Migraine.
- Loose skin texture (loss of elasticity).

Treatments should never aggravate any physical defect, be the cause of unnecessary client discomfort or enable cross-infection to occur. A golden rule to observe for contra-indications is that if in doubt, ask or don't proceed! There will always be someone more experienced than yourself who can give you an answer. In the case of some health conditions or treatments, ask the client's doctor for advice.

Questions 8.2

1   What is a contra-indication?
2   From the list of contra-indications above, make up your own guide of contra-indications specifically for the following beauty treatments:
   (a)   Body treatments.
   (b)   Waxing therapy.
   (c)   Electrical treatments.
   (d)   Epilation.
   (e)   Ulra-violet treatments.
   (f)   Lash and brow treatments.
   (g)   Make-up.
   (h)   Facials.
   (i)   Nail care.
   (j)   Sauna or steam baths.
3   Why is record-keeping important in the beauty salon?
4   What should you do if you are unsure about the safety of a treatment on a particular client?

8.3   Hygiene precautions during beauty treatments

'Be seen to be clean' should be every beauty therapist's maxim. Explain to the clients why you use disposables; they will appreciate your professional approach to your work. Although it is more expensive to follow hygienic procedures, the public will pay that little bit extra for safety if they can see it happening. Hygiene aspects of specific treatment areas are given below.

Applying creams and make-up

The hygiene problems in these areas concern the use of a product on the skin without contaminating the rest of the product still in the container. At home where the same person uses a product this is not important, so the fingers or a brush can be allowed to come into contact with the skin and with the product in its container. But the therapist must use an intermediate procedure to cut out contamination. Disposable wooden spatulas can be used to remove creams from a pot on to some form of palette, or to drop the cream on to the skin without skin contact. If contact with the skin is made, the wooden spatula should be discarded and replaced with a fresh one. Wooden spatulas are cheap and avoid the necessity for sterilisation that metal or plastic spatulas entail.

   If you are using a palette the fingers, brushes or cotton buds can be used to collect the product. Load the palette with enough material to complete a treatment, or reload using a fresh spatula. Thoroughly wash the palette before its next use. Many therapists use the back of their hands as a palette, as shown in Figure 8.1. They find this an easy method of application, but hands must be clean and the product should

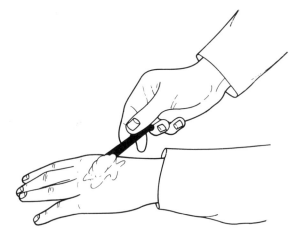

Fig. 8.1   Using the back of the hand as a palette.

not cause skin irritation. A gloved hand is more hygienic but many creams tend to run easily from the smooth surface. Any powders used can be sprinkled from their containers on to cotton wool, for application to the client.

Where the fingers cannot be used to apply the product, try to use disposables such as cotton buds rather than brushes which are difficult to sterilise adequately without damaging them. Some clients will bring their own brushes, especially if you give them tips on applying make-up and show them it can be done with their own set! Manufacturers will eventually come up with alternatives that work.

Wax treatments

Wax treatments may be used therapeutically (paraffin wax) or to remove hair (depilatory). Because wax adheres to the skin and will therefore pull out some hairs, body fluids may also be brought to the skin surface. The therapist should wear disposable gloves for protection from this. Used wax is a contaminated material and should be disposed of unless it can be sterilised. In the past it was filtered and used again. Heating wax to a high enough temperature to sterilise it adequately is not possible in most heaters, so it is better to play safe and dispose of it.

Manicure and pedicure

There is a danger with these treatments when using cuticle nippers, knives, orange sticks and nail files, that blood may accidentally be drawn. Non-metal implements such as orange sticks and emery boards should be treated as disposable after use on one client. Metal instruments should be of solid stainless steel so that they can undergo sterilisation by heat, preferably in an autoclave or a glass bead steriliser. If these are not available, as might be the case in a smaller establishment, use disinfectants produced specifically for use with metal tools. Seventy per cent alcohol is an effective disinfecting agent, but remember that tools will not be totally sterile. More than one set of instruments will probably be required.

The nails should be cleaned with disposable cotton wool pads, and disposable gloves should be available where there is a danger of drawing blood (although they only need to be put on in the event of an accident). If there is bleeding, care should be taken not to draw blood on to the nail varnish with the stroking action of the brush. If this should occur, dispose of the brush and bottle.

Other treatments

Showering facilities are important in beauty treatments, to either clean skin before or after a treatment. Shower trays are more hygienic than tiles as they are easier to clean. Suitable disinfectant and detergent solutions should be used. It is more hygienic to provide individual small bars of soap for each client (the type provided in hotels). Paper towel can be provided for clients to step on to dry themselves, primarily in order to avoid the possibility of infection from plantar warts and athlete's foot. Fabric towels should be washed after use by each client.

Couches for body treatments should have disposable paper towel coverings, and paper towel next to the couch for the client to stand on barefooted. Blankets should be lightweight so that they can easily be washed. The genital area should be covered with paper towel which should be properly disposed of after treatment.

Exercise equipment is used by clients wearing leotards and there is little risk of cross-infection as long as exercises are not performed in bare feet. Where towels are provided, such as on exercise benches, they should be either for the exclusive use of one client or disposable. Vibro-belts should not be used on bare skin. The surfaces of equipment should be washed regularly.

Saunas should be washed down with large quantities of water; a drain should be installed in the sauna floor for this purpose. Clients should wear bikini bottoms or bathing trunks, and the sauna should not be so overcrowded that clients are touching each other. Clients can sit on disposable paper towels. The same precautions apply to individual steam cabinets except that because of their fibreglass construction they are easier to wash properly. The insides should be wiped over with disinfectant solution. Either disposable paper towel or a fresh towel should be placed on the floor of the cabinet to absorb condensed steam. Paper mats should be placed outside the sauna or steam cabinet.

Spa pools are popular in a number of larger beauty establishments. Water is circulated under pressure and a number of people may be in the pool at one time. Water should be passing through a filtration system and being chemically treated at the same time. Chlorine and bromine are often used as the disinfecting chemicals in the water to prevent cross-infection. Sometimes the chemical treatment is automatic, but water should be manually tested once or twice daily to make sure it is working. Vigilance is necessary with spa hygiene because of bacterial infections of the skin caused by some species of Pseudomonas (a species of bacteria found in water). Follow manufacturers' instructions on cleaning materials for pools, as ordinary detergent could drain into the water recirculation equipment and affect the efficiency of automatic disinfection.

Spa baths are for individual use so they do not contain disinfecting solutions as they are cleaned out after each use.

Clients using sunbeds should shower first and wear bikini bottoms or swimming trunks. The bed should be wiped down with a suitable disinfectant such as cetrimide.

Electrical epilation and ear piercing will be looked at separately in Section 8.5 because they involve serious hygiene and safety issues (AIDS and hepatitis B).

Questions 8.3

1   What do you understand by the saying 'Be seen to be clean'?
2   What are the hygiene problems associated with the application of creams and make-up from their containers?
3   How can these problems be overcome?
4   Why is it difficult to use brushes hygienically?
5   Why should wax be disposed of after use on a client?
6   What is the main danger associated with manicure and pedicure?
7   How can it be overcome?
8   How should the nails be cleaned?
9   Describe the hygienic use of the shower in the beauty salon.
10 How can the use of the beauty couch be made hygienic?
11 What is the main risk of infection during exercise?
12 How are towels used hygienically in the beauty salon?
13 Describe the hygiene precautions that should be taken with the sauna and steam cabinet.
14 What is the main difference between the operation of a spa pool and a spa bath?
15 How is this reflected in the way that they are maintained?
16 What is the main health risk from a spa pool?
17 What hygiene measures should be followed with sunbeds?

8.4   Safety precautions during beauty treatments

This section examines the safety precautions that should be undertaken for specific beauty treatments, excluding electrolysis and ray therapies which are dealt with in Sections 8.5 and 8.6.

Faradic treatments

Faradic treatments should have few dangers if performed correctly. Like any electric treatment there is a risk of electric shocks. Also, rashes may develop from over-treatment or if the client has an allergy to the rubber pads. (If a client does have an allergy to rubber, place a buffer layer of damp sponge pads between the rubber pads and the skin.) There is also a possibility of muscle exhaustion during treatment.

Before switching on, always check that intensity dials have been zeroed. You should also check the surge interval and length, single or dual polarity and the frequency of the current. With new clients, explain the noises and sensations or they may find the treatment more unpleasant than is necessary. The client should have no jewellery or clothing on the area to be treated, and the skin and pads should be moistened with a 1% salt water solution. Increase the current slowly up to contraction, time the treatment carefully, and always turn the current down slowly before switching off or removing pads from the client. Minor shocks can be prevented by the moistening of the pads to provide good skin contact, and maintaining this contact with adequate strapping. There must be at least two electrodes in use, and one of them (the indifferent electrode) should always be in contact with the skin and should not be moved. The other active electrode (or electrodes) may be used on different areas. The client should be still during the treatment.

Galvanic treatments

As with faradic treatments, always check that the controls are at zero before use and before removing electrodes from the skin. On a new client, check skin sensitivity with a pin and some cotton wool so that too much current is not given to the client. Both client and therapist should remove jewellery as it can attract current and cause burns. Also, the client should not be in contact with metal, from say a couch frame. Some couches are fitted with a rubber sheet to insulate the client as any current escaping to earth would cause a burn.

Electrodes should not be allowed to break contact with the skin as the current will jump the gap, spark and cause skin burns. Electrodes which become cracked should be discarded for the same reason. The electrodes must be covered with viscose sponge covers which should be in good condition. There should be no creases as the folding can increase the current in the localised area. The skin should be cleaned before the treatment begins. The sponge covers should be soaked evenly in a 1% salt solution. The electrodes must be in close contact with the skin; rubber straps are available for this, and some therapists use crêpe bandages with a rubber strip between the bandage and sponge. Care should be taken that connections made with crocodile clips do not touch the skin. The polarity of the electrode (positive or negative) should match that specified by the manufacturers of the various solutions and gels used in treatments. Also, follow the treatment times recommended by the manufacturers of the solutions and gels. During the treatment, acids or alkalis may form on the skin and these must be cleaned off using warm water on the body or cleansers on the face. The sponge coverings of the electrodes will have absorbed these acids and alkalis so they must be washed quickly to stop them deteriorating.

High frequency

As for faradic and galvanic treatments, burns and electric shocks can result from poor technique. The skin and the area in which the treatment is carried out should be free from alcohol, as alcohol vapour could ignite. Also, the client should not come into contact with metal or moisture during the treatment, as they concentrate the current which could cause a burn. For the same reason jewellery must not be worn by the therapist or the client for indirect treatment.

A new client should be told what to expect as the sound and feel of high frequency can be frightening. Start the treatment with dials at zero and increase the intensity gradually until it is at a level the client can stand comfortably. For indirect treatment it is important that the client does not let go of the saturator bar and that one hand of the therapist stays in contact with the client's skin at all times, otherwise shock will result. When giving direct treatment, the electrode must be in contact with the skin when the machine is turned on and off. Any fabric used between the electrode and skin should be made of natural fibres, as synthetics may melt when sparking occurs and cause skin burns.

Manicure and pedicure

As stated in Section 8.3, the main danger involved in these treatments is cutting the client. Cuticle nippers should always be sharp as the cuticle is more likely to be torn with blunt blades. Some clients may be allergic to nail varnish; check for rashes. Care should also be taken when pushing back the cuticle as the growing nail plate could be damaged by pressure, showing as cross ridging when the nail grows. Always check water temperature before using it on the client and add antiseptic to foot baths used in pedicure. The client's hands should be wiped with antiseptic before the service is started.

Paraffin waxing

The dangers associated with this treatment are burning of the skin and the possibility of fires. Suitable wax heaters which are thermostatically controlled must be used. Test the temperature of the wax on your own skin before applying it to the client. As the wax is extremely flammable, never use it near a naked flame.

Depilatory waxing

Most waxes are flammable so follow the same rules as for paraffin waxing. Again, test the temperature of the wax before applying it to the client. The top layers of the epidermis are more liable to be pulled away if the skin is tanned or the client has just undergone solarium or heat treatment. In fleshy areas always stretch the skin so it is less likely to bruise. When tearing off muslin strips keep the angle of pull horizontal to the skin surface; this reduces hair breakage and bruising. Never allow hot wax to cool completely as it can become brittle, causing pain and broken hairs on removal.

Vacuum suction

There is some danger of bruising and tissue damage. Lubricants used should be non-absorbent by the skin and the treatment should not be painful.

- Test the pressure on yourself before using it on the client.
- Break the seal between the cup and the skin with the finger.
- Select the correct size of applicator and cup.

Saunas and steam baths

Dangers associated with these treatments involve heat. Besides possible skin burning or scalds, the client may pass out from excessive heat, and physical injury could result. Checks should be made on equipment temperatures before use, and clients should not have access to the thermostatic controls in case they adjust them too high. Clear instructions should be given to clients on the use of equipment; posters can reinforce this. Heaters or steam inlets should have a guard fitted. Overheating could result if a client is not used to a treatment, or if the treatment is too long. There should be a non-slip floor covering on to which paper towel can be placed to avoid slipping. The client should be able to rest after these treatments in case tiredness leads to fainting.

Showers

Showers present a danger from scalding and falling. The shower controls should be explained to the client before use and the thermostatic control should be checked regularly. A non-slip surface should be incorporated into the floor of the shower. Some form of hand-rail to aid balance would be useful, particularly if there are older clients (especially as they are more likely to break bones in falls). Clients should never walk on floors with wet feet as they could easily slip. A notice outside the shower to this effect, encouraging the wiping of feet, would be sensible.

Eyebrow shaping

This is carried out using tweezers. The jaws of the tweezers should be at an angle instead of straight, to help prevent the pulling of skin and possible skin damage (including bleeding). Use the fingers of the other hand to stretch the skin taut while plucking hairs in their direction of growth – this is less painful. Apply a soothing antiseptic lotion before, during and after the treatment. It reduces the possibility of infection and makes the treatment less painful.

Eyelash and eyebrow tinting

Skin tests should be given 24 to 48 hours before the service is to be given (see Section 3.3), just in case the client is allergic to the tint to be used. If the test is positive, do not proceed with the treatment. Contact lenses should be removed before treatment commences. Tint should be mixed with hydrogen peroxide that is not stronger than 10 volume or 3% (this is also the strength of hydrogen peroxide that should be used in the skin test). The resulting mixture should not be runny, as it is more likely to enter the eyes. Protect the surrounding skin from staining with petroleum jelly, and the underneath of the eye with a damp pad of cotton wool. The client should be told not to open their eyes until told to do so. Tint is removed from lashes with downward strokes on to the protective cotton wool pad, and from the brows with firm wiping strokes. Follow manufacturers' instructions on timing.

Questions 8.4

1 What are the dangers associated with faradic treatments?
2 How would you prevent the client developing allergic reactions to rubber?
3 What checks should be made before switching on the current for a faradic treatment?
4 Describe any other safety precautions you would observe during the faradic treatment.

5   What safety precautions need to be observed with a new client for a galvanic treatment?
6   Describe, with reasons, the safety precautions you would observe during the galvanic treatment.
7   Why are the sponge covers soaked in a 1% salt solution before use on the skin?
8   How would you know what polarity an electrode should be?
9   Why should the skin be free from alcohol before the high frequency service is started?
10   Describe, with reasons, the safety precautions you would observe during a high frequency treatment?
11   Why should only natural fibres be used in fabrics used for high frequency treatments?
12   What is the main danger associated with manicure and pedicure?
13   What measures would you observe to minimise the dangers of infection in manicure and pedicure?
14   Why are thermostatically controlled wax heaters used in salons?
15   How would you test paraffin wax before application to the client?
16   Describe how you would prevent skin damage when depilatory waxing.
17   What precautions would you observe when performing vacuum suction treatments?
18   What dangers are there for clients when using saunas and steam baths?
19   How would you prevent client injuries when using saunas and steam baths?
20   If you were having a shower installed, what safety features would you insist on and why?
21   How would you minimise discomfort for the client when eyebrow shaping?
22   Why is a skin test given before tinting?
23   What would you do if the test was positive?
24   Describe how the skin is protected from staining during eyelash and eyebrow tinting.

8.5   *Ear piercing and electrolysis*

Many hair and beauty salons offer ear piercing and electrolysis as services to their clients. Both can involve piercing the skin, so precautions must be taken to avoid possible infection. Cases of hepatitis B and blood poisoning have been attributed to ear piercing, so strict codes of hygiene are essential. In the future this could also be a route for AIDS to be transmitted. Under no circumstances should ear piercing or electrolysis be carried out by untrained people.

Ear piercing

The recommended methods of ear piercing use special guns, and the ear-rings are sold pre-sterilised and sealed in plastic capsules. This ensures that they cannot be contaminated. The following procedure should be followed for ear piercing and has been adapted from *A Guide to Hygienic Skin Piercing* by Dr Norman D. Noah, published by the PHLS Communicable Disease Surveillance Centre.

● Ask clients about their skin healing. Some clients develop excessive scar tissue or keloids (especially negroid clients). Never re-pierce the skin of a client with keloids if the hole has closed up, as the scarring will only get worse.

- Seat the client comfortably and clip the hair back, away from the ears.
- Wash and dry your hands.
- Place a paper towel on the client's shoulder.
- Clean the client's ear with a spirit swab.
- Clean your own hands with a fresh spirit swab.
- Mark the earlobes of the client with an appropriate skin marking pen. (Get the client to agree the exact position where they want the holes pierced.)
- Explain to the client what you are about to do in case they move with the shock and tear their ear.
- Open the sterile plastic capsules, and pierce the ears. If the ears are being re-pierced, do not pierce over previous scar tissue as it will not heal as quickly.
- Using clean tissue, adjust the tightness of the ear-rings.
- Dispose of the plastic capsules, swabs and tissues in a plastic bag, preferably in a pedal bin.
- Clean your hands with a spirit swab.
- Advise the client to keep the ears clean and dry, and if they should become wet to dry them with a clean paper tissue. Only surgical spirit should be used on the ear if it irritates, and if infection should occur the client should seek medical advice.
- The stud should be left in place for six weeks. Explain to the client that gold ear-rings will not cause the skin reactions that might be caused by cheap ear-rings. Also that ear-rings should be worn at all times for several months, to stop the holes from healing over.

Never pierce noses with your equipment. Asian women who traditionally have nose studs actually screw them into the nose flesh, without going through into the inside of the nose. As the nose is full of bacteria, piercing right through the nose would be inviting infection.

Electrolysis

What many salons refer to as electrolysis is in fact electrical epilation based on diathermy (the heating effect of the electric current). True electrolysis involves the use of a galvanic current which is connected to a fine needle that acts as a cathode. This needle is inserted into the hair follicle to be destroyed. The anode is placed on a small pad of cotton wool, soaked in a 1% salt solution, at the skin surface near to the hair which is to be destroyed. An alkali (sodium hydroxide) is produced which should destroy the hair. Electrolysis is illustrated in Figure 8.2.

Care must be taken to connect the needle holder to the negative pole, or scarring may result. Chemical burning may also result if too much sodium hydroxide is produced in the follicle, and this could cause deep scarring.

This is true electrolysis since it is a chemical reaction produced by an electric current. The rate of hair removal is slower than in diathermy.

In diathermy a high frequency or short wave source of electric current is passed through a fine needle which is inserted into the hair follicle until it reaches the hair bulb and papilla (the needle is inserted with the current switched off). When the electric current is passed through the needle it produces heat which damages the

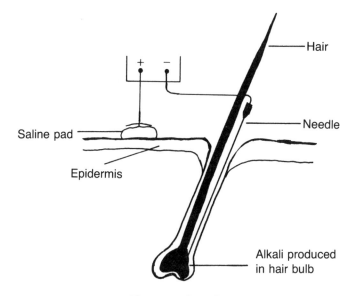

Fig. 8.2   Electrolysis

papilla and blood supply. The hair can then be removed. This is a much quicker method than true electrolysis so is very popular in salons.

Unless very expensive sterilisation procedures, such as autoclaving, are carried out, it is recommended that only sterile disposable needles are used for electrolysis (or any other procedure where a needle is inserted into the skin). AIDS and hepatitis B have been transmitted among drug addicts by the use of unsterilised needles.

The following procedure, again adapted from *A Guide to Hygienic Skin Piercing* by Dr Norman D. Noah (published by the PHLS Communicable Disease Surveillance Centre) should be followed for both methods of electrolysis:

- Wash and dry your hands.
- Place a clean paper towel on the worksurface.
- Clean the area to be epilated with a spirit swab.
- Clean your hands with a fresh spirit swab.
- Open the needle packet without touching the shaft or sharp end of the needle. If you do, dispose of the needle.
- Insert the needle into the electrolysis machine and begin to epilate hairs.
- The needle must be inserted at the correct depth. Too deep and the subcutaneous tissue will be destroyed, too shallow and the surface of the epidermis will be burnt.
- Turn on the current when the needle is fully inserted. To have the current on when inserting or withdrawing the needle will cause burning of the epidermis.
- Do not epilate hairs which are too near each other, to avoid infection of nearby follicles. Do not work for too long a time on any one client as tiredness can lead to mistakes being made.
- After completing work on the client, dispose of the needle into a sharps box (be

careful not to touch the shaft or sharp end of the needle). A sharps box is a container with a small top opening into which sharp objects such as blades or needles can be placed. Its use prevents accidental touching of infected sharp objects which could cut and possibly cause infection. The boxes are disposed of by specialist rubbish collectors. If you do not have a sharps box the needle should be sterilised by heating in a flame until red hot, before being disposed of.

● Clean the epilated skin with a spirit swab and dispose of used tissues and swabs in a plastic bag in a pedal bin.

● Advise the client to keep the epilated area clean and dry. Only surgical spirit should be used on the skin. If infection should occur, medical advice should be sought.

The *high frequency tweezer method* of electrolysis presents fewer dangers of spreading infection or causing skin damage as it does not involve entering the skin. The hair itself is used as a conductor of current. Hairs should not be searched for with the current switched on. The foot pedal controlling the current should only be depressed while a hair is being held.

Questions 8.5

1 Why is strict hygiene essential for ear piercing and electrolysis?
2 How are modern ear-rings sold for ear piercing?
3 What advantage does this have?
4 What are keloids?
5 Describe the hygienic ear piercing process.
6 What advice would you give to the client after ear piercing?
7 Why is it not recommended to pierce noses?
8 How does true electrolysis work?
9 How does diathermy work?
10 Why should only sterile needles be used in this process?
11 Describe the hygienic routine that you would follow when giving electrolysis.
12 How can skin tissue be damaged during electrolysis?
13 Why is the tweezer high frequency method a safer method of epilation than electrolysis or diathermy?

8.6 Infra-red and ultra-violet ray treatments

Intensity of treatments

Energy is brought to the skin surface during exposure to infra-red or ultra-violet radiation. The amount of radiation reaching an area of the skin surface per second is referred to as the intensity of the radiation. If the source of radiation is moved closer to the skin the intensity will increase, while if it is moved further away the intensity will decrease. This is because the radiation travels from the lamp source in straight lines which spread out or diverge. The further the radiation travels from the lamp, the more thinly spread it will be. If you are close to a radiator you feel more heat

A = Area
I = Intensity

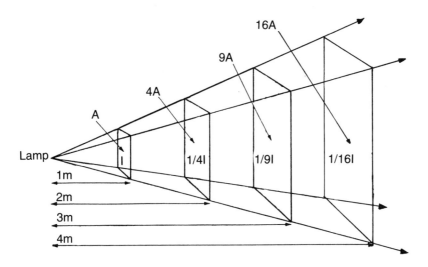

Fig. 8.3 The inverse square law.

than if you are further away. This is explained by the inverse square law which states: 'The intensity of radiation at a surface depends on the inverse square of the distance from the source'. Like most scientific laws, it requires further explanation. A few examples and Figure 8.3 will help explain the use of this law to the beauty therapist.

At a distance of 1 m from the lamp, the intensity of the radiation on the skin can be seen as 1. It thus follows:

- Double the distance from the lamp and the intensity is ¼ (2^2).
- Treble the distance from the lamp and the intensity is ⅑th (3^2).
- Quadruple the distance from the lamp and the intensity is ¹⁄₁₆th (4^2).

To achieve the same dose of radiation on the skin that would be delivered in one minute with the lamp 1 m away:

- At 2 metres it would take 4 minutes.
- At 3 metres it would take 9 minutes.
- At 4 metres it would take 16 minutes.

If you want to give the same exposure of radiation to a client but wish to alter the distance of the lamp from the skin, use the following formula:

$$\text{New time} = \text{old time} \left(\frac{\text{new distance}}{\text{old distance}}\right)^2$$

Example
If the exposure time for a client was 10 minutes with the lamp 1.5 m away from the skin, the new time for the same treatment with the lamp 1 m away would be:

$$\text{New time} = 10 \times \left(\frac{1.0}{1.5}\right)^2$$

$$= 4.4 \text{ minutes}$$

From this you should see the importance of noting lamp distance and exposure time on the record card of your client for each exposure to infra-red or ultra-violet radiation. Timers and tape measures should be used to check accuracy of observations.

Infra-red treatment

The main dangers associated with infra-red treatment in the beauty salon are skin burns, electric shock, eye damage and the possibility of fires. The client should be checked for sensitivity to heat and cold before treatment is given, as some skins have less sensitivity and may burn without feeling. The lamp should be allowed to warm up for several minutes before use (refer to the manufacturer's instructions). The lamp should be placed at least ½ m from the client and the treatment should be warming but tolerable. Tell the client to inform you if their skin feels too hot. If treatment is given near the eyes, goggles should be worn or damp cotton wool pads used to protect the eyes. Prolonged exposure to infra-red can cause cataracts in the eyes (a cataract is an area of opacity on the eye which does not allow light to pass through it). Lamps should be in a good state of repair and flammable materials should be kept away from the lamp when it is operating or they may ignite. Remember to switch the lamp off after use.

Ultra-violet treatment

Ultra-violet treatment in the beauty salon is given with either a ray lamp or a sunbed. The dangers associated with ultra-violet treatment are burning of the skin, and eye damage.

There are three types of ultra-violet radiation, according to wave lengths. These are UVA, UVB and UVC (see Figure 8.4). Sunlight contains all three wavelengths but the upper atmosphere of the earth absorbs UVC which converts oxygen into ozone, forming the ozone layer around the earth. Laws governing pollution in countries around the world are being changed to stop holes from developing in this layer. UVC is used in ultra-violet sterilising cabinets found in many hair and beauty salons to destroy microbes, but it has no place in use on the skin as it is too strong.

UVA produces melanin from melanosomes which have been left in the skin from previous tannings. This immediate tanning appears quickly but does not last. UVB is much stronger and causes the melanocytes to produce new melanosomes, the melanin produced from these causing delayed tanning. This takes longer to produce but lasts longer. Immediate tanning may last a few days while delayed tanning will

	UVA	UVB	UVC
Wavelength	Long. Close to violet in visible spectrum	Medium	Short
Effect on living tissue and cells	Beneficial	Beneficial	*Destroys life*
Increase of melanin in epidermis	Slight	Causes maximum pigmentation or sun tanning	Slight
Erythema	Some	Maximum erythema (also skin peeling)	Some
Vitamin D manufacture	None	Maximum amount produced	None
Beauty uses	Sunbeds	UV lamps	UV sterilising cabinet

Fig. 8.4   The three types of ultra-violet radiation.

last around a month. Natural sunlight contains much less UVB than UVA, but it takes around 1000 times more UVA than UVB to produce a tan. In normal exposure to the sun the UVB will also cause skin burning, so exposure must be strictly controlled. This is why suntan preparations are designed to block out ultra-violet rays, the higher the factor number, the more protection gained.

Sunbeds use tubes which give off almost pure UVA, so that a tanning effect can be achieved with little chance of burning. The exposure time can be up to 30 minutes on a sunbed depending on skin type. Ultra-violet lamps contain a hot quartz tube (high pressure mercury vapour) which gives off UVA and UVB and they are used in other treatments: they stimulate healing of the skin and are often used for acne treatment. UVB produces an erythema in the skin, a superficial inflammation of the skin appearing as rose-coloured patches. There are four degrees of erythema which can be produced with sunlamps, the greater the exposure to ultra-violet, the higher the degree of erythema produced. The beauty therapist only uses the first two. The four degrees are:

(1) A slight reddening of the skin which fades within 24 hours without skin irritation or soreness.
(2) A more marked reddening of the skin which fades in two or three days. There is also slight skin irritation (mild sunburn).
(3) Red and swollen, it is painful and will last about a week (sunburn).
(4) Similar to third in looks and duration except that blisters are also formed (severe sunburn).

There is also some skin peeling associated with the erythema, which increases with the degree.

UVB (and UVC) can cause two harmful effects on the eye, keratitis and con-junctivitis. Keratitis is inflammation of the cornea while conjunctivitis is inflammation of the outer covering of the cornea. Keratitis makes the eyes sensitive to light and they become painful and weep. It disappears within a few days. Conjunctivitis is often referred to as 'red eye'; it irritates and the eyes should be bathed in sterile water. (Conjunctivitis can also be caused by bacterial infection.) Eye problems can be prevented by not wearing contact lenses and always wearing protective goggles when on the sunbed or when exposed to ultra-violet light. Note that the therapist should wear these as well if near the ultra-violet source as the rays can be reflected off walls. Goggles should be cleaned with a disinfectant between treatments.

There are several safety precautions that should be taken with clients using sunbeds:

- The skin should be washed to cleanse it of cosmetics, deodorants and perfume, as some preparations may sensitise the skin, causing burning.
- Check that the client is not taking medication which might act as a photo-sensitiser (sensitiser to ultra-violet). Examples are insulin (for diabetics), anti-biotics (teracycline), tranquillisers, diuretics and blood pressure treatments. Seek medical advice.
- Time treatments and if the client needs to turn over half-way through a treatment, do not rely on them doing so themselves – many fall asleep! Timers should ring loudly and be kept away from clients so that they cannot be turned off without moving.
- Check natural skin colouring to determine exposure times. Fair skin is highly sensitive so should only be exposed for about 10 minutes. Olive or tanned skin can be exposed for up to 30 minutes. Record exposure times and skin reactions for each treatment on the client record card.

Ultra-violet lamps and solaria (multiple lamps) need to be more strictly controlled in terms of exposure. Timings and the distance of the lamp from the client must be calculated from a skin (patch) test. This is carried out as follows:

- Take a piece of dark paper about three inches wide and punch four holes in it about 2 cm (¾ in) apart. Wrap the paper round the client's clean forearm so

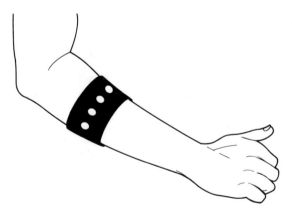

Fig. 8.5 Performing a skin test for ultra-violet.

that four small patches of skin can be seen. The rest of the skin should be covered. This is illustrated in Figure 8.5.

- Set the lamp up 0.5–1 m above the skin. This will be the distance you intend for the treatment. Let the lamp warm up and then place the client's arm under the lamp.
- Cover up three of the four holes with pieces of paper and time the exposure of the first patch for one minute. Then expose the second patch of skin and after a further minute expose the third patch. After a further minute expose the fourth patch and continue exposure for one more minute. This will give four patches of exposure, of one minute, two minutes, three minutes and four minutes.
- Mark each of the holes with a pen so you know which patch is which when you remove the paper; (1,2,3 and 4 is probably the simplest thing to mark and also refers to the number of minutes).
- After eight hours, erythema should be checked for. If only the four minute patch has reddened, this indicates that the selected exposure time for the client should be three minutes (that is one minute less than the first patch to show an erythema). If the three minute patch has an erythema, so will the four minute patch. The time selected would then be two minutes.
- If the patch which had a one minute exposure has produced an erythema, the skin test must be carried out again with the lamp further away from the skin. Perform the test on the client's other arm.
- Later, treatment times can be increased by 25% for each following session (4 minutes would be followed by 5 minutes and so on). Sessions should be every second day for between 20 to 24 days (10 to 12 treatments).

Questions 8.6

1   What does intensity refer to with ultra-violet and infra-red rays?
2   What happens to this intensity the further away someone is from the source of ultra-violet or infra-red rays?
3   Explain the inverse square law in your own words.
4   How does it affect a treatment to move a lamp closer to the skin?
5   How could the same treatment be given to a client if the lamp was set at two different distances?
6   What are the main dangers associated with infra-red?
7   How should the eyes be protected from infra-red?
8   What are the main dangers associated with ultra-violet?
9   How many types of ultra-violet are there?
10   Which are used in treatments?
11   What are the main differences in the effects of treatments with a sunbed and an ultra-violet lamp?
12   Describe the four degrees of erythema.
13   List the precautions to be taken when using sunbeds.
14   Describe how to carry out a skin test for ultra-violet.

9

Personal Health and Hygiene

This section of the book is intended to be a guide on how to look after your body, so that your appearance is always what is expected by the public.

9.1 Care of the hands

Hands are very important to the hairdresser, but unfortunately can easily suffer because of the chemicals that are used in the business. Chemicals such as perm lotions, tints, straighteners and shampoos can cause dermatitis (see Section 3.3). Observe the following routine:

- Wash your hands before starting the service to a client (or before eating food). This will help reduce the risk of spreading infection if you have been to the toilet, or have touched a source of infection on yourself (such as a cold sore) or another client.
- If you are using chemicals such as perms, tints or straighteners, you must wear rubber gloves. This should prevent dermatitis and damage by burning (from strong sodium hydroxide straighteners or bleach).
- Shampoos contain soapless detergents which may degrease the skin – that is, remove the natural oils. The oils of the skin (sebum) help prevent it drying by reducing moisture loss. Shampoos may cause not only dry skin, but also dermatitis (see Figure 9.1). When the skin begins to inflame and crack it could also become infected. This will happen particularly where there are rings or bracelets, as moisture gets trapped next to the skin.

Avoid dermatitis by:

- Wearing gloves *if possible*. (Some employers will not allow them to be worn for shampooing and clients may also complain.)

150

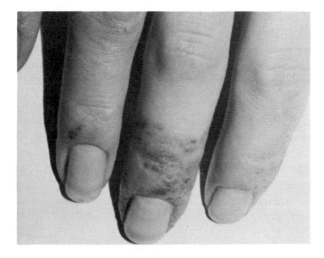

Fig. 9.1   Shampoo dermatitis.

- Rinsing hands thoroughly to remove all shampoo from them. This will reduce degreasing of the skin.
- Drying hands well as evaporation of moisture from the skin can help cause it to crack. (Think of chapped lips in windy weather.)
- Using moisturising cream as often as required and trying different brands to find the one that is most effective for you. Barrier creams do not offer much protection as shampoo easily removes them.
- Not wearing jewellery on your hands as this can trap moisture, causing skin to break.
- Keeping the fingernails clean and well manicured. This will avoid providing a possible breeding ground for germs. Short nails are less likely to scratch the client's scalp, or even catch in the client's hair.
- Wearing nail varnish. Otherwise nails can lose oils, leaving them weak and brittle, and making them more likely to be infected. Use clear varnish if you do not like colours.
- Keeping any cuts on the hands covered with plasters. This avoids possible infection being caught or spread.
- Having any warts on the hands removed in case they are cut and spread.

Questions 9.1

1   Which chemicals cause dermatitis in the salon?
2   When should you wash your hands in the salon?
3   How should you protect your hands when using perms or tints?
4   How do shampoos affect the skin?
5   List five things that will help prevent shampoo dermatitis.
6   Why should the fingernails be kept short?
7   Why should plasters be placed over cuts on the hands?

9.2 Care of the mouth

This is important so that you do not cause offence to clients through bad breath, and also so that your own teeth last without the need for major dental work. Remember these points:

- Bad breath or *halitosis* gives offence and may lose you not only clients but friends! It is caused by strongly smelling foods such as garlic, onions, spices and even oranges – so avoid them when you are working. Bad breath can also be caused by smoking. Brush the teeth regularly and remember that eating mints to mask the smell could help rot your teeth! If bad breath is caused by digestive troubles, see your doctor.
- Most of us want to keep our teeth as long as possible and can do this with proper care:
  Brush the teeth in the morning and evening, paying particular attention to the backs of the teeth. Small head toothbrushes are recommended for this. Regular brushing, particularly after eating, will help prevent tooth decay, or *caries*. Brushing is the most effective way to remove food particles.
  Massage the gums with the toothbrush at the same time. If your gums bleed when you brush your teeth they are not healthy and an infection might result. Visiting a dental hygienist will correct this. Gum infections could cause you to lose *all* your teeth so see a dentist if you suspect that you might have one.
  Use dental floss if your teeth are very close together and food gets trapped between them.
  Never try to crack nuts or open things with your teeth, it might crack the enamel or break the tooth.
  Avoid eating sweets. Sweets are almost pure sugar, and help tooth decay. Eat fruit instead.
  Use a toothpaste with fluoride as this strengthens teeth.
  See the dentist as soon as possible if you get toothache.
  Have check-ups as recommended by your dentist. These should be at least once a year.

Questions 9.2

1 What is halitosis?
2 How can bad breath be caused in the salon?
3 When should the teeth be brushed?
4 What does bleeding of gums indicate when brushing teeth?
5 Why is eating sweets bad for the teeth?
6 Why are fluoride toothpastes good for the teeth?
7 Should you have a dental check-up even if you think your teeth are in good condition?

9.3 Care of the hair

This does not mean simply having a fashionable style as many hairdressers may think at first. The hair can provide a breeding ground for germs and can also be a salon safety hazard. Here are a few points to keep in mind:

- Keep the hair tied back if it is long. This will prevent it getting in your eyes (causing possible accidents) or getting caught in the back of a hairdrier.
- Wash the hair as often as necessary, daily if required. You are then less likely to get scalp infections.
- If your scalp becomes itchy, possibly from an allergy to a shampoo, either use the shampoo diluted with water or change shampoos. Shampoos are very strong detergents and most of us use far too much. One wash is enough!
- If you have dandruff, treat it! See Section 3.4.
- Brush the hair regularly so that tangles do not develop. Brushing will also discourage attacks of head lice (see Section 4.1). As it encourages the secretion of sebum, however, brushing should be restricted if your hair becomes greasy quickly.
- Do not use other people's unsterilised equipment on your hair in case it is contaminated.
- If you come into contact with head lice, treat yourself (see Section 4.1).
- To avoid damaged hair, and maintain condition:
  Avoid harsh treatment (backcombing).
  Avoid too many alkaline processes (tints, perms or bleaching).
  Avoid over-hot hairdriers and the use of heated rollers, tongs and crimping irons.
  Condition as necessary and have split ends cut off.
- A good diet is necessary for healthy hair (see Section 9.7). Protein is essential daily as it is not stored in the body.
- Use brushes and combs which cannot scratch the scalp (bristles should be rounded, teeth should be blunt) or infection may result.

Questions 9.3

1 Why is it important to look after the hair?
2 How can accidents with long hair be avoided?
3 When should you wash your hair?
4 What should you do if you develop an allergy to a shampoo?
5 Why is regular brushing of hair important?
6 What conditions of the scalp and hair should you treat?
7 How can hair damage be prevented?
8 What type of brushes or combs should be used on the hair?
9 Why is diet important in having healthy hair?

9.4 Care of the feet

Since hairdressers spend their working lives on their feet, it is important that the feet should be healthy and not cause unnecessary pain or discomfort.

Most important of all in this is footwear. Shoes should be the correct size, closed and have a low heel. Comfort should be your main consideration when buying working shoes, not style! If shoes are the wrong size:

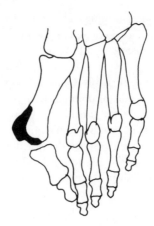

Fig. 9.2 The formation of a bunion. Bunions can develop when the big toe is turned inward by constant pressure of a tight shoe. This causes excess growth of the big toe bone and a sac of fluid forms over it.

- Corns may develop where tight-fitting shoes put pressure on the epidermis. The pressure causes a thickening of the skin to form a horny, painful hard cone. They may be relieved by using corn pads, but their removal is best carried out by a chiropodist.
- Ingrowing toenails result from pressure on the nails. It is usually the big toenail that penetrates the skin, causing an infection. Avoid these by cutting the nail straight across. Some people require operations to relieve them.
- Bunions are caused when the joint of the big toe becomes inflamed, causing pain on walking and an unsightly bulge at the side of the big toe. Figure 9.2 shows the formation of a bunion. The big toe is turned inward by constant pressure of a tight shoe, causing excessive growth of that toe bone (shown in black). People inherit the tendency for bunions to form, but wearing tight footwear causes bunions to develop. Men do not get bunions as often as women because they usually wear broader fitting shoes, but during the 1950s when winkle-pickers were in fashion, many more men had bunions because their feet were cramped into tightly-toed shoes. High heels can also cause bunions as they help push the toes to the front of the shoe where they are cramped (see Section 9.5). Bunions can be operated on, but the operation is painful and several weeks off work may be required. Wear lower heels to ease discomfort and prevent the bunions from becoming more inflamed.
- Bursitis is the term given to swelling and inflammation. It is found on moving joints and also on the back of the heels. It is often combined with bunions and may have to be dealt with surgically.
- Callouses occur where the skin thickens through pressure from weight and work. You usually find them on your heels and balls of the feet, but sometimes on the hands where you grip the scissors. This is the one problem that you will get even if you go barefooted!

- Blisters develop where there is 'rubbing' from shoes. It is usually when new shoes are worn that this problem is at its worst. Try to 'break' shoes in by wearing them around the house for short periods. Wearing a plaster will relieve blisters; take care not to burst them as you can easily get infection.
- Shoes which are too large can also cause problems. The toes are used to try to grip the shoe; this can lead to claw toes and their rubbing can cause blisters.

Looking after the feet

- Flat feet or fallen arches may be inherited, but continual standing can cause the ligaments which maintain the arch to stretch and the arches to fall. The condition may be treated by exercises and artificial arch supports can be worn. It will otherwise be extremely painful to stand all day, so see a chiropodist to get expert advice.
- Athlete's foot is an infectious fungal condition which must be treated, and precautions should be taken to stop its spread (see Section 2.5).
- Plantar warts or verrucae are caused by viruses and are infectious. They should be treated and precautions should be taken to prevent them from spreading (see Section 2.7).

Following a daily routine to care for your feet:

- Wear clean socks, tights or stockings daily.
- Wash and dry your feet each morning and evening as required.
- Cut toenails regularly, straight across.
- Wear correctly fitting shoes with low or medium heels.
- Wear closed shoes in the salon, or hair may enter the skin and cause infection. Closed shoes also protect the feet from falling objects such as scissors.
- Treat infectious conditions when they arise and take care that you do not spread them.
- Wear high heels for short periods of time, not for walking or working in.
- Wear arch supports if you need to.

Questions 9.4

1   How do corns develop?
2   What are ingrowing toenails and how should they be avoided?
3   What is a bunion?
4   Why do more women get bunions than men?
5   What is bursitis?
6   Where would callouses be found?
7   How can blisters be avoided?
8   Should blisters be burst?
9   Why are shoes which are too big bad for the feet?
10   What can be done for fallen arches?
11   What should you do if you have either athlete's foot or plantar warts?

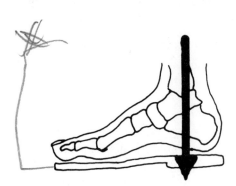
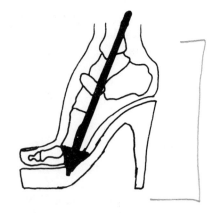

With a low heel, the weight of the body is put on to the ankle and the heel of the foot.

With a high heel the weight of the body is thrown forward on to the toes.

Less energy is required to keep balance properly.

More energy is required to keep balance so fatigue can result more quickly. Also, the toes are compressed so that bunions are more likely to develop.

Fig. 9.3 The effects of shoes on feet.

12   Why should shoes with open toes not be worn in the salon?
13   Look at Figure 9.3. What type of heel should be worn in the salon and why?

9.5 Posture

Posture is how you 'hold' yourself when standing, sitting or walking. Most of us recognise bad posture in someone else because their clothes do not seem to hang properly. Good posture will help you work longer without becoming tired and will also improve your looks!

Posture depends on the skeleton, the ligaments which hold the bones in place, and the muscles which enable movement to take place. Good posture means that the muscles do as little as possible to hold the body, so they do not tire.

In a good standing position the body is stretched upwards and held comfortably, with the spine assuming its natural curve. The stomach muscles are contracted and firm, and the weight of the body is distributed on both feet so that the shoulders are level. Low heeled shoes make most of the body's weight bear down on the ankles, whereas high heels push it forward on to the toes. This is shown in Figure 9.3. Bunions can result from high heels (see Section 9.1) and so can bad posture.

High heels push the body forward and cause pain in the tendons of the calf. Because the weight is thrust forward a hollow develops in the back and the resulting bad posture can cause problems with breathing, circulation and digestion. It also causes fatigue or tiredness, thereby increasing the risk of accidents. Try to avoid working in a bending position, and stretch up as often as possible. Try not to work

Hollow back
This may be caused by wearing shoes with very high heels.

Lateral curvature
This may be caused by standing with your weight on one leg.

Fig. 9.4 How bad posture can affect the spine.

with your weight on one leg as this curves the spine (see Figure 9.4). Your feet should be slightly apart when working, with your toes pointing forwards.

Questions 9.5

1 What is posture?
2 Why is posture important?
3 Describe good posture.
4 How can high heels give bad posture?
5 How should you stand when working?
6 What effect can standing on one leg have on the spine?

9.6 Personal hygiene

It is important that you look after your body. We have already looked at how you should look after your hands, mouth, hair and feet in this chapter, and the importance of posture. To avoid body odour or *bromidrosis*, it is important that you follow a regular hygiene routine. Body odour is a result of two things: apocrine sweat, and the bacteria that break it down to cause body odour. If we eliminate or reduce one or both of these causes we will keep body odour under control.

Anti-perspirants contain chemicals, such as aluminium chlorhydrate, which reduce the size of the sweat pore, so that we sweat less. If you think of a bath and a basin tap, the reason the bath tap gives out more water is because the pipe is wider

(22 mm as opposed to 15 mm). Although sweating in the armpits is reduced by anti-perspirants, we still sweat with eccrine sweat glands over the rest of the body. Many people wrongly believe that anti-perspirants are bad for you because they think the body will not cool properly.

Deodorants are similar to antiseptics – they inhibit the growth of the bacteria that break down the sweat. They do not mask body odour or destroy it as the name implies. An unperfumed brand will work as well as a perfumed one. It is important that you wash properly every day to remove stale sweat – soap will also kill bacteria. To avoid body odour it is important also that you wash your clothes regularly, particularly heavy woollen sweaters.

Discontinue the use of anti-perspirants or deodorants in aerosol form if you get an allergic reaction or start to develop tenderness in the armpit. Although aerosols are convenient, some people cannot use them because they develop painful abscesses (deep bacterial infections that may require antibiotics and lancing) in the armpit, because the chemicals are driven down into follicles and sweat pores and cause inflammation. This may be avoided by using roll-ons.

If you are unsure whether to use a deodorant or an anti-perspirant alone, use a combined product. Very few people do not get body odour once they reach puberty; just because you think you don't smell does not mean that you don't!

Overalls should be worn over your clothes to protect them. They should be comfortable and easy to wash as they will get dirty and smell quickly. They must allow you to lose heat as the salon will be warm. They must withstand frequent washing and drying, and for this reason you should have at least two sets.

Natural fibres such as cotton will feel cool to wear and will absorb sweat. This is why cotton underclothes are so suitable. Cotton has the disadvantage of creasing, but can be treated so it is crease-resistant. A number of mixes are available with cotton, and a polyester and cotton combination is particularly suitable as it is so easy to wash.

Man-made fibres such as nylon and polyester are easy to wash but can be uncomfortable to wear, as they do not absorb sweat and may help you retain heat. Nylon underwear is not recommended because it causes sweating and encourages germs to breed.

Since hairdressers are on their feet all day, resting with the feet raised will be beneficial and will help reduce swelling. Try to sleep for eight hours a day and take some form of regular exercise such as walking or swimming.

Questions 9.6

1   What is the common name for bromidrosis?
2   How is body odour caused?
3   Describe how an anti-perspirant works.
4   Describe how a deodorant works.
5   Besides using anti-perspirants and deodorants, what else can be done to prevent body odour?
6   Why can't some people use an aerosol on their armpits?
7   What would you look for in your choice of overall?
8   How can you reduce the swelling of your feet after standing all day?

9.7 Diet

This section explains what you should eat to be healthy rather than what you should eat to lose weight.

Most hairdressers do not have regular lunch breaks. Food is often rushed and of the convenience kind. Many hairdressers are also obsessed with dieting, which can be extremely harmful. This section will examine what should be in a balanced diet, and will give some ideas on healthy eating.

A balanced diet is one which will provide just the right quantity of each of the six essential dietary nutrients – proteins, carbohydrates, fats, minerals, vitamins and water. Roughage, also called fibre, should also be present if the digestive system is to function properly. Figure 9.5 lists the sources and functions of the main nutrients.

Proteins are required for the growth of new body cells and the replacement of old ones. Skin, hair and nails are made of the protein keratin. Proteins are composed of twenty-two amino acids, eight of which are said to be essential because they must be taken into the body in the form of food. The other fourteen can be synthesised by the body. Excess protein is converted into glucose or fat. Protein cannot be stored. It provides about four calories of energy per gram. Eating a lot of protein does not give you muscles unless you exercise to produce them!

Carbohydrates are required as a source of energy and are converted into glucose. If taken in excess they are converted into glycogen and fat. Glucose is the energy source for the brain. It provides about four calories of energy per gram. Sugar is present in large quantities in sweets and helps to cause tooth decay, so should be avoided.

Fats provide energy for the body, and a gram of fat produces about nine calories of energy. The body converts fat into fatty acids and glycerol. It is stored as fat. Most of us consume far too much fat and this has been associated with heart disease. It should be safe to cut down on fat without any harmful effects. Figure 9.6 shows the fat content of common cheeses.

Minerals and vitamins do not provide energy but are used in the regulation of the body's metabolism. Some are involved in the action of hormones, and Figure 9.5 indicates the results of a lack or deficiency of them. They are needed in relatively small quantities, and the average diet does contain enough. Many people who take vitamins do not need to, and take them in excessive amounts, thinking that they will do them good. Vitamin C, for example, cannot be stored by the body, so taking it in excess provides no extra benefits.

Water is an essential part of every diet and we cannot survive for long without it. It is the basic constituent of all body cells and tissues. It is needed for the transportation of substances around the body and in the control of body temperature. Water is also produced during the course of tissue respiration.

Roughage or fibre provides no energy but helps in digestion. Fibre in food is composed of cellulose, which we cannot digest, and is part of fruit, vegetables and cereals. Most people do not eat enough dietary fibre. When you go to the toilet, your faeces should 'float' if you have enough fibre in your diet.

Figure 9.7 shows a table of ideal weights for different heights for men and women. The table is a guide only. The 'acceptable' weight is a *range* of weights which are considered healthy for each height, depending on one's body type. The 'ideal' weight

Nutrients	Sources	Functions
Proteins	Animal: meat, fish, dairy products. Vegetable: peas, beans, nuts, wheat, carrots, cabbage, lentils.	Basis of all body cells; used for growth and repair. *Cannot be stored by the body.*
Carbohydrates	Sugars: jam, honey, syrup, sweets. Starches: bread, cake, potatoes.	Provide energy and heat, used by brain. Excess is stored as body fat.
Fats	Animal: dairy foods, fatty meat, cooking fats. Vegetable: cooking oils, salad oils, nuts, margarines.	Provide heat and energy. Excess is stored as body fat. Too much fat can cause obesity (overweight) and lead to heart disease.
Minerals Calcium	Milk, flour, cheese.	Builds strong bones and teeth.
Iron	Meat, especially liver and kidney, eggs, flour, green vegetables.	Needed by all cells especially red blood cells; present in haemoglobin. Lack causes anaemia.
Iodine	Fish, shell fish, iodised salt.	Controls the rate at which energy is used by the body, (in the hormone thyroxine).
Sodium chloride	Milk, cheese, butter, eggs, meat, fish, vegetables.	Needed by all cells and for making acid in the stomach.
Vitamins Vitamin A	Fish liver oils, fish, liver, butter, carrots, tomatoes, all green vegetables. Vitamin A poisoning is possible from excessive amounts of this vitamin.	Needed for normal growth, healthy skin and vision and protection against infection. Lack causes night-blindness.

Nutrient	Source	Function
Vitamin B complex Thiamine (B1)	Wheat embryo, yeast, peas, beans, brown rice, liver, pork, fish and eggs.	Destroyed on cooking. Needed for release of energy from food and healthy nerves. Lack causes beri-beri disease.
Riboflavine (B2)	Milk, cheese, yeast, meat, fish, eggs and vegetables.	Needed for healthy skin, mouth and eyes. Lack causes stunted growth and inflamed tongue.
Nicotinic acid (Niacin)	Green vegetables, yeast, eggs, milk, cereals, liver and other meats.	Needed for the release of energy from food. Lack causes pellagra.
Cyanocobalamine (B12)	Liver, milk, meat and fish.	Needed for the production of red blood cells and haemoglobin. Lack causes pernicious anaemia.
Vitamin C (ascorbic acid)	Fresh fruit, especially citrus fruits, and fresh uncooked vegetables.	Needed for healthy skin; helps in the absorption of iron. Lack causes scurvy.
Vitamin D	Fish liver oils, butter, fish and eggs; ultra-violet rays in sunlight build it up in the body.	Needed for healthy bones and teeth. Helps the absorption of calcium. Lack causes rickets.
Vitamin E	Wheat germ, green vegetables, peanuts, eggs and bread.	Prolonged lack is thought to cause sterility.
Vitamin K	Spinach, cabbage; made by intestinal bacteria.	Needed for healthy skin and the clotting of blood.
Water	All liquid drinks and in food.	Needed for all cell processes transport, temperature control.
Roughage	Undigestible plant cellulose in fruit, vegetables, cereals, especially bran and nuts; wholemeal bread.	Prevents constipation and helps to regulate absorption of food.

Fig. 9.5 The essential nutrients of a balanced diet.

Type of cheese	Fat content %
Cottage	4
Cheese spread	23
Edam	23
Camembert	23
Danish blue	29
Cheddar	34
Stilton	40
Cream	47

Fig. 9.6 Fat in cheese.

applies to an average-sized person and should not be taken as the perfect weight for everyone at that height. The term 'obese' is generally applied to anyone who is 20% over their ideal weight. However, there are some very muscular athletes who are over 20% heavier than their ideal weight! To stick to a weight you are satisfied with, weigh yourself regularly at the same time once a week. Wear the same clothes (or none at all) and use the same weighing scales. If you are overweight for your height, do not starve yourself, but cut down generally on the size of food portions and try not to eat between meals. Dieting is a temporary measure taken to lose weight, and many people tend to put the shed weight back on again very quickly after losing it. A *sensible* diet should be a way of life. A female hairdresser needs an average of 2500 calories per day to maintain body weight; a male would need about 2900 calories. If you take in more energy than this you will put on weight; if you take in less energy you will lose weight. Dieting should mean taking in slightly less energy than required each day, so that the body must use up its store of energy.

Diet and disease

- Heart disease is almost certainly associated with too much fat in the diet.
- Diabetes and tooth decay may be linked with too high an intake of sugar.
- Bowel cancer, constipation and diverticulosis (a bowel problem that is becoming common) may be associated with too little dietary fibre.
- High blood pressure and strokes may be linked with too much salt in the diet.
- Obesity may be linked with too much carbohydrate and fat, and too little fibre.
- Obesity is associated with high blood pressure, diabetes, heart disease and strokes. It is dangerous to be overweight, so much so that you will have to pay more for life insurance.
- Smoking, drinking and lack of exercise will also increase the risk of illness and premature death.

There are a number of things you can do to have a positive effect on your health through diet.

You can eat more fibre by eating wholemeal bread, flour and pasta; eat high

Men

Height			Weight										
	(in shoes)		Acceptable				Ideal			Obese		
m	ft	in	kg↔kg	st	lb↔st	lb	kg	st	lb	kg	st	lb
1.575	5	2	50.8–64.0	8	0–10	1	54.9	8	9	77.7	12	1
1.6	5	3	52.2–65.3	8	3–10	4	57.6	9	1	78.5	12	5
1.626	5	4	53.5–67.1	8	6–10	8	59.0	9	4	80.7	12	10
1.651	5	5	54.9–68.9	8	9–10	12	60.3	9	7	82.7	13	0
1.676	5	6	56.2–70.8	8	12–11	2	61.7	9	10	84.6	13	5
1.702	5	7	58.1–73.0	9	2–11	7	63.5	10	0	88.6	13	11
1.727	5	8	59.9–75.3	9	6–11	12	65.8	10	5	90.3	14	3
1.753	5	9	61.7–77.1	9	10–12	2	67.6	10	9	92.5	14	8
1.778	5	10	63.5–78.9	10	0–12	6	69.4	10	13	95.3	14	13
1.803	5	11	65.3–81.2	10	4–12	11	71.7	11	4	99.3	15	5
1.829	6	0	67.1–83.5	10	8–13	2	73.5	11	8	101.1	15	11
1.854	6	1	68.9–85.7	10	12–13	7	75.3	11	12	102.9	16	3
1.88	6	2	70.8–88.0	11	2–13	12	77.6	12	3	106.0	16	9
1.905	6	3	72.6–90.3	11	6–14	3	79.9	12	8	108.4	17	1
1.93	6	4	74.4–92.5	11	10–14	8	82.1	12	13	110.3	17	7

Fig. 9.7 Desirable weights (in indoor clothing) for adults aged 25 and over.

Women

Height			Weight									
	(in shoes)		Acceptable				Ideal			Obese		
m	ft	in	kg↔kg	st	lb↔st	lb	kg	st	lb	kg	st	lb
1.473	4	10	41.7–54.0	6	8– 8	7	46.3	7	4	58.7	10	3
1.499	4	11	42.6–55.3	6	10– 8	10	47.2	7	6	66.2	10	6
1.524	5	0	43.5–56.7	6	12– 8	13	48.5	7	9	68.0	10	10
1.549	5	1	44.9–58.1	7	1– 9	2	49.9	7	12	69.4	10	13
1.575	5	2	46.3–59.4	7	4– 9	5	51.3	8	1	71.1	11	3
1.6	5	3	47.6–60.8	7	7– 9	8	52.6	8	4	81.0	11	7
1.626	5	4	49.0–62.6	7	10– 9	12	54.4	8	8	75.3	11	12
1.651	5	5	50.3–64.4	7	13–10	2	55.8	8	11	77.1	12	2
1.676	5	6	51.7–66.2	8	2–10	6	58.1	9	2	79.4	12	7
1.702	5	7	53.5–68.0	8	6–10	10	59.9	9	6	81.6	12	12
1.727	5	8	55.3–69.9	8	10–11	0	61.7	9	10	83.5	13	3
1.753	5	9	57.2–71.7	9	0–11	4	63.5	10	0	86.2	13	8
1.778	5	10	59.0–73.9	9	4–11	9	65.3	10	4	89.0	14	0
1.803	5	11	60.8–76.2	9	8–12	0	67.1	10	8	91.6	14	6
1.829	6	0	62.6–78.5	9	12–12	5	68.9	10	12	94.8	14	12

Fig. 9.7 cont.

Food	Fibre content %	Food	Fibre content %
Wheatbran	44	Brown bread	5
Bran cereal	27	Boiled sprouts	3
Puffed wheat	15	Boiled carrots	3
Almonds	14	Baked potatoes	3
Shredded wheat	12	Boiled runner beans	3
Rye crispbread	12	Bananas	3
Boiled frozen peas	12	Pears	3
Cornflakes	11	White bread	3
Wholemeal flour	10	Lettuce	3
Wholemeal bread	9	Apples	2
Peanuts	8	Oranges	2
Baked beans	7	Tomatoes	2
Blackberries	7	Grapefruit	1
Muesli	7	Boiled potatoes	1
Boiled spinach	6	Porridge	1
Digestive biscuit	6		

Fig. 9.8.   Fibre content of foods.

fibre foods such as rice, potatoes, beans, fruit and vegetables. Figure 9.8 shows the fibre content of a number of foods.

To reduce the fat content of your diet, trim excess fat off meat and grill rather than fry food. Eat fish and poultry rather than red meat. Use skimmed milk, as milk accounts for one-eighth of all the fat that we eat. Use low fat cheese, such as cottage cheese. Try to use less butter and margarine. Try vegetarian food to see if you like it. Use plain low fat yogurt rather than cream.

To reduce your sugar input, cut down on sweets, cakes, sweet drinks and fruit in syrup. Use a sweetener in place of sugar where possible. Most of us eat almost one hundred pounds of refined sugar each year.

On average, most of us eat two teaspoonfuls of salt each day. A lot of salt is present in processed food. It is possible to reduce the amount of salt that we put on food or in cooking. Try to cut down on highly salted crisps, nuts and other types of snacks.

Eating in the salon

In the salon, wash your hands before handling food. Wash up cups and plates in the staff room sink. If food or drink is prepared either for yourself or clients, it should be done under hygienic conditions. It is particularly hygienic to use disposable plates, cups and cutlery.

If you cannot eat a cooked meal while you are working, try to eat wholemeal sandwiches rather than cakes and sweets. Try to stick to one weight if you diet. Many girls keep reducing their target weights and slimming becomes an obsession. The slimmer's disease, anorexia nervosa, can end in death. If people start to tell you that you are looking like a 'skeleton' and you still think that you are fat, believe them and seek help.

Questions 9.7

1   What is a balanced diet?
2   Why are proteins needed in the diet?
3   Does eating protein produce muscles?
4   What is the function of carbohydrates in the diet?
5   Why should sweets be avoided?
6   Why is too much fat in the diet a bad thing?
7   Which types of cheese have the highest and lowest fat content?
8   From Figure 9.5, list the functions of the minerals and vitamins.
9   Besides drinking, where else does the body get water from?
10 How can you tell if you have enough fibre in your diet?
11 Using the table in Figure 9.7, do you consider yourself to be the correct weight for your height?
12 How does dieting help you lose weight?
13 What disease is associated with too much sugar in the diet?
14 How would you increase the amount of fibre in your diet?
15 How would you decrease the amount of fat in your diet?
16 How would you cut down your daily intake of sugar?
17 How and why would you cut down the amount of salt you eat?
18 Why are disposable plates and cups a good idea in salons?

9.8   Can we avoid cancer?

Scientists are continually searching for answers to what causes cancer and how to prevent it from starting. It is a difficult question as a very long time often elapses between the cause of cancer and its subsequent development. Exposure to asbestos dust, for instance, can induce cancer many years afterwards. Asbestos is now being removed from buildings and replaced by other materials. Scientists estimate that about 80% of cancers are caused by something in our everyday life: the atmosphere, food and drink, chemicals and infections to which we are exposed.

Cancer is caused by exposure to radiation. Among the survivors of the atomic bombs of Hiroshima and Nagasaki there was an increased incidence of leukaemia, breast cancer, and cancer of the brain and bowel. There is speculation that there is a higher incidence of cancer and malformed babies in places near nuclear power stations. Avoid X-rays unless they are necessary, as over-exposure makes damage to living cells more likely, with serious consequences later.

Diet is possibly one of the biggest causes of cancer, particularly the amount of fat in the diet. As fat is also linked with coronary disease it is important that we reduce our dietary fat intake. The proof that fat is linked to cancer is shown by what happens to the Japanese when they live in the United States. In Japan, bowel cancer is rare, but it is common in the United States. However, when Japanese people migrate to the United States their rate of bowel cancer increases; this is also true for breast cancer. The prime suspect for this happening is the change of diet from fish and rice to a more fatty, meat diet.

To reduce fat in your diet try not to eat more than one meat meal per day. Cut out (or at least cut down on) butter and cream. Reduce the amount of cakes, biscuits, eggs, cheese, ice-cream and chocolate that you eat. Do not be afraid to eat starchy foods such as bread, potatoes, rice and pasta. As lack of fibre contributes to cancer of the bowel and rectum, try to eat wholemeal bread and pasta, and brown rice. Eat jacket potatoes rather than fried. Grilling food rather than frying will remove a lot of excess fat. Avoid meat products such as sausages, pies and burgers, which have high fat contents.

Eating plenty of fresh fruit and vegetables will stimulate the production of enzymes in the liver which help to destroy toxins and cancer-causing chemicals in food. Recent research has shown that mouldy foods produce cancer-causing substances (mouldy peanuts produce the chemical aflatoxin which does cause cancer in animals). Do not eat mouldy bread or cheese; even if you cut off the mould that you can see, it has already penetrated deeply.

Avoid food additives where possible, especially colours. They have been shown to cause hyperactivity in some children. If you both smoke and drink, you are fifteen times more likely to get cancer than those who do neither. Cigarettes are not called 'cancer sticks' and 'coffin nails' without reason. The cancer-causing chemicals (carcinogens) in cigarettes are in the tar, and this is why it is better for you to smoke cigarettes with low tar. Pregnant women who smoke increase the risks of miscarriage or having stillborn children. Giving up smoking decreases your chances of cancer and coronary disease, gives you more resistance to infections, your sense of taste improves, you become fitter and you save money!

At work, avoid inhaling hairspray and keep chemicals off your skin.

Questions 9.8

1   What proof is there that what we eat can help stop cancer?
2   What kinds of food would you eat to reduce the possibility of cancer?
3   What type of cancer does fibre in the diet discourage?
4   Why are cigarettes also known as 'cancer sticks'?
5   What should the hairdresser avoid at work to reduce the possibility of developing cancer?

10

First Aid

First aid is the first action that should be taken in an emergency. First aid should be given as quickly as possible to minimise injury.

You should familiarise yourself with the action to be taken for each event, so that if the need arises you will do the right thing almost without thinking. In every salon, someone should be responsible for first aid and the upkeep of the first aid box.

10.1 Bleeding

Most bleeding results from a wound to the skin but it may be internal (inside the body) or external (outside the body). The obvious first aid action is to stop or reduce the bleeding. You may also, however, have to treat for shock and help reduce the risk of infection occurring.

In the salon you may occasionally snip the skin rather than the hair! For a small cut the bleeding can be stopped by applying pressure to the damaged skin. This allows the blood to form a clot, which is the body's natural defence mechanism. (When platelets in blood are exposed to air they break up and cause the blood to thicken and eventually stop flowing.) If you cut someone's ear, apply pressure by pinching the skin. Do the same, for example, if you cut your finger.

The risk of infection from the AIDS and hepatitis B viruses has created the need for extra safety measures when giving first aid for bleeding. The following rules should be followed:

- Wear rubber gloves when applying pressure to a cut yourself.
- Take care not to get blood on to damaged skin (dermatitis on the hands). Any cuts on the hairdresser or beauty therapist should be covered with a plaster.

If the cut is small:

- Give the client a piece of sterile cotton wool to apply pressure themselves.
- Once bleeding has stopped get the client to place the cotton wool into a plastic bag which can then be sealed and disposed of.

- Sterilise the tool which cut the client.
- Wipe up any spillage of blood with household bleach.

When shaving, it is easy to nick small spots on the skin. Avoid this by 'marking' such spots with your finger through the lather, otherwise you won't be able to see where they are until the lather is bright red! A styptic pencil is available (it looks like a lipstick) especially for shaving cuts. This reduces the bleeding by helping to constrict (reduce the size of) the blood vessels. However, as this could help to spread infection from one person to another, its use should be restricted to one person. An alternative to the styptic pencil is alum powder. It works in the same way, but is more hygienic because the powder is only used once.

If the bleeding is more serious, apply direct pressure to the wound using dressing pads, bandages, clean handkerchiefs or tissues. If you can raise the wounded area it will lower the blood pressure there, and help to slow the bleeding.

If someone has a large stomach wound, possibly from falling through a glass door or on to a coffee table with a glass top, hold clean towels tightly against the wound. As for all serious bleeding, get medical help as soon as possible. If you bandage a wound and the bandage becomes wet with blood, do not remove it, but apply another bandage over it.

If something becomes lodged in a wound, such as a piece of glass, do not remove it but make a ring dressing over the wound. This will stop the glass being pushed deeper into the wound until such time as it can be removed with medical supervision. Removing a piece of glass could increase bleeding.

Many people suffer from nosebleeds which often result from blowing the nose hard or from picking it. There are many old remedies for stopping the bleeding – putting something cold on the bridge of the nose, plugging it with tissue, putting the head back, etc. If someone has a nosebleed, they should take these three steps:

(1) Lean the head forward (this stops blood from going down the throat).
(2) Pinch together the nostrils at the very bottom of the nose (this allows the blood to clot and stops the blood flow). (It is now recommended that the very bottom of the nose is pinched and not just below the bone as you will see in many books.)
(3) Do not blow the nose for some time afterwards, as the clot could be dislodged before the damaged veins have healed, and bleeding would start again.

All the bleeding mentioned so far has been external, and although it is less likely that you will see internal bleeding while working in a salon, you might encounter this in a car accident or serious fall. It is not obvious that someone has internal bleeding, unless there are external signs. These include coughing or vomiting of blood; discharge of blood from the mouth, nose or ear; blood being passed in urine or faeces; bruising. As much as four pints (over two litres) of blood can be lost into the body cavities. If you suspect internal bleeding, reassure the casualty, get him or her to rest in a comfortable position (sitting upright if it is a chest injury) and get to a hospital as soon as possible.

When someone is injured and has to be taken to hospital, it can be of benefit to know how the pulse changes. A pulse is a throb in an artery that occurs every time

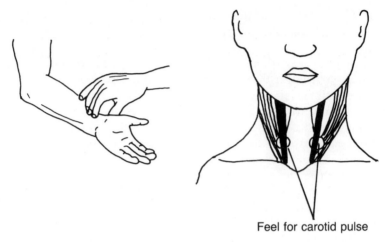

Feel for carotid pulse

Fig. 10.1 The two areas to feel for a pulse.

the heart beats. The pulse is best found on either the underside of the wrist (thumb side) or the side of the neck below the jaw (see Figure 10.1). Count the number of pulses every 30 seconds and double this number to arrive at the number of pulses per minute. Try this on yourself; if there are 36 pulses in 30 seconds, the pulse rate is 72 times per minute. The following are normal pulse rates per minute: 60 to 80 for adults, 90 to 100 for children and 100 to 140 for babies.

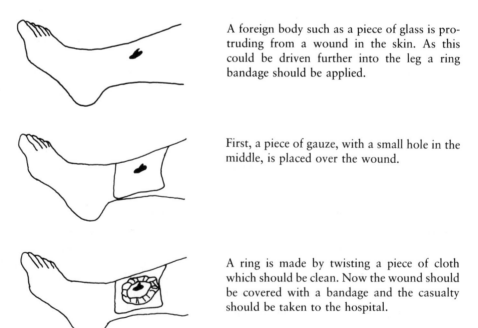

A foreign body such as a piece of glass is protruding from a wound in the skin. As this could be driven further into the leg a ring bandage should be applied.

First, a piece of gauze, with a small hole in the middle, is placed over the wound.

A ring is made by twisting a piece of cloth which should be clean. Now the wound should be covered with a bandage and the casualty should be taken to the hospital.

Fig. 10.2 How to make a ring dressing.

In all wounds to the skin try to keep the damaged area clean and covered. This prevents possible infection. If someone is cut on something dirty, check if he or she has had a tetanus injection. If not, send him or her to hospital for one.

If something protrudes from the wound, do not remove it but make a ring dressing as shown in Figure 10.2.

Questions 10.1

1   What is first aid?
2   What is the purpose of all first aid given for bleeding?
3   Why must the first aider be safety conscious when giving first aid for bleeding?
4   How should the bleeding from a small cut be stopped in the salon?
5   How can shaving cuts be prevented?
6   Why is alum powder preferable to a styptic pencil?
7   How should more serious bleeding be stopped?
8   What should you do to stem the flow of blood from a large stomach wound?
9   Should a large piece of glass be removed from a wound?
10 How do you make a ring dressing and when should it be used?
11 What is the first aid for a nosebleed?
12 What would make you suspect that a casualty had internal bleeding?
13 If a cut has been caused on something dirty, what extra precaution should be taken?

10.2   Burns and scalds

A *burn* is an injury to the body tissues caused by dry heat, which could be something hot, fire, friction or electricity. A *scald* is caused by moist heat which could be hot liquids, steam or hot fat.

In the salon some chemicals burn; they are corrosive. Most of us have been burnt by hydrogen peroxide, but there are other chemicals which could cause a more severe burn.

A superficial or surface burn will result in blisters and reddening of the skin. These usually heal within a few days, but are painful because the nerve endings are irritated. A partial-thickness burn goes deeper than the epidermis, so that a red weeping area of small blood vessels (capillaries) is exposed. There will also be blisters, and it will be painful. Although such a burn will heal within 1 to 4 weeks, with little or no scarring, the skin may be red for longer. A full-thickness burn will result in the complete destruction of the skin, and the hair follicles it contains. Because nerve endings have been destroyed, there will be no pain following the burn.

The extent of a burn can be calculated by the 'rule of nine'. This divides the body into areas which are each approximately 9% of its whole. This is shown in Figure 10.3. In adults, if a burn covers 15% or more they must be taken to hospital (10% in children).

Burnt tissue retains heat and will do further damage unless it is quickly cooled. Cooling will relieve pain and prevent further damage to the tissue. *The first aid for a burn or scald is to flood the area with water for up to 15 minutes. If you have to use a wet cloth, hold it against the burn but do not rub the skin. The treatment for a*

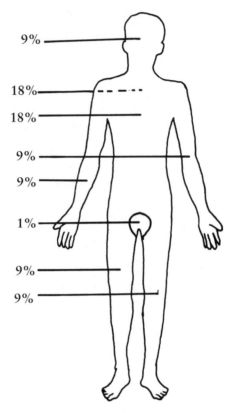

9%

18%

18%

9%

9%

1%

9%

9%

Fig. 10.3 The 'Rule of Nine' shows how the body is divided to calculate the area of skin burnt.

chemical burn is the same – in this case, however, water dilutes and removes the chemical.

Remember the following points:

- If clothes or hair are on fire, smother the flames with towels or put out with water if available. Remove smouldering clothing by pulling at a non-burning piece of material.
- Remove any clothing that has been soaked in boiling fluid.
- Remove any constricting items such as footwear or jewellery (ring on a burnt finger, etc.) as swelling will result from burns.
- *Do not remove burnt clothing which has cooled* – it will be sterile from the heat which has caused the burn.
- Cover the burnt area lightly with sterile gauze, or failing this, a clean piece of cloth. This is important on a large burn to prevent infection before medical help can be obtained. Do not use materials which are fluffy.
- *Never* handle the burnt area (it could cause infection).
- *Never* pick blisters (they protect skin from infection).

- *Never* remove skin or pieces of clothing which are stuck to the burn (it will cause more damage).
- *Never* apply lotions or ointments to the burn (it will be sterile from the heat of the burn).

If a burn is severe (twice the size of the palm of the hand) fluid can be lost from the tissues and the casualty may go into shock (see Section 10.12). Until he or she can be taken to hospital, give the patient the following drink to replace lost fluid: half a teaspoon of salt plus half a teaspoon of sodium bicarbonate in a litre of water.

Questions 10.2

1   What can cause a burn?
2   What is the difference between a burn and a scald?
3   Besides heat, what else could cause a burn?
4   Describe the different types of burn and how long the skin would take to heal.
5   How can the extent of a burn be worked out?
6   What is the first aid for a heat burn or scald?
7   What is the first aid for a chemical burn on the skin?
8   Why should rings be removed if a hand is burnt?
9   How should the burnt area of skin be protected from infection?
10 How would you know if a burn was severe or not?

10.3 Epileptic fits

Epilepsy is a condition in which the sufferer can go into uncontrollable convulsions. These may occur within hours of each other, or may be days, weeks, months or years apart. If a client or hairdresser is epileptic, they should ensure that other people know in case of an attack. Many epileptics carry a medic alert card (about the size of a credit card) or bracelet saying that they are epileptic. Our brain cells work by electrical activity, in a controlled way. When an epileptic has a fit a lot of uncontrolled electrical impulses occur at once, resulting in jerking of the limbs.

There are two types of epileptic fit – minor and major (given the French names 'petit mal' and 'grand mal'). Minor epilepsy usually occurs in children, and at its worst results in loss of consciousness. Often a child will just be dazed for a few moments and will carry on as if nothing has happened. Major epileptic fits usually occur in four stages:

(1) *Aura* This is a warning that a fit is about to occur; it usually lasts a few seconds but does not always happen.
(2) *Rigidity* The muscles tighten and the epileptic falls to the ground. Often in this stage the epileptic may urinate or defecate. Breathing may stop as well, but this stage lasts less than a minute.
(3) *Shaking* This is the stage where the epileptic shakes violently (termed convulsions). This stage may last several minutes.
(4) *Coma* After the shaking the epileptic often stays unconscious for about 30 minutes. They may vomit, or breathing can be obstructed.

Fig. 10.4 The recovery position. This is used with any unconscious casualty to allow easy breathing and prevent choking or suffocating on vomit.

What to do

First, remain calm. Do not try and hold the epileptic down or try to restrain the jerking. If there are any sharp objects nearby, try to move them or stand in front of them, in case the casualty should be injured on them. Do not put anything in the casualty's mouth or between the teeth. The mouth will probably be firmly shut.

When the convulsions stop, place the casualty in the recovery position (see Figure 10.4). Call for an ambulance if the casualty has been hurt while falling, or goes into a series of fits without recovering consciousness. If it is the first time someone has had a fit, further medical investigation will be necessary. Remember:

- An epileptic is usually of normal intelligence.
- Epilepsy does run in families but its exact cause is unknown. It can be acquired following head injuries or high fevers.
- Do not put things into an epileptic's mouth during an attack – epileptics are unlikely to bite their tongues.
- A British driving licence will only be granted to someone who has been free of epileptic attacks (except in sleep) for three years.
- A fit can be triggered off by flashing lights, such as a strobe light in a discotheque or a faulty fluorescent tube.

Questions 10.3

1   What might an epileptic carry on them to show that they suffer from epilepsy?
2   How many types of epileptic fit are there?
3   Describe the four stages of a fit.
4   What would you do if someone had an epileptic fit?
5   What could set off a fit?
6   Why are unconscious casualties placed in the recovery position?

10.4 Hysterical fits

Hysteria is a word which causes confusion; it has nothing to do with epilepsy. An hysterical fit usually occurs as a reaction to some kind of stress or upset. The fit can range from simply a temporary loss of control, with screaming and shouting, to a dramatic rolling on the ground, crying and tearing at the clothes. The fit's purpose (although the sufferer is unaware of this) is to appeal to a sympathetic audience and it is rare for sufferers actually to hurt themselves.

If a client should have a hysterical fit, perhaps following some salon disaster in which the hair is damaged, remember three things. Be very firm with them and try to reassure them. Get them away from an audience which could make them worse. Do not express sympathy in case it starts them off again, but try to give them something to do to keep them occupied. Remember:

- Hysteria is not more common in women than men.
- Slapping a client having a fit can be considered an assault.

Questions 10.4

1   Are hysterical fits related to epileptic fits?
2   How do hysterical fits vary?
3   What are the three things that you should do if someone has an hysterical fit?

10.5 Fainting

Fainting is caused simply by a lack of oxygen to the brain, which can result in a period of unconsciousness. Causes include a lack of air in a room, hunger, standing in one position for too long, heat, tiredness and fright.

When someone feels faint, they may become giddy and unsteady on their feet. They may start to sweat and feel sick. If a client feels faint, get them to put their head down between their knees, as this will increase the blood flow to the brain (see Figure 10.5). Also, try to get them into fresh air (open a window if possible). Give them a few sips of water. If a client has fainted, put their feet up higher than their head (on a stool, books, pillows, etc.) and loosen their clothing (see Figure 10.6). Try to get them into fresh air. They should start to recover within a few minutes, so reassure them as they may not know exactly what has happened. Give them a few sips of water once they are sitting up again. When someone faints, the skin becomes pale and the pulse weakens, but both return to normal on recovery.

Cutting out breakfast can often result in fainting. If you want to diet, eat less, but do not starve yourself.

Fig. 10.5   Put the head down between the knees if you feel faint.

Fig. 10.6   Raise the legs of the casualty who has fainted.

Questions 10.5

1   What causes fainting?
2   How does someone feel just before fainting?
3   What is the first aid for someone who feels faint?
4   What is the first aid for someone who has fainted?

10.6   Diabetes

Diabetes is a condition in which unconsciousness or coma results from too little or too much insulin in the blood. Insulin is the hormone made by the pancreas to control our blood sugar (glucose) level. Its job is to keep the blood sugar content controlled by directing it into the cells, where it is used to provide energy. Without insulin, the body's cells are starved of sugar, despite a high level in the blood.

Affected people pass abnormally large quantities of urine, and as result have an abnormal thirst. The urine of someone with this type of diabetes can be sweet, and it is called *diabetes mellitus* ('mellitus' means 'like honey'). In a few rare cases the urine is not sweet (insipid) and results from a failure of the pituitary gland; it is called *diabetes insipidus*. About 1% of the population in Britain have diabetes. In a tribe of American Indians nearly half the population have diabetes (the Pimas of Arizona).

The main danger for a diabetic under treatment with insulin is actually having more insulin than they need. This could be due to the sugar level falling because of a missed meal or too much exercise, or from too large an injection of insulin. Low blood sugar is called hypoglycaemia.

A coma caused by *too much insulin* results in:

- pale and moist skin;
- shallow breathing;
- no smell on breath (of acetone);
- rapid pulse.

Before going into a hypoglycaemic coma the diabetic may behave aggressively or as if drunk. Such an attack could develop in a matter of minutes and can be easily stopped by taking sugar.

A coma caused by a *lack of insulin* (i.e. too much sugar in the blood or hyperglycaemia) results in:

- face flushed (red);
- deep breathing;
- a smell of acetone on the breath (odour of nail varnish remover).

A high blood sugar level can take hours or days to develop, and may take hours to cure (by injection of insulin). As the sugar level rises, the cells are starved of 'fuel' so start to break down fat instead. This results in waste products called ketones being produced – acetone on the breath.

If the person is still conscious, try and ask them what to do. If they cannot tell you, give them a sweet drink (with two tablespoons of sugar in it) or sugar lumps to eat. As many diabetics carry these, check the pockets for them. Also check the wallet or handbag for a diabetic card, or the neck or wrists for a medic alert bracelet (this is a piece of jewellery with information about the condition).

If the person is unconscious, place them in the recovery position and call for medical help (either an ambulance or phone the number on the diabetic card, if one is found).

- A diabetic can lead a virtually normal life.
- They may develop arterial disease so should not smoke.
- Cuts etc. often take longer to heal.
- Pumps are becoming available which can be worn on a belt and give injections automatically.
- Diabetic foods are sweetened without sugar as it would be rapidly absorbed by the stomach and lead to a rapid increase in blood sugar.
- Remember that glucose is the energy source for the brain. If it is deprived of it, the brain cannot function properly.

Questions 10.6

1 What is diabetes?
2 What is the function of insulin in the body?
3 What are the two types of diabetes called?
4 Describe the coma caused by secretion of too much insulin.
5 How might someone behave before going into a hypoglycaemic coma?
6 Describe the coma caused by secretion of too little insulin.
7 What should you do if someone has a diabetic attack?

10.7 Heart attacks (cardiac arrest)

A heart attack occurs when the blood supply to the heart or cardiac muscle is reduced. Because the cardiac muscle must work constantly in order for the heart to pump blood, it cannot do its work properly if the oxygen supply to a section of cardiac muscle suddenly ceases (caused by a blood clot stopping the flow of blood). That muscle will die. Heart attacks are most likely to occur in middle-aged or elderly people, but can also occur in the young. Heart disease is the biggest cause of death in Britain and most Western countries. Those most at risk are those who

- smoke;
- are overweight;
- get little exercise;
- have a high dietary fat intake.

Before a heart attack commences there are often severe chest pains which spread to the arms and neck. The casualty will become short of breath, the pulse will become weak and irregular and he or she may become unconscious.

The aim of first aid at this stage is to reduce the work of the heart so that it does not stop.

- Do not move the casualty unnecessarily. Support them in a sitting position, using cushions or towels. (See Figure 10.7.)
- Loosen clothing around the neck, chest and waist.
- Phone for an ambulance once the casualty is comfortable. (If this happens when other people are around, ask someone else to phone.)
- Ask the casualty to breath deeply.
- Do not ask the casualty to lie flat as it will be more difficult to breath and it may cause the heart to stop.

What should I do if the heart stops?

If the heart stops, the casualty will become unconscious, no pulse will be felt, there will be no sign of breathing, the pupils of the eyes will dilate (enlarge) and the skin colour will become paler or blue. In effect, they are dead. First aid must be given within three minutes as the brain receives no oxygen once the heart stops. *Without oxygen there will be brain damage after three minutes.* You must act quickly; you have no time to phone for an ambulance if you are alone.

- Lay the casualty on a hard, flat surface (the floor).
- Clear the airway by removing false teeth, blood etc. from the mouth. Tilt the head backwards so that the nostrils are in the air. (See Figure 10.8.)
- Pinch the nostrils closed, cover the mouth with yours, and give a sharp breath into the body. The chest should rise. (See Figure 10.9.)
- Now begin cardiac massage to restart the heart. Place one hand on the sternum (breast bone), and the other on top of it; push down. The aim of this is to press

Fig. 10.7   Supporting the casualty with towels or cushions.

Fig. 10.8   The blocked airways can be cleared by tilting the head back.

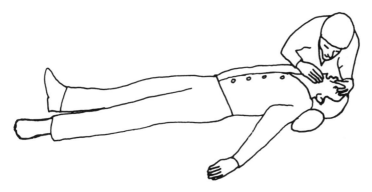

Fig. 10.9   Mouth to mouth artificial respiration.

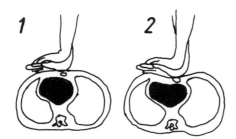

Fig. 10.10   The compression of the heart between the spine and sternum.

the heart between the sternum and the spine (backbone). (See Figures 10.10 and 10.11.)

- You must give one breath to six compressions of heart massage.
- Check the carotid pulse (see Figure 10.1) every few minutes.
- If there are two people available to give first aid, share the two tasks as you will tire easily.
- Keep this up until an ambulance arrives or until casualty recovers.

What is angina?

Angina is a very painful condition of the heart where the arteries of the heart have become too narrow for an adequate supply of blood to get to the cardiac muscle.

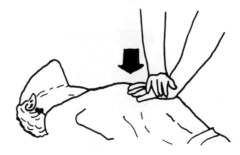

Fig. 10.11 Cardiac massage.

Excitement or over-exertion can bring on an attack of severe chest pain, together with pain in the left shoulder and arm. It is relieved by rest, and should last only a few minutes. People who suffer from angina often carry tablets which help to prevent attacks before they start.

Questions 10.7

1 What causes a heart attack?
2 What happens to cardiac muscle in such an attack?
3 Who is most at risk of a heart attack?
4 What signs of heart trouble might someone show before a heart attack?
5 Describe the first aid that should be given to someone at this stage.
6 Describe the first aid that should be given to someone if the heart stops.
7 What is angina?

10.8 Strokes

This is the term used when the brain is damaged by bleeding from a burst blood vessel in the brain, or by blockage of a blood vessel due to a blood clot. The symptoms vary from loss of feeling in a limb to unconsciousness. If the right side of the brain is damaged it will be the left side of the body that will be affected. The casualty may be paralysed down that side, and the speech may be slurred. If only a small blood vessel is involved there may be complete recovery. Those most at risk are the middle-aged to elderly, people with high blood pressure, or those with a weakness in a blood vessel wall since birth (who could have a stroke when young). Other names for strokes are seizures or apoplexy.

There is usually a sudden collapse, sometimes following a headache. Breathing may be noisy, and there may be some frothing at the mouth.

- Clear the airway (see Figure 10.8).
- Loosen tight clothing and place in recovery position (see Figure 10.4).
- Phone for an ambulance.
- If breathing should stop, give mouth-to-mouth artificial respiration.

Questions 10.8

1   What is a stroke?
2   What symptoms might the victim of a stroke show?
3   Who is most at risk of suffering from a stroke?
4   What other names are there for strokes?
5   Describe the first aid for a stroke.

10.9   Sprains and fractures

Sprains or fractures could occur in the salon as the result of a fall, or simply turning an ankle.

A sprain is the result of tearing ligaments round a joint, usually the ankle or wrist.

- Apply a crêpe bandage to support the joint.
- Wet it with cold water (immersing if possible) to reduce swelling.
- If the sprain is severe take the casualty to hospital for a precautionary X-ray in case a bone is broken.

A fracture is a broken or cracked bone. A fracture can be either open or closed. An open fracture is when there is a wound leading down to the fracture, or when the end of a bone sticks out of the skin. A closed fracture is when the skin covering the bone is not broken. If there is bleeding, treat the casualty for that first. A fracture may not be obvious, and must be confirmed by an X-ray. Call for an ambulance as soon as possible. Look for these points:

- pain and tenderness in the injured area;
- swelling and bruising;
- loss of power in the limb;
- an unnatural movement of the limb;
- a grating sensation on moving the limb;
- deformity of the limb.

Figure 10.12 illustrates the types of fracture that could occur.

The first aid for a fracture is to immobilise the injured part, by using the body as a splint where possible (tying an injured leg to an uninjured one) or a wooden splint which can be padded. If an arm is injured it can be tied to the body or put into a sling (made from a triangular bandage) to support it. Try to move uninjured parts of the body to the injured part. If no bandages are available, use ties, belts or pieces of towel – whatever is to hand in the salon.

- *Don't* tie knots over the injured part.
- *Don't* have a bandage directly over a fractured limb.
- *Don't* give any food, drink (including alcohol) or tablets to the injured person as they may require an anaesthetic to ease the pain when a bone is set at the hospital.

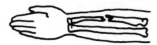

Simple fracture The bone is broken cleanly with no fragmentation.

Compound fracture The bone is broken in more than one place.

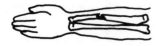

Greenstick fracture The bone is only partially broken, with no 'clean' break.

Open fracture The broken bone punctures the skin and becomes exposed. This can make a limb look abnormal.

Complicated fracture The broken bone damages nerve or blood vessels in the damaged area.

Fig. 10.12   Types of bone fracture.

Dislocation of a joint is very similar in appearance to a fracture. It is a severe twist or wrenching of a movable joint, displacing the bones from their normal position. Treat as if it were a fracture and prevent the casualty from moving it. Call for an ambulance.

Questions 10.9

1   How do sprains or fractures occur?
2   What is a sprain?
3   Describe the action to be taken if someone sprains an ankle.
4   What is a fracture?
5   Describe the five types of fracture.
6   What would you look for if you suspected a fracture?
7   What is the first aid for a fracture?
8   What is a dislocated joint?
9   How should it be treated?

10.10   Eye injuries

Any injury to the eye should be dealt with quickly, as damage to the eye could lead to either loss or impairment of vision. The two most common eye injuries in a salon are caused by small objects or chemicals.

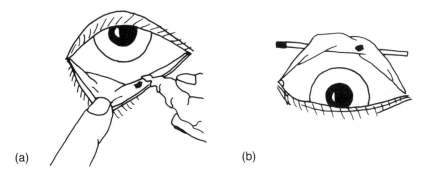

(a)   (b)

Fig. 10.13   Removing an object from the eye (a) with the corner of a handkerchief (b) by
folding the upper eyelid back over a matchstick.

If a foreign body, such as hair or grit, enters the eye, locate it by pulling down the
lower eyelid. Remove the object with the corner of a handkerchief as shown in
Figure 10.13(a). If the foreign body is under the upper eyelid, first try to place the
upper lid over the lower lid so that the object comes off on the lower lid. If this fails,
take either a matchstick or a hairgrip, and flip the upper eyelid over it so that the
object can be removed (see Figure 10.13b). If you cannot remove the object from
the eye, cover with an eyepad and seek immediate medical help.

For any injury to the eye caused by chemicals, the first aid is to flood the eye with
cold water to dilute the chemical. Use either the salon water spray or a jug to flood
the eye with water. Cover the unaffected eye with your hand to prevent chemicals
being washed into it. If irritation persists, seek medical advice.

Questions 10.10

1   Why must eye injuries be dealt with quickly?
2   How would you remove an object from the eye?
3   What should you do if you cannot remove an object from the eye?
4   How would you deal with a chemical entering the eye of a client?
5   What should be done if irritation persists?

10.11   Choking

A small piece of food may be inhaled into the windpipe when eating. Most people
are able to cough it up at once but if this is not possible, help will be needed. Stand
behind the person as shown in Figure 10.14 with your arms clasped just under the
sternum. Give a sharp bear hug. The food should be coughed out.

Questions 10.11

1   What is the cause of choking?
2   How would you give first aid to someone who was choking?

10.12 Shock

Shock is caused by a drop in blood pressure. It may be due to loss of blood (internal or external bleeding), loss of fluid (from burns), loss of pumping power from the heart (as in heart attack), severe fright or pain, or a severe allergic reaction. It will deprive the body tissues of oxygen and energy. Such a condition could cause death if not treated. It has been known for people to die of minor injuries because they went into shock. These are the symptoms to look for:

- Pulse is fast and weak.
- Breathing is rapid and shallow.
- Skin becomes pale, cold and clammy.
- Mouth becomes dry.
- Sweat appears on forehead.
- If conscious, casualty will feel weak, sickly and thirsty.

Quick action is vital:

- Phone for an ambulance.
- Lay the casualty flat with the legs slightly raised. (This will allow blood to get to the heart and brain easily.)
- Cover with blankets (or coats or towels) to keep warm.
- Tight clothing should be loosened to allow easy breathing.
- Don't give any drink, food or tablets to the casualty.
- Be careful what you say in case the casualty becomes more anxious.

Questions 10.12

1   What causes shock and when might it occur?
2   What effect does shock have on the body?
3   List the symptoms that someone in shock would display.
4   What action should be taken if a casualty suffers shock?

10.13 Cramp

Cramp is a sudden tightness and pain in the muscles. The leg muscles are the most often affected. It can be very painful. In hot weather it can be due to a lack of salt. As salt is lost in sweating it is important for those taking part in sport to take sufficient salt in their diets.

   Stretch the affected muscle, e.g. if it is the calf which has cramp, straighten the knee and pull the foot up towards the shin. Eventually, the pain will go away.

Questions 10.13

1   What is cramp?
2   Which muscles are commonly affected by cramp?

Fig. 10.14 First aid for someone who is choking.

3   How can hot weather cause cramp?
4   What is the first aid for cramp?

10.14   Electrocution

If the casualty is still in contact with the source of electricity, your first aim is to break that contact. In Figure 10.15 the easiest thing to do is to remove the plug from the socket, or yank it from the socket by pulling the cable. It should be safe to do this because both the plug and cable are made from insulated materials which cannot conduct electricity. If for some reason you cannot do either of these things, then use a non-conductor (such as a wooden broom handle) to knock the appliance from the hands.

Now check if the casualty is breathing and if not clear the airway and give mouth-to-mouth artificial respiration (See Figure 10.9). Once the casualty is breathing, treat any burns with cold water. Make sure there is no further chance of electrocution during this. Call for an ambulance as soon as possible.

Questions 10.14

1   What is the first thing that you should do if a casualty is still being electrocuted?
2   What should you do if the casualty has stopped breathing?
3   If the casualty is breathing, what action should be taken?

Fig. 10.15 Electric shock casualty.

10.15 Poisoning

Anyone who accidentally or otherwise takes a poison or overdose of tablets should be rushed to hospital. Do not wait for an ambulance if a car is available. Try to take the container that they may have eaten or drunk from. If there are chemical burns around the mouth, you may wash any remaining chemical off the skin.

- Do not make the casualty sick.
- If they have been sick take a sample of vomit to the hospital.
- Only give a drink (milk or water) if you know that a corrosive liquid such as bleach or peroxide has been taken. This will help to dilute it.
- If the casualty stops breathing give artificial respiration (see Figure 10.9).

The reason that you do not make the casualty vomit is two-fold: if a corrosive poison has been taken it will burn the throat and mouth as it comes up, and it could also be breathed into the lungs.

Questions 10.15

1 What action should be taken if someone is poisoned?
2 When should drinks be given to someone who has been poisoned?
3 What should be taken to the hospital with the casualty?
4 Why should you not make the casualty vomit?
5 What should you do if the casualty stops breathing?

Item in first aid box	Number of items	
	(a)	(b)
First aid guidance card	1	1
Individual sterile plasters	20	40
Medium sterile dressings	2	4
Large sterile dressings	2	4
Extra large sterile dressings	2	4
Sterile eye pads/bandages	2	4
Triangular bandages/slings	2	4
Sterilised wound coverings	2	4
Safety pins	6	12

Fig. 10.16 Minimum contents of first aid box for number of employees between (a) 1–10 or (b) 11–50.

10.16 The first aid box

All salons should have a first aid box which is available in the event of an accident. This legal requirement varies with the number of people on a premises and is governed by the Health and Safety (First Aid) Regulations of 1982. Many first aid boxes are marked with a red cross on a white background *or* a white cross on a red background. However, the most modern first aid boxes are *GREEN WITH A WHITE CROSS*. The box should close tightly so that it is dust and moisture free. All employees should know where it is kept.

Figure 10.16 shows minimum amounts of items if the number of employees is between (a) 1–10, or (b) 11–50. These are the minimum recommended contents. Because of the risk of AIDS and hepatitis B several pairs of disposable rubber gloves should be kept in all salon first aid boxes. It is also useful to have some cotton wool and tissues; surgical adhesive tape; a crêpe bandage for a strain and a bowl for pouring water. The first thing to run out in a first aid box is plasters. As it makes sense to keep cuts covered, have a supply of waterproof ones for protection. If you want to learn more about first aid, phone your local St. John's Ambulance who regularly run courses.

Figure 10.17 shows the procedure for telephoning the emergency services. Make yourself familiar with this so that you can act quickly if ever an emergency occurs. One day it could help gain vital seconds to save someone's life.

Never give alcohol to anyone who is feeling ill or who has been hurt in case they should need an anaesthetic on entry to hospital. If you do, they will have to wait longer for treatment.

Questions 10.16

1 How would you recognise a modern first aid box?
2 How would you recognise an older first aid box?

Emergency calls to these services are free

- **Call operator by dialling 999** or as shown on your telephone number or in your dialling instructions.

- **Tell the operator the emergency service you want:** Fire Brigade, Police, Ambulance.

- **The operator will ask you for your telephone number (as shown on your telephone) and will then put you through to the emergency service wanted.**

- **When the emergency service answers, give the full address where help is needed and other necessary information** such as landmarks which will assist in finding the location quickly.

- **Wait for the emergency service to arrive.** You may be needed as a witness.

  Remember!

- Speak clearly and calmly so that valuable time is not wasted repeating information.

- Get to know the position of the '9' hole or button on your telephone and practise trying to find it with your eyes closed. This will help if you have to make an emergency call in the dark or a smoke-filled room.

Fig. 10.17 Telephoning the emergency services.

3	What regulations govern the minimum contents of a first aid box?
4	Where is the first aid box in your salon?
5	From the number of people in your salon, what should be in the first aid box?
6	What other useful items could be in a first aid box?
7	In salons, what is usually the first thing to run out in a first aid box?
8	Where would you find out about first aid courses?
9	Describe how you would phone for an ambulance.

11

Mainly Female

This chapter describes a number of conditions that are either exclusive to females or generally tend to affect women more than men.

11.1   Thrush

Thrush is a fungal infection that is caused by the yeast-like organism, *Candida albicans*. Thrush is also known as *moniliasis*. An attack of thrush will produce itching and irritation, often accompanied by a thick white discharge. The same yeast causes nappy rash. It is not 'caught' in the normal sense of the word, because *Candida* is already present in the vagina and bowel of many women, along with many other types of bacteria and fungi. The yeast is not a natural inhabitant of these areas, but vaginal thrush has been known since the time of the Ancient Greeks. If these yeast cells are already present in the vagina, it is usually a change in pH which triggers an attack.

The natural pH of the vagina is acid and this inhibits the growth of both bacteria and fungi. A number of things can upset the pH and lead to an attack of thrush.

Some causes of thrush

- During menstruation (bleeding from a period) the pH may rise from the normal of between 4.0 and 5.0 to between 5.8 and 6.8, because of the alkalinity of the blood.
- Antibiotics given for other infections may allow thrush to take hold. They are not specific enough and kill bacteria that help to keep thrush in check (these are the lactobacilli which break down glycogen to lactic acid and help to maintain an acid pH in the vagina). If you get thrush when you are given antibiotics, tell your doctor to see if an alternative treatment is available, or if you can be given treatment for the thrush before it develops.
- Pregnant women often get thrush, mainly because of a change in the glycogen

content of vaginal mucus. The increased amount of glycogen cannot be broken down into an acidic form and provides conditions for the yeast to multiply.

- Some women on the pill get thrush for the same reason (this will be the type containing oestrogens), or because of an increase in vaginal secretions (progesterone pills).
- Women who use intra-uterine devices (IUDs) may get attacks of thrush because of increased bleeding caused by them.
- Older women who have gone through the menopause will have less vaginal secretions and physical damage caused by intercourse can result in thrush infections. Medical advice should be sought.
- The semen of some men is more alkaline than others. If this is the reason for an outbreak of thrush, it is possible to use special acid jellies during intercourse (or a sheath).
- A man may be a carrier of thrush; if one person gets thrush both sexual partners should be treated for it, or they may reinfect one another.
- The yeast that causes thrush flourishes in warm, moist environments. An attack could be triggered by wearing tight jeans, tights or nylon briefs.
- The yeast is more likely to breed where there is broken skin, which could be caused by scratching an irritation. Many women get irritated skin because they are allergic to the ingredients of vaginal deodorants, bubble baths or highly perfumed soaps.

How is thrush treated?

Although there are a number of ways to treat yourself at home, it is important to seek medical advice. You will not be the first woman patient the doctor has seen with thrush, so don't be embarrassed.

Your doctor will probably give you pessaries to clear it up. These are very large pills, usually of an antibiotic, which are inserted high into the vagina at night. They are made of a wax which melts (wearing a minipad helps stop any mess at night). Some of the pessaries used are based on the antibiotic econazole, and this should not be used within the first three months of pregnancy. These only have to be used for one week. Those based on nystatin, another antibiotic, may have to be used for up to a month. You will usually be given a cream to help reduce irritation and control fungal growth on the skin surrounding the vagina. Use the full course of treatment you are given; you will then be less likely to have another attack.

Although these are the likely treatments that you will be given, you might also be given a gel to use internally, or even special medicated tampons. Because these tampons remain in close contact with the infected area they seem to work quickly. However, many doctors do not prescribe them because of cost.

One of the most successful home remedies is plain unpasteurised yogurt (this is the natural type, not filled with fruit). The Ancient Greeks used this remedy without knowing how it worked. It contains cultures of lactobacilli, which break down the glycogen in vaginal secretions into lactic acid. This produces a 'hostile' environment for the yeast. One of the easiest ways of applying it is on tampons. Eating natural yogurt during a thrush attack will also help stop the yeast breeding in the intestine.

You could also use an organic acid such as diluted white vinegar (it does not contain sugar) or lemon juice in water. This can be applied on a tampon and can help to get rid of the infection in many women.

How do I prevent an attack?

- Avoid tights, tight jeans and nylon briefs. Wear stockings or popsocks, cotton briefs and skirts.
- Use pads instead of tampons when you have a period. They are less likely to upset the pH of the vagina.
- Avoid antibiotics as far as possible. Remember to tell your doctor that you are prone to thrush attacks.
- Avoid perfumed soaps, vaginal deodorants and bubble baths.
- Shower rather than take a bath.
- Wipe from 'front to back' after going to the lavatory. This will help to avoid contamination with any yeast that might be present in the bowel.
- If the pill is the cause of your thrush, change brands or try another form of contraception.
- Make sure that your sexual partner is also treated at the same time as you, or reinfection will occur.

Questions 11.1

1   What micro-organism causes thrush?
2   Describe the symptoms of thrush.
3   What usually triggers an attack of thrush?
4   List some of the possible causes of an attack of thrush.
5   What is the medical treatment for thrush?
6   What home remedies are there for treating thrush?
7   List the things that you can do to prevent an attack of thrush.

11.2   Cystitis

The term 'cystitis' means inflammation of the bladder. It occurs when the urethra or bladder becomes infected. Anyone with a bladder infection feels like going to the lavatory every few minutes, although there may be little urine to pass. Urination is extremely painful, because the urine burns and stings. Blood may be present in the urine. If sufferers force themselves to urinate it is possible to damage the urethra, producing small tears that make passing urine even more painful. Cystitis will affect over half the women in Britian at some time during their lives. Many will have attacks of it at regular intervals. The main symptoms of cystitis are:

- A stinging or burning pain when passing water.
- Wanting to 'spend a penny' more than usual, even if there is little urine to pass.
- An ache, lower than the usual stomach ache.
- Passing urine which is darker than usual, and may be streaked with blood.

What causes cystitis?

The most frequent cause is the entry of bacteria into the urethra, usually through its entrance. The bacteria responsible are Escherichia coliform (E. coli for short). E. coli are found in the bowel where they help in digestion and cause no problems. E. coli are also present on the skin surrounding the anus, and as the opening to the urethra is so close they can easily spread forward to cause infection. This is the reason women get cystitis more often than men. The bacteria can be spread during sexual intercourse, either from around the anus of the woman or from the penis of the man. Cystitis is dangerous because an untreated infection could spread to the kidneys. This is why it is important not to ignore the early symptoms of an attack. Girls in their mid-teens are most likely to get kidney infections from cystitis.

How can I get rid of cystitis?

As soon as you feel the first twinges of an attack, begin to drink a lot of water, or bland liquids such as weak tea or milk. For the first three hours try to drink about a half pint every twenty minutes. This will help to flush out the bacteria that cause the infection.

See your doctor as soon as possible. He will prescribe you antibiotics to kill the bacteria, and the symptoms will begin to clear up within a few days. Take the full course of tablets to prevent its immediate return.

When you have cystitis the burning can be relieved by taking a teaspoon of bicarbonate of soda in water. This is alkaline and helps to reduce the acidity of the urine. Besides taking painkillers for the pain, some relief can be obtained by holding a hot water bottle against the stomach.

Taking antibiotics for cystitis has one nasty side effect – it can bring on attacks of thrush (see Section 11.1).

How can I prevent cystitis?

- Keep yourself extra clean around the anus and vagina. Keep an extra flannel to wash this area in the morning and at night. Wash with plain warm water and a mild soap without any additives. Work gently from front to back.
- Whenever you move your bowels, use soft toilet tissue and wipe from front to back. Wash if at all possible.
- Avoid bubble baths, bath oils and vaginal deodorants. As daily bathing can cause inflammation of the urethra, try to have a quick, shallow bath or a shower instead.
- Before sexual intercourse, both you and your partner should wash in plain warm water.
- Try to pass water soon after sexual intercourse to flush out any bacteria which have entered the urethra.

Questions 11.2

1   What is the meaning of the term 'cystitis'?
2   When does it occur?

3　　What are the symptoms of cystitis?
4　　What are the possible causes of cystitis?
5　　Why should cystitis be quickly treated?
6　　How can you get rid of cystitis?
7　　What could be done to prevent an attack of cystitis?

11.3 Varicose veins

In Britain, one person in five will have varicose veins. Women are far more likely to develop them than men. A varicose vein is, in fact, a vein which has lost its elasticity. Because of this it is weakened and will dilate (expand) easily. One of the first signs of a varicose vein is that it becomes swollen with blood when you stand up.

What causes varicose veins?

It is the surface veins of the legs that become varicose. Veins have simple valves (see Figure 11.1) to prevent the backflow of blood. The surface veins are connected to deeper veins in the leg. Each is guarded by a valve that allows blood to flow only from the surface veins to the deep veins – in normal veins at least.

Surface veins contain more muscle than the deep veins, because they must be able to react to changes in their environment. For example, they contract in response to injury or cold, and expand in response to heat and some hormones. The deep veins have a much more stable structure. Basically, they are tubes which are emptied by the squeezing effect of surrounding leg muscles when they contract.

If the valve of one of the veins joining the surface and deep veins should fail, the part of the surface vein that is normally protected by this valve will be flooded with blood from the deep vein. This is because that blood is under higher pressure so backflow will occur. The walls of the surface vein expand to cope with influx of extra blood. This puts extra pressure on the other valves which, in turn, also fail because their outside edges can no longer touch each other. This is illustrated in Figure 11.2, but the whole process can take place over a number of years rather than days.

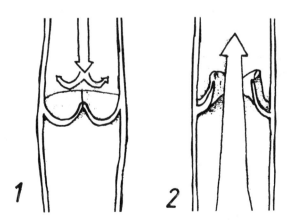

Fig. 11.1 Valves in veins: (1) closed; (2) open.

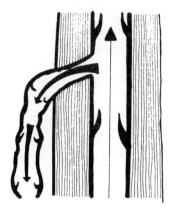

Fig. 11.2   Backflow of blood into a surface vein of the leg. The surface vein is seen as a varicose vein.

Why do we get varicose veins?

This is a question that cannot be fully answered because all the reasons are not known. Here are the most likely reasons for their occurrence in different people:

- In the young there is probably an early defect in one or more of the valves. Some people have fewer valves in their surface veins, so the remaining valves have to withstand more pressure.
- When thrombosis (a blood clot) occurs in a vein, following an accident, childbirth or an operation, it can damage the valves in the deep veins. This causes a build-up of pressure in the surface veins which results in their eventual failure.
- If you are on your feet all day, like many hairdressers throughout their working lives, you are no more likely to get varicose veins than the next person – if your veins are perfectly healthy. If, however, they are defective, the high pressure generated in the deep veins from standing will cause the collapse of surface valves.
- Varicose vein formation has always been a fear to pregnant women. Those women who already have varicose veins claim that they protrude more during pregnancy. The enlarged womb causes the return of blood from the legs to the heart to be slowed down, and this results in increased vein pressure in the legs. This could cause the formation of new varicose veins and could also cause the old ones to protrude more. The female hormones (oestrogens) which are at higher levels during pregnancy also cause the veins to expand and hold more blood.

What can be done for varicose veins?

A doctor will do one of four things:

- If the veins are mild and give little trouble, he will do nothing at all. It takes a good deal of time for them to become worse. The other forms of treatment are all aimed at keeping the affected veins empty of blood.

- The veins in your legs can be supported and compressed by the wearing of elastic stockings. This is useful for pregnant and overweight women, as these situations can be changed. They should not be worn at night. Many hairdressers wear support tights during the day to help avoid varicose veins. These are of benefit, but many complain of their toes being squeezed by the tights!
- Varicose veins can be treated by injection. The surgeon finds the weak valves and injects an irritant solution into these points. This sets up intense local inflammation. The weak area is closed off by the formation of scar tissue and the vein will not fill up with blood. As it takes a number of weeks for the scar tissue to form, the legs are bandaged for about six weeks to prevent blood from entering the veins.
- Two types of operation are available for varicose veins. In the first a piece of wire is passed along the length of the vein and is used to pull out a whole segment of vein. In the second operation, the vein is separated and tied off so that it cannot fill with blood.

Questions 11.3

1   How common are varicose veins?
2   What is a varicose vein?
3   What is the first sign of a varicose vein?
4   How does a varicose vein develop?
5   What are the most likely reasons for someone developing varicose veins?
. 6   How can a hairdresser help avoid varicose veins?
7   What can be done to get rid of varicose veins?

11.4   Premenstrual tension (PMT)

For up to eight days each month some women experience increased irritability, depression and tiredness, with stomach cramps – mainly in the few days before a period begins and perhaps for the first few days of a period. There may also be physical changes associated with this: water retention can cause an increase in weight and make a woman feel bloated. There may also be backache, joint pains and headaches. In 1931 the term 'premenstrual tension' was first used to describe the symptoms.

The menstrual cycle refers to a series of changes that occur in the uterus and ovaries. The average menstrual cycle lasts for 28 days. Menstruation itself is the sloughing off of the cells of the lining of the uterus (the lining of the womb) and the rupturing of the tiny blood capillaries supplying the tissue (resulting in bleeding).

What causes PMT?

The chief culprit appears to be the changing levels of the female sex hormones, oestrogen and progesterone. Oestrogen reaches its highest level about midcycle, and again at day 21 of a 28-day cycle. Progesterone begins to be secreted near midcycle and reaches its peak about day 21 to 24, after which its level quickly diminishes.

When PMT occurs, the levels of both hormones are falling rapidly. PMT seems worse when the level of oestrogen is higher in relation to the level of progesterone.

A high percentage of women who commit suicide or criminal acts do so at this time. PMT is now taken into account by the law in France as an extenuating circumstance even where murder is concerned.

What can be done for PMT?

There is medical help available for PMT, but recognising the symptoms will help minimise the effects.

- Your doctor may consider putting you on a course of female hormones, as it has been shown that PMT is associated with low levels. Do not expect it to work quickly; it may take two months before it begins to work. Taking female hormones does not necessarily give birth control protection, so check with your doctor if you require it.
- Another treatment available from doctors are tranquilisers to help control down-turns of mood. It is better to avoid this treatment as you might become dependent on them.
- A natural remedy is oil of primrose. This does help some women, so check with your chemist. It will take a few months to have an effect.
- You can keep a chart of your menstrual periods over six months to get an idea when the symptoms of PMT occur. On the days before a period take things more slowly, avoiding things you know cause tension.

Questions 11.4

1   What are the symptoms of PMT?
2   What is the menstrual cycle?
3   What causes PMT?
4   If you suffer from PMT, how can the effects be minimised?

11.5   Dysmenorrhoea (painful menstruation)

Girls and young women often suffer spasmodic pain at the beginning of each period. Dysmenorrhoea is accompanied by high levels of progesterone. Usually the first periods a girl has are painless, because ovulation (the release of eggs from the ovum) has not yet occurred. Once ovulation occurs the following period may be accompanied by cramp-like pains in the lower abdomen, as well as the sides of the thighs. The pain usually comes in waves, so is not continuous. The pain can cause the skin to become very pale, and may be severe enough to cause either fainting or vomiting.

Can anything be done to ease attacks of pain?

Some things can be done to help sufferers cope with pain:

- If possible, curl up and hug a hot water bottle.
- During the first part of an attack, relax fully and breathe slowly. As the wave of pain reaches its height breathe a little more quickly and less deeply. As the pain dies away, breathe more slowly again.
- Self-massage can also help; gently massage across the stomach or back, depending on where the pain is.
- Some girls find that the pain can be eased by wearing an elasticated pair of briefs that are designed to 'give control', rather like girdles do.
- *Remember that this condition usually lessens with age, and it is young women who suffer from it.*
- Try different pain killers to see which one gives you the most relief.

Pain killers are freely available over the counter without a doctor's prescription. Nearly all of them contain one or more of the following three ingredients:

Aspirin (acetyl salicylic acid) relieves pain, reduces fever and inflammation but can irritate the stomach lining and cause gastric bleeding. It should therefore *not* be used for a stomach upset. Soluble aspirin acts more quickly.

Paracetamol relieves pain, reduces fever, but does not relieve inflammation. It does not irritate the stomach lining and can therefore be safely used for pain where gastric upset is involved, such as hangovers from drinking alcohol. Long-term use could cause kidney damage.

Codeine is the strongest painkiller of the three but it does not reduce fever or inflammation. It is included in many products based on aspirin or paracetamol, making them more effective pain relievers, while still reducing fever.

Questions 11.5

1   What are the symptoms of dysmenorrhoea?
2   What can be done to ease the pain during an attack?
3   Describe the action of the 3 common painkillers.

11.6   Migraine

Migraine has been known since ancient times, so it cannot be blamed on modern city life. It is defined as a headache that comes at intervals with complete freedom between attacks. It may be accompanied by nausea (feeling sick) or vomiting with disturbances (shimmering and zig-zags) in the field of vision. It affects twice as many women as men and it can be very disruptive to work or home life.

What causes migraine?

Migraine appears to run in families, but there is usually a particular triggering factor that causes an attack. This could be a type of food, such as cheese, chocolate, red wine, citrus fruits or fatty foods. They all contain substances that affect the blood vessels. Missing meals can also bring on an attack.

Any type of change can also trigger an attack. This could be a change in the weather, in hormone levels, in sleep patterns or even going on holiday. A powerful trigger is the arousal caused by something pleasant or unpleasant.

These triggering factors influence the constriction and dilation of blood vessels in the head. The stress hormones, adrenaline and noradrenaline, have an effect on blood vessels as well. This is why they too can trigger off attacks.

What can be done for migraine?

- Try to find out what foods trigger off attacks and avoid them.
- Drink white wine rather than red.
- Try to avoid stressful situations. If your job puts you under stress, learn how to relax.
- During an attack, massage on the back of the neck will help. Also avoid too much light (so lie down in a dark room). Try different painkillers to see which is the most effective in easing the pain during an attack.

Questions 11.6

1   How would you know you had migraine and not a normal headache?
2   Which sex is most likely to suffer from migraines?
3   List some of the things that can trigger migraines.
4   What can the migraine sufferer do to prevent attacks?
5   What should the sufferer do during a migraine?

11.7   Lumps in the breasts

It is important for women to check their breasts each month to ensure that no change has occurred in them. Fourteen thousand women die from breast cancer every year in Britain. When a woman discovers a lump in her breast she will not be comforted by the fact that four out of five lumps are benign and not cancerous. She will be flooded with anxiety until she knows if she is that unlucky one in five.

Even if a lump is cancerous, it may not be as bad as you might think provided that the lump is found quickly. *Don't hope that a lump will go away if you ignore it – see your doctor as soon as possible.* If you notice something unusual in one breast, check the other breast to see if it feels the same. If it does, it's probably nothing to worry about. All breasts are different, so the way to recognise if something is wrong is to check your breasts regularly.

The best time to examine the breasts is just after a period, when they are soft and no longer tender. If you have stopped having periods, choose a regular day each month to check them, such as the first or last day of the month.

To examine your breasts properly, first *look* and then *feel.*

Looking

Stand in front of a mirror, undressed to the waist. You are looking for the following:

- Any change in the size of either nipple or breast.
- Any bleeding or discharge from either nipple.
- Any unusual dimpling (inversion) or puckering on the breast or nipple.
- Any veins standing out more than is usual for you.

Check your breasts with your arms hanging loosely by your side and with your arms raised above your head. Turn from side to side to see your breasts from different angles.

Feeling

It is best to do this lying down on the bed, with a pillow under the head and a folded towel under the shoulderblade on the side of the breast being examined. This helps to spread the breast tissue, and makes it easier to examine. Use the left hand to examine your right breast and vice versa. Keep the free hand under the head.

Keep the fingers together and use the flat of the fingers (not the tips) to examine the breast. Starting above the breast, trace a continuous spiral around the breast until reaching the nipple. Move the fingers in small circles. Self breast examination is shown in Figure 11.3.

Examine the armpit for any lumps as well, and finish the self examination by squeezing the nipple to check for any discharge.

Most breast lumps turn out to be cysts which are relatively harmless. If you are unfortunate enough to develop a cancerous lump, it might be possible to remove it

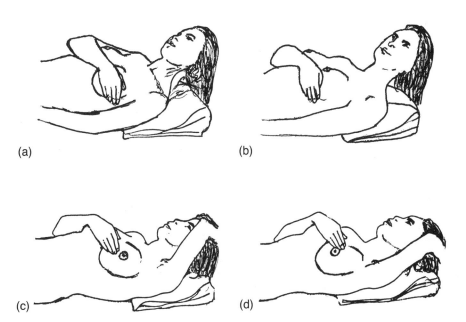

(a)   (b)

(c)   (d)

Fig. 11.3 Self breast examination. In (a) and (b) the underarm and side of the ribcage are examined with the flat of the fingers. In (c) and (d) the fingers are used to trace a continuous spiral around the breast stroking from the edge towards the nipple.

alone, without removing the whole breast. This is most likely if the lump is found soon after it develops, and receives prompt medical treatment. Always ask about a 'lumpectomy'.

Although it is rarer, men can also develop breast cancer.

Questions 11.7

1   Why should women examine their breasts regularly?
2   How many lumps are malignant on average in this country?
3   When is the best time to examine your breasts?
4   List the main points to look for during breast examination.
5   Can men develop breast cancer?

If you are female start giving yourself regular examinations

11.8   Cancer of the cervix

Although cancer of the cervix (the neck of the womb) is fairly rare it is the second most common cancer affecting women after cancer of the breast. Cancer of the cervix kills 2000 women a year in Britain. The disease can be detected early by a smear test in which a small wooden spatula is simply wiped around the neck of the womb to collect some surface cells and secretions. This cervical smear sample is then examined under a microscope to see if there are any abnormal cells. Fortunately, the cancer takes a long time to develop, so any abnormality can be detected before it becomes cancerous (malignant) if a smear test is performed. If it is detected at a precancerous stage all traces of harmful cells can be removed by a simple operation under local anaesthetic.

Women over the age of 35 who have not had a test are considered to be at particular risk, over 90% of deaths from cancer of the cervix occurring in women in the 35-plus age group. The cervical smear should be taken every three years. Although this may seem a long period, the cancer is slow to develop. If you do have a smear test it is essential to ask for the results. In Canada, the number of women dying each year from cervical cancer has decreased by 40% as a direct result of an advertising campaign to inform the public.

Questions 11.8

1   What is the cervix?
2   How can cancer of the cervix be detected?
3   At what age are women considered to be at particular risk of developing cancer of the cervix?
4   How often should smear tests be performed?

11.9   Hysterectomy

Hysterectomy is the removal of the uterus (womb). It is a common operation and about 50 000 are performed every year in Britain. The operation requires about ten days in hospital followed by several weeks of rest. Because the uterus is so important to a woman it can be difficult for her to accept the loss psychologically. If a woman still wants to have children she must consult with her doctor to see if there are any alternative treatments. The reasons a hysterectomy are performed may vary, and these are some examples, along with alternative treatments:

- *Fibroids* are growths in the uterus which can cause heavy periods and pain. They are not cancerous. They could be removed by surgery, although a hysterectomy may be necessary at a later date.
- *Endometriosis* is a condition in which the endometrium, or lining of the uterus, begins to grow outside the uterus itself. Mild cases may be successfully treated with hormones. Diathermy, a form of heat treatment, or surgery may also be used.
- *Prolapsed uterus* occurs when the pelvic muscles and ligaments fail to hold the uterus in place and it slips down into the vagina. It can occasionally be corrected by surgery.
- *Pelvic infections* are infections of the uterus, fallopian tubes and ovaries. The term 'pelvic inflammatory disease' is often used. Such infections can be treated with courses of antibiotics.
- *Menstrual disorders* may vary but usually involve excessive bleeding. Hormone treatment is often successful in dealing with this. A 'D and C' – the spreading of the cervix (*dilation*) followed by the gentle scraping of the uterine tissue (*curettage*) – is another alternative treatment which is frequently used. Excessive bleeding may result in anaemia but lost iron can be replace by eating liver or kidneys, or by taking iron tablets.
- *Cancer* could include the ovaries as well as the uteus. Many doctors will want to perform surgery as quickly as possible and remove the uterus. Treatments for cancer without surgery are available, such as anti-mitotic drugs or radiation treatment.

Removal of the uterus means that a woman will no longer menstruate and that she cannot become pregnant. The operation is carried out under general anaesthesia and may be performed through the vagina or through an abdominal incision. Hysterectomy may involve the removal of the fallopian tubes and ovaries. For a woman who has not yet begun the menopause, the removal of the ovaries may lead to menopausal symptoms. This is because the ovaries are involved in the production of oestrogen and progesterone, the secretion of which by the ovaries eventually stops in the natural menopause, to be taken over by other tissues (see Section 1.12). Because the withdrawal of female hormones is so sudden, hot flushes, night sweats and vaginal dryness may occur. If this does happen, the doctor may prescribe HRT (hormone replacement therapy).

Questions 11.9

1   What is a hysterectomy?
2   What reasons are there for a hysterectomy to be performed?

3   When will a hysterectomy cause early development of menopause?
4   What can be done to treat the symptoms?

11.10   Rubella (German measles)

Rubella is a mild illness caused by a virus. It is highly infectious, symptoms of the infection being a slight pink rash and fever. The glands may be swollen and you may feel off-colour. The danger of the disease is catching it when you are pregnant, as it can damage the unborn child.

If a woman catches the disease during early pregnancy there is high risk that the baby will be miscarried or stillborn (born dead). If the baby is born alive it may suffer physical or mental handicaps, such as deafness, blindness, heart defects and mental retardation.

If you have had German measles when you were young this will give you a natural immunity against the disease and you need never worry about catching it when you are pregnant. However, if you have not had the disease you are putting the life of your unborn baby at risk. Each year many women become pregnant unexpectedly, so do not think it could not happen to you. Rubella vaccination is the only sure protection. In Britain it is now offered to schoolgirls between the ages of 10 and 13. There is a simple blood test that your doctor can perform to check if you have had the disease. If you are in doubt and are of childbearing age, put your mind at rest and have the test. The vaccination itself is harmless but should be delayed if you are unwell or already pregnant. As for all vaccinations, tell your doctor if you are allergic to antibiotics or to rabbits (they are used to produce the vaccine). It is very important that you do not get pregnant for three months after the vaccination.

Questions 11.10

1   What is the cause of rubella?
2   What is the common name for rubella?
3   Why is it dangerous to have rubella when you are pregnant?
4   How is a natural immunity to rubella developed?
5   When should a female be vaccinated against rubella?

11.11   VDUs (video display units)

This is included in this chapter because of an apparent risk to women from the radiation emitted from computer monitor screens.

Research conducted in 1986 showed that pregnant mice that were exposed to the magnetic fields from computer screens, of the type used in schools, colleges and salons, had severely deformed babies or dead foetuses.

This research indicates possible dangers to pregnant women who work with computers. In a salon the only person at risk is probably the receptionist, if client records and cashflow are kept on a computer. Special protective aprons are now available to be worn when using a VDU.

If you are pregnant check with your doctor for safety.

Questions 11.11

1   What is a VDU?
2   What are the possible dangers of using VDUs?
3   What should a pregnant woman who uses a VDU do?

11.12   The menopause

This is often called 'the change of life'. It marks the end of a woman's ability to have children and is a period of physical and emotional turmoil for most women.

It usually occurs between the early forties and late fifties. The periods become increasingly irregular and finally they stop. Sometimes they may stop quite suddenly. A number of different symptoms are caused by the hormonal changes that trigger the menopause. Symptoms vary from slight nuisances such as tiredness, headaches, dizzy spells, irritability, loss of concentration, pins and needles, constipation and flatulence, to the following more serious problems:

Depression

This often accompanies the menopause. There will be feelings of lethargy, weepiness, lack of energy and general unhappiness. Much of this may be due to the fact that menopause is a sign of increasing age. Also, children may be at the age where they are leaving home. If depression is severe, medical help should be sought.

Hot flushes

These are often the worst symptoms. Blood vessels suddenly expand and more blood comes close to the surface of the skin so that the woman appears flushed. This is because the skin becomes warmer and the body reacts by perspiring. Hot flushes are unpredictable, lasting seconds or minutes, recurring on the same day or weeks apart. At night there may be 'drenches' – sudden heavy sweating. These may be brought on by alcohol, spicy food, hot drinks or even embarrassment. Many women simply put up with them, but see a doctor if they persist for more than a month or so.

Reduced vaginal lubrication

This is a distressing symptom that makes many women worry about their sex life. Oestrogen creams may be prescribed to increase secretions, but the use of lubricant creams enables a normal sex life to be enjoyed. Hormone replacement therapy (HRT) is used to combat symptoms of the menopause but it can cause increased risks of blood clots and cancer in women with such histories.

Questions 11.12

1   What is the other term used to describe the menopause?
2   At what age does the menopause usually start?
3   What are the symptoms of the menopause?

4   If depression is severe, what action should be taken?
5   What can bring on hot flushes?
6   Why might a doctor prescribe oestrogen creams?
7   Can all women be given hormone replacement therapy?

11.13 Contraception

Contraception is the prevention of pregnancy, as opposed to birth control which can include the termination of a pregnancy (abortion). The reason contraception is included in this chapter is twofold:

- Many young women get pregnant each year through ignorance.
- The majority of men in this country think it is the responsibility of the woman to take precautions against getting pregnant.

Although no method of contraception is completely problem-free at present, if it is seen as the responsibility of the couple, rather than the woman alone, there should be a suitable method from one of the following types. Some methods do carry slight risks for the woman because of side effects, so read on and take note.

The pill

This is used by 4 out of 10 fertile women. The combined pill (this contains the two female hormones oestrogen and progesterone) is the most popular one in the UK, and works by raising hormone levels so that an egg is not released (it prevents ovulation). The pill is the preferred method for young women who have no family history of high blood pressure or heart or circulation problems. Women who suffer from heavy or painful periods may benefit from this type of pill. There are health risks from side effects for women who smoke, who are overweight or who suffer from migraines or liver disease. The pill is prescribed by either your doctor or family planning clinic. A six-month supply is usually given so that check-ups can be given at this time.

   Side effects may include headaches, increased blood pressure, depression, reduced sex drive, and weight gain. Breast size often increases. There may also be spotting of blood between periods (breakthrough bleeding). There is an increase in the frequency of thrombosis (blood clots) in regular pill takers. Mothers who are breast feeding cannot take the combined pill because it causes decreased milk production.

- If you have any side effects seek medical advice. Your prescription may be changed to a pill with a different combination of hormones. Do not ignore side effects just because you are frightened that you will be taken off the pill.
- If you are ever placed on antibiotics check with your doctor or pharmacist whether or not it will affect your pill. Sometimes another method of contraception will be necessary for a few weeks.
- You must take your pill regularly each day, or it may not work. Some women take it after having sex only, which will not give protection.

- Coming off the pill can lead to several months where ovulation (releasing an egg) does not take place. Other methods of contraception should be used as you can still fall pregnant within weeks of coming off the pill.
- After giving birth women may take some months before they start having periods, particularly if breast feeding. This *does not* mean that you cannot become pregnant in this time, so take precautions.

The progesterone-only pill (commonly called the mini-pill) is intended for those who cannot take oestrogen. Mothers who are breast feeding can take it without decreasing milk production. It is important that it is taken regularly and at the same time. It works by thickening the mucus at the entrance of the cervix, which prevents penetration by sperm. It also stops eggs from implanting in the womb. The side effects include irregular periods and spotting of blood between periods. Health risks are fewer than for the combined pill.

The morning after or post-coital pill is intended for women who had inadequate or no contraception. It must be taken within 72 hours of intercourse. The pill contains high doses of progesterone and oestrogen, usually taken in two separate doses. It makes the lining of the womb hostile to implantation of the egg so prevents the pregnancy from developing. Because of the high hormone doses involved it is only used as an emergency method of contraception (women who have been raped may take it to prevent unwanted pregnancy).

Intra-uterine device

This is also known as the coil or IUD. It is a device made of plastic, or covered with copper wire, which is inserted into the womb through the vagina. While it is in position, it prevents a fertilised egg from becoming implanted. It is recommended for women who cannot take the pill but it may not be suitable for very young women, those who have not been pregnant, or those who have suffered from pelvic infections. Depending on type, it may need to be replaced every two years or more. It can be fitted in a doctor's surgery and you will be shown how to check that it is still in position. Side effects include increased bleeding and pain during periods as well as a slight risk of pelvic infections and ectopic pregnancy (pregnancy outside the womb).

Barrier methods

A barrier method of contraception is any device that prevents sperm from entering the womb and fertilising an egg. The methods used by women include the diaphragm, cervical cap and contraceptive sponge. These devices are all placed over the entrance to the cervix. Because they need to be inserted in advance of intercourse, such methods may not be suitable for the very young or for those for whom sex is unplanned. Many couples find them off-putting. The cap and diaphragm need to be of the correct size so it is best to go to a family planning clinic who will teach you how to use them properly with a spermicide (a chemical that creates a hostile environment for sperm). Sponges can be bought over the counter and need no special training. These methods are not as reliable as the pill or IUD.

The male barrier method is the sheath or condom (also referred to as rubbers, Johnnies or French letters). It is pulled over the erect penis prior to intercourse and prevents the ejaculate from being deposited in the female. It has recently gained in popularity because of the protection it can afford against AIDS. Please note however that it is not a 100% efficient method of contraception so cannot give full protection against AIDS or any other sexually transmitted disease.

Condoms are available in many colours and forms but many men claim decreased sensitivity so do not like using them. They are obviously an added protection if you are not sleeping with a regular partner, even another form of contraception is being used.

The ovulation or rhythm method

These methods involve the woman knowing when ovulation occurs so that she can abstain from intercourse while she is fertile. It involves keeping a daily body temperature chart and observing the consistency and appearance of the mucus produced by the cervix. It is often used by Roman Catholics who observe the church law that contraception cannot be used. It is not suitable for anyone who does not have regular periods or who cannot abstain from intercourse for several days. A doctor or family planning clinic should be consulted for advice on this method.

Sterilisation

This method of contraception involves an operation to cut and seal off the sperm tubes (vas deferens) in a man or to clip or tie off the fallopian tubes in a woman. The male operation, vasectomy, is a simpler operation than the female sterilisation. It is only recommended for those over 35 years of age or those who are certain they do not want any more children. Both operations have no effect on sex drive or performance but can be damaging psychologically if counselling is not sought before reaching a final decision. It can be irreversible as many couples have found out to their despair.

The future

The 1990s will probably bring a one-off vaccination as a form of contraception for the female. It will be reversible by another antidote injection when the woman wants to become fertile again. Research is also advanced on a male pill.

Termination

Each year many women find themselves with unwanted pregnancies for a wide variety of reasons. If you are in this position you should discuss it with your doctor immediately. If you cannot face your own doctor there are charitable organisations that will help you. Termination, or abortion as it is better known, is best carried out before the fourteenth week of pregnancy, when the procedure is similar to that of a

D and C (see Section 11.15). After 14 weeks hormones are often used to stimulate contractions to expel the foetus. Many women suffer attacks of depression after an abortion so support may be necessary from family or partners.

Questions 11.13

1   What is contraception?
2   How does this differ from birth control?
3   Which type of pill is the most popular one in the UK?
4   How does the combined pill work?
5   Who should not take the combined pill?
6   What risks or side effects are there involved with taking this pill?
7   Why is it not suitable for women who are breast feeding?
8   What should you do if you are placed on a course of antibiotics?
9   What is the mini-pill and who is it suitable for?
10 How does the mini-pill work?
11 What side effects does it have?
12 What is the morning after pill?
13 How does it work?
14 How does an IUD work?
15 Who is it suitable for?
16 What are the side effects of IUDs?
17 What barrier methods are available for females?
18 What barrier methods are available for males?
19 What extra protection can be afforded by sheaths?
20 Why are barrier methods not popular with some people?
21 How does the rhythm method work?
22 Who is sterilisation suitable for?
23 How does it work?
24 What methods of contraception are being developed for the future?
25 By what time should a termination be carried out?
26 How are terminations carried out?

11.14 Infertility

Many men and women never imagine that they will have problems becoming pregnant. If a couple has been having regular sexual intercourse for more than 12 months without contraception and do not become pregnant, then there are possibly fertility problems. The infertility can be either with the woman or the man. Specialist medical help is required, and an appointment should be requested with a consultant who specialises in infertility problems. With many couples who have been childless for years there is sudden pregnancy when they have given up trying, thinking they were infertile. This could possibly be linked to tension when trying to conceive. Once a couple are in their thirties medical help is definitely required as the time left to conceive with medical help will be running out.

Female infertility is usually due to a failure to produce eggs, or to a blockage in the fallopian tubes. Causes include:

- Long-term illnesses such as diabetes, thyroid disorders or chronic infections.
- Having intercourse less often than three times a week (the chances of sperm being in the womb when an egg is released are reduced).
- Having intercourse more than seven times a week (this may make the number of mature sperm too few to fertilise the egg).
- Irregular or infrequent periods (this may be due to hormone imbalance so that ovulation does not occur or the frequency of ovulations is decreased).
- Previous pelvic infections, ovarian cysts, abortions or ectopic pregnancies (these may cause blockage of the fallopian tubes so that eggs cannot be fertilised).

Investigation of the condition is often carried out by a simple operation called a laparoscopy. Under general anaesthetic two small slits are made in the abdomen. Carbon dioxide is passed through a hollow needle in one slit to distend the abdomen. An endoscope is passed through the second slit, enabling the surgeon to see inside and find the trouble. Ultrasound scanning may be used to look for abnormalities, as well as injections of dyes to check for fallopian tube blockage. Male partners will be asked to undergo a sperm count to see whether or not they are infertile. The male is asked to abstain from sex for two days before giving his sample. Some couples may be helped to conceive by being placed on fertility drugs (increasing ovulation, but sometimes resulting in multiple births), by tubular surgery or by other techniques (test tube babies, etc).

One of the commonest causes for failure to conceive is basically not knowing how to achieve the best chance for fertilisation. The following points should increase the chances of conception:

- Having intercourse about three times a week (this gives a good chance of having intercourse on a fertile day, and keeps the number of sperm high).
- Having intercourse on the woman's most fertile days. These can be worked out from temperature, charts, available from the doctor.
- The position of intercourse should be with the man on top. This allows sperm to be deposited closer to the womb. The woman should remain laying down for 15 minutes to allow the maximum number of sperm to enter the womb.
- Men should not wear tight underpants as this can increase the temperature of the testicles and damage sperm. Boxer shorts are more suitable underwear.
- Both partners should be in good health. Smoking, drinking and being overweight can all decrease the chances of conception.

Questions 11.14

1 When should couples suspect fertility problems?
2 Why should help be sought by couples in their thirties if they cannot conceive?
3 What are the two main causes of female infertility?
4 List some of the causes of infertility.
5 What is a laparoscopy and how is it carried out?
6 How can male fertility be checked?
7 What can couples do to increase their chances of conception?

11.15   D and C

This stands for dilation and curettage. It is a minor operation that is usually carried out to find the cause of heavy periods, and may sometimes cure them. It is also used to investigate infertility and as a method of abortion. The operation is carried out under general anaesthetic so usually requires two days in hospital. The neck of the womb (the cervix) is dilated (widened) and an instrument called a curette is used to scrape out the lining of the womb. The scrapings are then examined. Women who have D and C operations usually suffer bleeding for a few days and some pain in the lower abdomen.

Questions 11.15

1   What does D and C stand for?
2   Why is the operation usually carried out?
3   How is the operation carried out?

12

Revision and Examination Preparation

This revision chapter is here simply as an aid to passing hairdressing hygiene examinations. It is not supposed to be a quick way of looking up information so that you don't have to use the rest of the book! This chapter will help you remember the salient facts you have already covered. Beauty therapists should also read Chapter 8.

12.1 *Infectious diseases*

An infectious disease is one which can be passed from one person to another. Disease can be spread directly by touching, by infection from droplets or indirectly by coming into contact with an infected object – towels, brushes etc.

An infection can be caused by three different groups of micro-organisms: bacteria, viruses and fungi. Pathogenic bacteria cause disease whereas non-pathogenic bacteria do not. Bacteria are classified according to their shape:

- Round = *cocci*
- Round in couples = *diplococci* (e.g. pneumonia)
- Round in bunches = *staphylococci* (e.g. boils)
- Round in chains = *streptococci* (e.g. impetigo)
- Rod-shaped = *bacilli* (e.g. diptheria)
- Spiral-shaped = *spirochaetes* (e.g. syphilis)
- Comma-shaped = *vibrios* (e.g. cholera)

Bacteria can divide by cell division (*mitosis*) every 20 minutes in the correct conditions. They need six things:

(1) Food
(2) Moisture
(3) Oxygen
(4) Warmth

(5) Darkness (remember that the ultra-violet rays in sunlight kill them)
(6) Alkalinity (acidity acts as antiseptic – the natural pH of skin is acid).

Blood has all six of these.

If conditions are adverse, bacteria can form *spores* (so can fungi). Spores are the last things to die during sterilisation.

Bacteria that use oxygen from the atmosphere are *aerobic* – if they do not they are *anaerobic*. *Impetigo* is caused by streptococci which enter breaks in the skin. It is seen mostly in children as yellow crusty blisters around the mouth and is highly infectious. It is also seen on the scalp as a secondary infection following head lice infestation. It is spread directly or indirectly.

Furuncles or boils are due to severe infection of a follicle by staphylococci. The 'head' forms and a core of pus is seen. This leaves a cavity which heals with a scar. Boils are often seen where skin rubs (e.g. pressure of collar or neck).

Carbuncles occur when several follicles become infected to give a 'boil' with several heads.

Sycosis barbae or barber's itch (or rash) occurs in the beard area of men as small red pustules which itch. It is caused by staphylococci and is usually spread on infected razors and shaving brushes. To prevent, disinfect razors and brushes.

Folliculitis is the term given to the infection of a follicle by staphylococci.

Acne is due to blockage of the hair follicles with sebum and keratin. Usually there is infection by staphylococci. Acne starts at puberty and is seen in seborrhoeic areas (face, chest and back).

Viruses are very small and infections caused by them are much harder to control as antibiotics have no effect. They multiply inside living cells, destroying them. Viruses which are spread by droplet infection (coughing, sneezing) usually cause infections of the respiratory tract (e.g. colds ad influenza).

Herpes simplex or cold sores are usually seen around the lips. The virus can lie dormant, becoming active from time to time after a cold or when a person is over-tired, or has been over-exposed to the wind or sun. It can be spread, when blisters are present, by direct contact (kissing) or indirect contact (cup, towel).

Verrucae or warts show on the skin surface as a small external growth (except for plantar warts which grow into the skin). Warts often disappear without treatment. They can be removed by 'burning' off with dry ice or by diathermy. Hairdressers can easily cut warts on their hands so should have them removed. Plantar warts can be painful – as they are on the feet – and are often spread by people walking barefoot (e.g. in swimming pools).

Fungi are a group of plants including yeasts and moulds. The fungi affecting man live mostly on the skin surface and are parasitic. Ringworm fungus (tinea) consists of a series of fine branching threads known as a *mycelium*. The threads secrete a digestive juice with an enzyme that digests keratin. It can attack the skin, hair or nails. The ringworm spreads when portions of the mycelium break away and are carried directly or indirectly to another person. The antibiotic griseofulvin is used to treat ringworm. Ringworm can affect six body areas: (1) feet (2) body (3) groin (4) nails (5) beard (6) scalp. There are several types of ringworm:

(1)   *Tinea pedis* or athlete's foot is the most common type of ringworm. It is mostly seen in summer and starts between the fourth and fifth toes, where the skin appears sodden and broken. It is often spread on changing room floors or in swimming pools. Control with foot powders.
(2)   *Tinea corporis* appears on the body as a red 'ring' with a definite edge (unlike a rash).
(3)   *Tinea cruris* is found mostly in men, as a large red 'horseshoe' on the groin.
(4)   *Tinea unguium* affects the nails which become yellow and powdery. It takes several months to cure.
(5)   *Tinea barbae* is seen in the beard area and is usually caught from animals.
(6)   There are three types of ringworm of the scalp, the most common being *Tinea capitis*. This is usually seen in children under twelve as once puberty is reached sebum seems to give extra protection. It is seen as bald patches with broken hairs within, and the scalp is covered with greyish-white scales.
      Black dot ringworm causes bald patches which are studded with black dots (these are the tips of hairs broken off below skin level). There is no scaling.
      Favus or *honeycomb ringworm* has a characteristic yellow crust with a mouse-like odour. This leads to loss of hair, but the patches may have some normal hairs within.
      Note *the differences between these three forms of scalp ringworm.*

Thrush is a fungal disease of the mucosa (mouth, vagina) caused by single-celled yeasts.

Some bacteria and fungi are *saprophytes* which live on dead or decaying matter.

12.2   Infestations

A *parasite* lives in, or on, another living creature causing it *harm*. *Ectoparasites* live outside the host, *endoparasites* within.
The presence of small animal parasites on a body is known as an *infestation*.

●   *The head louse* (*Pediculus capitis*) is a six-legged insect that causes the infestation known as *pediculosis capitis* (note the spellings!). They are found on the hair close to the *occipital* area of the scalp. They live on blood and lay eggs called *nits* which are cemented to the hair (within an inch of the scalp). Head lice can be killed with shampoos containing insecticides such as malathion or carbaryl. Nits are loosened with vinegar and combed out with a fine-toothed comb.
●   *Pubic lice* cause the infestation known as 'crabs'.
●   *Body lice* are found in the seams of clothing. They only go on to the body to feed.
●   *The itch mite* causes an infestation known as scabies. It burrows into the epidermis. It is a mite and not an insect, because it has eight legs.

- *The bedbug* (*Cimex*) is found in furniture and skirting cracks and feeds on people's blood at night (do not confuse with harmless dust mites).
- *Fleas* (*Pulex irritans*) are insects with large back legs for leaping. They usually live on family pets, especially cats. Although cat fleas bite humans they will not live on them.

Advice on insect parasites and rats and mice should be obtained from the environmental health officer at the local town hall. Rodents can be discouraged by keeping bins covered and not leaving food about in the salon.

12.3 Non-infectious conditions

Some diseases or conditions are non-infectious so cannot be transmitted from one person to another.

Psoriasis is an abnormal formation of skin keratin. The thick silvery scales itch and when removed leave red-bleeding points and sore-looking skin. Nails may show 'thimble pitting'.

Pityriasis is over-production of epidermal cells, resulting in small scales which are shed and can be seen on the scalp and caught in the hair. Pityriasis is commonly known as *dandruff* and can be treated with shampoos containing *zinc pyrithione* ('Head and Shoulders') or *selenium sulphid* ('Selsun').

Alopecia is the term for baldness. There are many types:

- *Male pattern baldness* is seen in many men and can start in the late teens. It is due to genetic inheritance and the effect of androgens (male hormones). It starts at either the front hairline or the crown of the head. There is no proven cure.
- *Alopecia senilis* is baldness of old age.
- *Alopecia areata* starts as small bald patches which can join together to form larger ones. The sides of the patch may have exclamation mark hairs. Hair should grow back in three to four months and is often white, giving a 'piebald' appearance. It can be caused by shock. Medical advice should be sought, because it can lead to the following two types of baldness, *alopecia totalis* and *alopecia universalis* which can be permanent.
- *Alopecia totalis* is the complete loss of head hair.
- *Alopecia universalis* is the complete loss of body hair.

  Seek medical advice as these conditions can be permanent

- *Traction alopecia* is caused by too much pressure or tension on the hair. In pony tails the baldness would be along the front hairline. It can be seen with rollers. Correct by not using tension.
- *Cicatricial alopecia* is due to scarring, such as bad cuts or from boils. Medical advice should be obtained if due to an infected scalp.
- *Diffuse alopecia* is the loss of hair from an area gradually, so that the hair thins. It is often seen in women after pregnancy. It could be due to anaemia (lack of iron) or an underlying problem such as hypothyroidism or a tumour. Medical advice should be sought to eliminate serious causes.

Dermatitis means inflammation of the skin. It can be caused by perm lotion, tints (tints or para dyes can also cause cancer in laboratory animals and possibly in humans) or shampoos. It can be prevented by wearing gloves or by avoiding contact with the chemicals that cause it.

Shampoos degrease the hands so the hands should be dried and moisturised. The client should be protected by keeping chemicals off the scalp and giving a skin test before every application of tint (24 to 48 hours beforehand). Some people are allergic to their own sebum and suffer from *seborrhoeic dermatitis*. Do not confuse this with *seborrhoea* (overactivity of sebaceous glands). Excess production of sweat (feet and hands usually) is termed *hyperidrosis*. Body odour is caused by the breakdown of apocrine sweat by bacteria and can be controlled by *anti-perspirants* (which reduce the amount of sweating by making sweat pores smaller) or *deodorants* (which inhibit the growth of bacteria like an antiseptic).

Halitosis is the term for bad or unpleasant breath. It can result from digestive troubles, smoking or eating strong-tasting food (such as onions or garlic). Teeth should be cleaned regularly to prevent this and tooth decay (caries).

Defects of the hair shaft include *canities* (= grey hair); *monilethrix* (= beaded hair); *trichonodosis* (= knotted hair); *fragilitis crinium* (= split ends); *pili torti* (= twisted hair shaft); *trichorrexis nodosa* (= nodes in hair).

12.4 Disinfection

Sterilisation is the complete destruction of all living organisms on an object.

- *Dry heat* This will blunt scissors and is too hot for plastics etc. Used to burn infected hair.
- *Moist heat* Towels can be boiled at 100°C. If the pressure is increased to 15 lbs per square inch the temperature of boiling is raised to 121°C. This is done in an autoclave (a type of pressure cooker). Metal could rust; plastics melt.
- *Formaldehyde gas* Formalin is placed on a heating element in a cabinet to produce the gas. Used for combs, brushes, rollers etc. Instruments should be cleaned *before* sterilising. As it pits metal it should not be used on scissors.
- *Ultra-violet radiation* is available to use in the form of a sterilising cabinet. Tools must be cleaned to remove all dirt and grease which ultra-violet cannot penetrate. As ultra-violet rays travel in straight lines, tools must be turned. The cabinet is a good place for keeping tools between clients. Ultra-violet produces vitamin D in the skin (a lack of this vitamin causes *rickets*).
- *Quaternary ammonium compounds* or *quats* are cationic detergents such as *cetrimide*. Use as a 1–2% solution in bath for tools. An anti-rust ingredient can be added to use for razors, scissors, etc.
- A *disinfectant* kills germs if used long enough, and strong enough.
- An *antiseptic* will inhibit the growth of bacteria without necessarily killing them. If peroxide is used it should be less than 10 volume strength.

12.5 General salon hygiene

Remember the following points:

- Objects used in salons should be washed and sterilised regularly to prevent the spread of germs. Towels should be washed after each client, not just dried. Waste material should be disposed of in covered bins or burnt.
- Work tops should be non-porous (as bacteria may breed) and washable. Formica is suitable. Clean with a non-scouring product as scouring powders scratch.
- Floors should be non-slip and washable (vinyl), and not polished too much.
- Lacquer should be removed from mirrors with methylated spirit.
- Bins should be covered and pedal-type. Never leave food around the salon because it attracts vermin.
- Tools should not be kept in pockets because it spreads infection.
- Sinks should be fitted with traps to stop smells or air-borne infection. They can be either 'U' bend or bottle trap. The bottle trap type should be used on shampoo basins as it makes the removal of hair easy.
- Use two sets of tools, so that one can be sterilised while the other is in use.

12.6 Physical salon hazards

Remember the following points:

- The salon and staircase should be well lit.
- Floors should be made of non-slip material and left unpolished. Carpets should be fixed. Any spilt liquids should be dried immediately.
- Do not trail wires or leave things where people walk.
- Furniture should not have sharp edges or protruding handles. Instead it should have rounded corners and recessed handles. Doors should not fling open: use magnetic catches and sliding doors instead.
- Wall fittings should be above head height.
- Care should be taken where scissors are placed and when cutting near the ears or neck.

12.7 Preventing salon accidents

Remember the following points:

- Chemical containers should be clearly labelled and chemicals should never be placed in non-chemical containers such as lemonade bottles.
- Never pour chemicals into dirty bottles.
- Once chemicals are poured from storage bottles they should not be returned (peroxide, for instance, could otherwise decompose). Measure quantities; do not guess.
- Replace stoppers on bottles and jars, and avoid inhaling lacquer.

- Protect hands with rubber gloves when perming, tinting or straightening.
- Use base cream on the client when straightening, and backwash to keep out of the eyes.
- Do not play a jet of hot air on metal hair clips as it can cause burning.
- Fit diffusers on light fittings as glare can cause headaches – which can lead to accidents.
- Tie back long hair; it could get caught in the hairdrier.

See also *physical salon hazards* (Section 6.5).

12.8 Fire safety

Remember the following points:

- Care should be taken with flammable products such as lacquer. Store away from heat sources in small quantities. As peroxide can assist fires it should be stored away from heat and flammable substances, such as setting lotion.
- Use electrical equipment correctly as it can cause fires.
- Do not drape towels over heaters as they may cause the appliance to overheat.
- Provide adequate ash trays or have no smoking.
- In the event of fire, first get clients to leave, close windows and doors, call the fire brigade and/or deal (if possible) with the fire yourself. Do not endanger yourself but always get clients out of the salon first.
- Small fires may be extinguished with sand or fire blanket.
- Electrical fires may be extinguished with a carbon dioxide extinguisher.
- Never use a water extinguisher on an electric or oil fire.
- Aim the extinguisher jet just in front of the fire.

12.9 Electrical safety

Remember the following points:

- Wire the plugs correctly and fit the correct size fuse to protect the appliance.
- The earth wire must be used if available to protect the user from electrocution. If there is no earth a two-wired appliance must be double-insulated. Check to see that it has the double-insulated symbol.
- Replace broken plugs and flexes.
- Do not run too many appliances off one socket – it causes overloading.
- Do not use appliances near water.
- Join wires with insulated blocks and not tape.
- Never put wires directly into a socket without a plug; this is highly dangerous.
- Disconnect any appliance from the mains before opening to inspect.
- Do not trail a flex where people might walk.
- Do not run flex under carpets as it gradually twists and can come away from the back of an appliance.

- Do not knock nails into walls if there is any danger of hitting buried cable.
- If in doubt *consult an electrician*.

12.10   *Safety points of an electric plug*

(1) Plugs should be made of an insulated, unbreakable material.
(2) They should be fitted with a fuse of the correct size to protect the appliance.
(3) A plug should have a cord grip to stop the flex from being pulled away from it.
(4) The earth pin should be longer than the live and neutral pins – this will open up the socket holes. The socket design should prevent you from putting wires into the socket without a plug.
(5) The live and neutral pins should be insulated next to the lug so that a child cannot get his fingers against live metal if the plug is pulled out slightly from the socket.

12.11   *Ventilation*

Remember:

- The salon temperature should be 20°C (68°F) and the amount of oxygen in air 21%.
- When breathing we take oxygen out of the air and put in carbon dioxide and water vapour.
- Ventilation should replace air three or four times an hour without causing draughts. Natural air movement is by convection and diffusion.
- Hopper windows are placed above doors, and direct currents of air upwards so that it is heated before reaching clients. Cooper's discs and louvre windows can be used to aid ventilation and control the entry of air.
- Electric extractor fans should not be placed near air intakes (doors etc.).
- Humidity should be controlled as it encourages bacterial growth and infection, can cause condensation, or hair to drop (setting).
- Faulty paraffin heaters (or gas) can give off poisonous carbon monoxide gas.

12.12   *The first aid box*

A first aid box should contain the following:

(1) Sterile dressings; (2) gauze bandages; (3) crepe bandages; (4) triangular bandage; (5) adhesive plasters; (6) cotton wool; (7) antiseptic liquid or cream; (8) eye bath; (9) tweezers; (10) scissors; (11) safety pins; (12) eye pad.

12.13   *First aid*

- *Minor cuts* Apply pressure. For shaving, use alum powder and not a styptic pencil as this could spread infection. For *nosebleeds* pinch the soft part of the

nose and place the head forward till clots are formed. Do not blow the nose.
- *Major cuts* Try to stem the blood flow with a cloth. If there is very heavy blood loss from a limb, apply a tourniquet which must be released every few minutes.
- *Chemicals in the eye* Rinse with tepid water; an eyebath may be useful.
- *Fainting* If the client feels faint place the head between the knees. If she has fainted, raise the legs to get blood to rush to the head.
- *Minor burns and scalds* Run under cold water.
- *Major burns and scalds* If possible, cool with water and then cover with sterile gauze and seek immediate medical help.
- *Epileptic fit* Remove objects on which the sufferer could be hurt. After the fit, place the patient in the recovery or semi-prone position (on her side). This prevents choking on vomit or swallowing the tongue.
- *Hysterical fit* Get person alone, don't be harsh but be firm and express no sympathy.
- *Diabetic coma* This results from lack of insulin (flushed face, deep breathing and breath smelling of acetone) or an excess of insulin (skin pale and moist, breathing shallow). Seek medical aid; check pocket for diabetic card.
- *Electric shock* Turn off electricity before touching the person being electrocuted. If breathing stops, give artificial respiration.
- *Heart attack* The skin often turns blue. If the person is still conscious, support in a sitting position and loosen tight clothing. If the heart stops, alternate between breathing into the lungs (make sure your mouth is over theirs) and cardiac massage (pressure onto sternum or breast plate) until heart restarts and/or medical help arrives.

12.14 Care of the feet

- *Corns* are due to ill-fitting shoes; the skin thickens.
- *Ingrowing toenails* result from pressure on the nails. To prevent, cut nails straight across.
- *Bunions* are caused by incorrectly fitting shoes which make the joint of the big toe become inflamed.
- *Flat feet* may be due to continual standing or may be inherited. To treat, use an artificial arch support.
- Check for athlete's foot or plantar warts and treat them if possible.
- High heels push the body forward, leading to bad posture and fatigue.
- Low or medium heels are more comfortable. Correctly fitting shoes should grip at the heel and over the instep. If shoes are too large they could cause claw toes.
- Wash feet regularly and dry well.
- Keep toes covered as this prevents cut hair from entering the skin of the feet.

12.15 Health and Safety at Work Act 1974

- This legislation aims to secure the health, safety and welfare of all persons while at work.

- According to the Act, employers must provide a safe and healthy environment.
- It is employees' duty to take reasonable care for the health and safety of themselves and their clients.

If a client has an obvious skin infection or parasitic infestation they should be *tactfully* referred to a doctor and *no* hairdressing service given. If staff have begun service, finish as briefly as possible and disinfect tools, towels and gowns. Disposable paper towels and ear shields should be used where possible.

12.16 *Examination tips*

- Any examination that you take should allow you enough time to answer adequately the questions that you have been asked. *Don't panic*!
- If the question is of the multiple choice type, read the question first *without looking at the answers*.
- Do you know the answer? If you do, look to see if it is one of the four alternative answers you have been given.
- If you are unsure of the answer, check the four alternative answers and see if one seems familiar to you.
- If you are still unsure, check to see if you know that some answers are definitely wrong. This way, when you guess the answer, you have a better chance of being correct!
- *Never leave a multiple choice question unanswered.*

Sample question:

Which of the following terms means baldness?
(a) dermatitis   (b) trichology
(c) alopecia   (d) pityriasis

When answering short answer questions, where either a few words or a sentence are required, answer the questions in the order that they are given. Number each question, and if you are unsure of an answer leave a space so that you can return to it later. If you do this, you are less likely to forget to come back.

If you are unsure of a spelling, try to spell the word as it sounds to you. If you are asked 'What type of bacteria causes boils?' and you write 'staphylostreptococci', the examiner will know that you are unsure whether to write staphylococci or streptococci. When you think that there are two answers, put them. Some questions are rather vague and the answer the examiner requires may not be obvious to those sitting the examination!

When answering essay questions, read the whole question first and make sure that you understand what it is asking. Also, check that the last line does not have a bearing on the whole question. Students often neglect to read the part of the question that asks for 'advantages and disadvantages of each method'. This results in an uncomplete answer.

If the essay is in parts (a), (b) and (c) *or* (i), (ii) and (iii), *do not ignore the part numbers*! The examiner expects to see those numbers in the margin of your answer so that he can mark it accordingly. Before launching into an essay, jot down the important points on a piece of scrap paper first. This will help you not to forget points. If you remember a missing point, include it as a footnote at the end of your essay. The examiner will still give you marks.

Finally, always look through your paper a second time as you may spot mistakes.

Hygiene is not just an examination subject – it is important to your everyday working and home life.

Glossary

abscess: a bacterial infection, usually deep in the skin.

acne: the term used to describe 'spotty' skin usually seen in adolescents.

AIDS: this stands for 'acquired immunodeficiency syndrome', a viral disease which destroys the immune system so that the sufferer eventually dies of a variety of illnesses to which he or she has no resistance. See Section 2.8.

alopecia: the term used to describe baldness. There are many types of baldness, described in Section 3.6.

anagen: the part of the hair growth cycle in which the hair is actively growing. It lasts between 1.5 and 7 years.

androgens: the name given to male hormones which control the growth of underarm and pubic hair. Cause male pattern baldness and acne in sensitive individuals.

antibodies: the name of the particles produced by the immune system in response to an infection.

anti-perspirant: an agent that reduces the amount of sweat secreted. Used in the control of body odour.

antiseptic: a chemical that will inhibit the growth of bacteria without necessarily killing them.

apocrine gland: the type of sweat gland found attached to hair follicles in the armpits, pubic region and nipples. The decomposition of this sweat leads to body odour.

athlete's foot: the common name for ringworm of the feet, *tinea pedis*, the most common type of ringworm. See Section 2.5.

bacilli: a type of bacteria which are rod-shaped.

bacteria: a type of micro-organism that can be seen with a microscope. See Section 2.2.

basal layer: the bottom layer of the epidermis where cells are actively dividing.

blackhead: also known as a comedone, it is a plug of oxidised sebum and keratin which blocks the openings of pores. Often seen in acne.

boil: also known as a furuncle, it is a septic condition of a hair folicle with a characteristic single large head.

bromidrosis: body odour due to sweating. It is usually caused by the bacterial decomposition of apocrine sweat, but the same term is often used to describe the smell of sweaty feet which is due to eccrine sweat.

bunions: the term used to describe the deformity of the bone at the side of the big toe, usually caused by tight shoes.

burn: the name given to skin damage caused by heat or strong chemicals. To give first aid, hold in running cold water.

calorie: a unit of energy used for the energy values of foods.

carbohydrate: the type of foodstuff that gives energy. Examples: sugars and starches.

catagen: the breakdown period of the hair growth cycle which usually lasts for about two weeks.

cold sore: the common name for herpes simplex, a skin infection caused by a virus.

conjunctivitis: inflammation of the eyeball. Can be caused by bacteria or as a reaction to ultra-violet radiation.

cortex: the inner part of the hair, consisting of numerous strands. It is the part of the hair where melanin is found and it is changed during chemical processing of hair.

crabs: the common name given for the infestation caused by pubic lice.

cuticle: the outer part of the hair which consists of several layers of overlapping scales.

cystitis: a bacterial infection of the urethra which causes pain and 'burning' on the passing of urine.

dandruff: the common name for pityriasis, a non-infectious condition of the skin in which epidermal scales are produced too quickly.

deodorant: a chemical which inhibits the growth of bacteria, rather like an antiseptic. Used to control body odour.

dermatitis: the term given for inflammation of the skin caused by an external agent. Can be the result of an allergy. Common types of dermatitis in hairdressing include dye and shampoo dermatitis.

dermis: the second layer of the skin, containing nerves, blood vessels and connective tissue.

disinfectant: a chemical that will kill germs if used long enough and strong enough.

eccrine glands: the type of sweat gland that is found all over the body. The sweat consists of water and a little salt. It cools the skin by evaporation.

ectoparasite: a parasite found on the outside of the body.

eczema: inflammation of the skin with itching, caused by an internal agent, such as an allergy to food.

endoparasite: a parasite that is found inside of the body.

epidermis: the top layer of the skin, which protects the skin beneath it and makes both vitamin D and melanin in response to ultra-violet radiation.

epileptic fit: a fit involving uncontrollable convulsions. First aid is to stop the casualty from hurting himself. Place in the recovery position after the fit.

fainting: passing out due to an insufficient supply of oxygen to the brain. First aid is to raise the legs higher than the head so that more blood flows to the brain.

fat: a type of foodstuff made up of fatty acids combined chemically with glycerol. All animal fats and plant oils are fats; their main role is to store energy.

first aid: the first action that should be taken in the event of an emergency in order to minimise or lessen any harmful consequences.

follicle: a downgrowth of the epidermis from which hairs grow. Sebaceous glands are usually attached.

folliculitis: infection of a hair follicle by bacteria. Usually a hair is protruding from the pustule at the skin surface.

formaldehyde: the name of the vapour given off by formalin which is used to sterilise tools.

fragilitis crinium: alternative name for split ends, a condition caused by harsh physical treatment of the hair. The only remedy is to cut off the damaged ends.

fungi: these are a group of plant micro-organisms which contain no chlorophyl and cause several types of ringworm and other diseases such as thrush.

gangrene: the name given to the condition where the flesh decays and dies.

germinative layer: another name for the basal layer of the epidermis.

glands: tissue which produces a secretion. Examples include eccrine and sebaceous glands.

heart attack: the condition that arises when cardiac tissue is deprived of oxygen, usually caused by a blood clot. Will result in the death of all, or some, of the heart muscle. See Section 10.7.

herpes simplex: the scientific name for cold sores.

horny layer: the top layer of the epidermis, which consists of a lot of dead cells. The main function is to protect the cells underneath from physical injury and water loss.

hyperidrosis: the overproduction of sweat, most often sweating of the hands and feet. Usually a nervous condition.

impetigo: a bacterial skin infection where there are yellow, crusty blisters. May also arise as a secondary infection caused by head lice.

infectious: a disease that can be spread by direct or indirect contact – it can be 'caught'. Infectious diseases are caused by either bacteria, fungi or viruses.

infestation: describes somebody or something having living creatures living in or on them. A person can be infested with lice while a building can be infested with rats.

itch mite: the mite that causes scabies.

keratin: the name of the protein of which the skin, hair and nails are composed. Differs from many proteins in that it contains sulphur.

lice: the name of three different types of insect that live on human blood. One variety is found on the head, one on the body and one in the pubic region. They are killed with insecticides.

lymphocytes: the type of white blood cell which produces antibodies to help fight infection.

medulla: the name given to the hollow air spaces that form the centre of the hair. It may not be present in some hairs.

melanin: the dark pigment of the skin and hair. In the epidermis it absorbs ultra-violet radiation and prevents burning of skin.

melanocyte: cell which produces melanin. Located in the germinative layer of the epidermis.

menopause: the time when the periods of a woman cease and hormone levels change. It can have distressing symptoms.

minerals: chemical elements that are an essential part of the diet because of their functions. Mineral deficiency can cause serious conditions of ill health.

monilethrix: the production of beaded hair, which breaks off easily.

nits: the eggs of a louse. In head lice they are found attached to hairs, close to the scalp.

occipital: the part of the cranium that forms the back of the head. Often called the nape in hairdressing.

papilla: the part of the hair follicle from which the hair grows.

para-dyes: oxidation tints that contain para-compounds. These can cause dermatitis.

parasite: a living creature that lives in or on another creature, causing it harm.

pediculosis: the scientific name for an infestation of lice.

phagocyte: cell that ingests foreign bodies such as bacteria in the blood.

pityriasis: the scientific name for dandruff.

protein: a type of foodstuff that is made up of amino acids linked chemically together. Found in meat, fish and various vegetable sources. Needed for growth and repair of cells.

psoriasis: a non-infectious skin condition in which the epidermis is produced too quickly, resulting in severe scaling.

recovery position: the name given to the position in which any unconscious casualties should be placed to make sure that they don't choke or smother on vomit. Casualties should be laid on their side.

ringworm: also called *tinea*, it is the name of a group of fungal skin infections. See Section 2.5.

roughage: the name given to the part of the diet that provides bulk but no nutritional value. It helps prevent constipation and certain intestinal diseases.

scabies: the infestation caused by itch mites.

sebaceous gland: the gland that produces sebum and is found attached to the hair follicle. The development of these glands is controlled by androgens.

sebum: the oily secretion of the sebaceous gland.

staphylococci: round bacteria arranged in clumps.

sterilisation: the complete destruction of all living organisms on an object.

streptococci: round bacteria arranged in chains.

telogen: the resting part of the hair growth cycle which usually lasts between 3 and 4 months.

thrush: the name of a fungal infection of the genital tract, usually female. It is caused by a yeast. See Section 11.1.

tinea: scientific name for ringworm.

trichonodosis: knotting of the hair.

trichorrhexis nodosa: name given to swelling on hair caused by rough physical or incorrect chemical treatment.

trichotillomania: the name given to pulling out one's own hair – usually an obsessional or nervous disorder.

varicose veins: surface veins of the legs in which failure of some valves has caused slower circulation and swelling. See Section 11.3.

ventilation: the changing of the air in a room. Should take place 3 to 4 times an hour without the production of draughts.

verruca: the scientific name for wart, a viral infection of the skin.

vibrio: a comma-shaped bacteria.

virus: a minute micro-organism that can only be seen with an electron microscope. Causes skin infections such as cold sores and warts.

vitamins: accessory food factors needed in extremely small quantities by the body, without which it would not function properly.

Wood's light: type of ultra-violet radiation which causes ringworm to fluoresce. Used in diagnosis.

Index